From Pinochet to the 'Third Way'

From Pinochet to the 'Third Way'

Neoliberalism and Social Transformation in Chile

MARCUS TAYLOR

Pluto Press

LONDON • ANN ARBOR, MI

First published 2006 by Pluto Press
345 Archway Road, London N6 5AA
and 839 Greene Street, Ann Arbor, MI 48106

www.plutobooks.com

British Library Cataloguing in Publication Data
A catalogue record for this book is available from the British Library

ISBN   0 7453 2451 7 hardback
ISBN   0 7453 2450 9 paperback

Library of Congress Cataloging in Publication Data applied for

10   9   8   7   6   5   4   3   2   1

Designed and produced for Pluto Press by
Chase Publishing Services Ltd, Fortescue, Sidmouth, EX10 9QG, England
Typeset from disk by Stanford DTP Services, Northampton, England
Printed and bound in the European Union by
Antony Rowe Ltd, Chippenham and Eastbourne, England

For Susanne

Contents

List of Figures and Tables

Acknowledgements

Many people have been instrumental to the completion of this book. My fullest thanks go to Simon Clarke, for his instruction and close reading of earlier versions. Ronaldo Munck and Mike Neary also provided very useful commentaries at that stage. On the Chilean side, Daniel Chernilo supplied logistical support and delivered insightful and constructive critiques of numerous chapters. Octavio Avendaño offered lodgings and excellent companionship, and José Bengoa, Manuel Riesco, Cristián Paiva and Guillermo de la Peña all provided help or advice at various points during my research stays in Chile. On the Montreal side, Jean-Philippe Warren has been a source of constant and much-welcomed humour and enthusiasm, which greatly aided the final stages of writing. From other locations, Guido Starosta, Leigh Binford and Nancy Churchill gave much appreciated support in different ways. Last, but far from least, my partner Susanne Soederberg has provided bountiful inspiration and encouragement, and it is to her that I dedicate the book.

Acknowledgements

Introduction:
Neoliberalism and Social Transformation

The primary concern of this book is to provide a comprehensive and critical analysis of the emergence and unfolding of neoliberalism in Chile. This is undertaken as a way to deepen our understanding of the social transformations and consequences inherent to this political practice at a global level. Chile provides an excellent case study through which to examine the nature and impact of neoliberalism for several reasons. On the one hand, Chile was the first country in either the developed or developing world in which a thorough programme of neoliberal restructuring was initiated. The privileged position of neoliberal technocrats in the policymaking bodies of the Pinochet dictatorship between 1975 and 1989 gave them an unparalleled opportunity to undertake far-reaching reforms in conditions of political impunity. As a consequence, neoliberal restructuring proceeded further and more rapidly in Chile than in any other country. On the other hand, the Chilean experience of neoliberalism has since its inception played an extremely significant role in influencing international debates on development strategy. In spite of a tumultuous history over the last 30 years, the various permutations of neoliberalism in Chile have repeatedly been heralded as models of policy practice worthy of emulation throughout the developing world. Much like the East Asian 'model' of development, which was controversially lauded by international institutions such as the World Bank as proof of the virtues of market-led development (World Bank 1993a; cf. Burkett and Hart-Landsberg 2000), the Chilean experience has been a touchstone for international debates over the salience of neoliberalism at a global level (Drake and Jaksic 1999; Ffrench-Davis and Stallings 2001). It is useful to briefly overview the three primary incarnations of the Chilean model before introducing the analytical themes addressed in the body of the book.

THREE DECADES OF CHILEAN NEOLIBERAL MODELS

Two years after the violent overthrow of Socialist president Salvador Allende through a military coup led by Augusto Pinochet in September 1973, a pioneering group of economists introduced a new and radical policy orientation in Chile. Since the 1930s the Chilean political economy was characterised by a structuralist approach to development, prevalent across much of Latin America, which sanctioned the formation and expansion of state institutions aimed at promoting industrialisation, regulating social conflicts and reshaping social structures. The new policymakers in the authoritarian regime, however, professed the need to reverse this trend through a rapid and uncompromising restructuring of social institutions. By transforming the relationships between state and society and between social classes, the intention of these reforms was to strengthen the regulatory role that market forces played in the processes of capitalist development in Chile. The market, they argued, should be freed from external constraints in order to allow its self-regulatory dynamic to provide a more rational and efficient context for social interactions. Not only would this create a more prosperous economy, but would also promote human freedom and social harmony.

At the time, these proposals for reform – later given the title of 'neoliberalism' – were widely regarded as peculiarly unorthodox and profoundly misguided. This mistrust was due in no small part to the institutionally engrained Keynesian conviction that direct state intervention in the economy is the only means to ensure stable growth within capitalist societies. Indeed, two years before the introduction of this programme in Chile, US president Richard Nixon highlighted the global hegemony of Keynesian thought in his declaration that 'we are all Keynesians now'. Nonetheless, the programme of social restructuring undertaken in Chile – predicated on the teachings of Chicago School economists – attracted a small yet vocal set of domestic and international admirers and proponents who believed it offered a solution not only to the economic and social crisis in Chile, but also to the ills of capitalist societies on a global scale. Buoyed by the proclaimed successes of the strategy in Chile, which they claimed contrasted greatly with the socio-economic malaise afflicting other developing countries, proponents soon referred to it as the 'Chilean model' and claimed that it provided a blueprint for other countries to follow. Francisco Orrego, a leading regime ideologue and early proponent of the idea of a Chilean model, stated as early as 1975 that:

Chilean action can assume leadership characteristics ... and the Third World will be able to understand and benefit from the Chilean experience (cited in Frank 1975: 19).

In hindsight, Orrego's assertion of Chilean exceptionalism initiated a 30-year period during which at least three permutations of neoliberalism in Chile have been heralded as templates for other developing countries to follow. Although the initial application of neoliberal reforms in 1975 resulted in an expected deflationary period, the subsequent achievement of high levels of economic growth in the late 1970s led to the proclamation of an 'economic miracle' predicated on free market policies. On this basis, major figures within the tradition of neoclassical economics, which provides the theoretical rationalisation of neoliberal policy practice, visited Chile to extol the virtues of their worldview and draw international attention to a new 'model' country. Milton Friedman, for example, gave a master lecture on state television and Friedrich von Hayek was made honorary president of the Centre for Public Studies, a leading Chilean think-tank of the neoliberal ilk (Valdés 1995). This first incarnation of the Chilean model was further nurtured by adulation from advocates located in US institutions and universities and by the self-aggrandising pronouncements of the Chilean reformers themselves.

The impact of the Chilean experience was particularly important within the international organisations of the World Bank and the International Monetary Fund (IMF). The IMF had been undergoing a period of redefinition since the early 1970s when the abolition of fixed exchange rates not only undermined its established means of crisis management but also obliterated its original raison d'être (Helleiner 1994). The presumed virtues of the Chilean experience proved a useful resource with which to legitimate the organisation's ideological shift toward Chicago School monetarism and to establish a new function for the organisation, namely, the global propagation of neoliberalism as a solution to global economic woes. Concurrently, the World Bank underwent its own internal reconfiguration in the late 1970s when signs of widespread stagnation and crisis undermined its previous support for structuralist models of state-mediated capitalist development. By 1982, under strenuous pressure from the United States executive, the World Bank had undertaken an ideological house cleaning and installed proponents of the new orthodoxy into all major positions (Green 1995; George and Sabelli 1994). The importance of these power shifts in international organisations became manifest in the response of these two organisations to the 1982 debt crisis. Both organisations reacted by promulgating 'shock therapy' reforms in afflicted countries that closely mirrored the Chilean strategy of 1975.

However, at the very moment that the Chilean model was being globally propagated in the guise of structural adjustment through the coercive power of international financial institutions, the 1982 debt crisis hit Chile particularly severely. As positive growth rates dissipated into a mire of the deepest recession experienced by Chileans since the 1920s, the triumphalism of the first generation of model proponents was cut short. In the face of a massive collapse of firms and banks and rapidly escalating unemployment, the original cadre of Chilean neoliberal technocrats was banished from the regime and large-scale state interventions were implemented to uphold the crisis-stricken institutions of Chilean capitalism.

Notwithstanding this dramatic setback, the Chilean model rose phoenix-like from the ashes of the debt crisis when, in the late 1980s, an export-led boom opened up a decade of dramatic economic expansion in Chile. With annual GDP (gross domestic product) growth rates averaging above 8 percent between 1987 and 1997, it appeared that the Chilean reforms had again been vindicated and advocates once more extolled the virtues of Chilean neoliberalism. Moreover, the return to liberal democratic forms of government in 1990 offered observers an opportunity to argue that the successes of the Chilean restructuring could be maintained and even improved within the framework of liberal democracy. Whereas during the 1970s and 1980s the US State Department, the World Bank and the International Monetary Fund were prepared to overlook the authoritarian character of the Chilean state owing to Cold War considerations, the 1990s marked a changed international climate and led to a new emphasis on the propagation of liberal democracy (Robinson 1996).

Indeed, for Chile, the perceived successes of the post-dictatorship period were soon to be attributed by international organisations such as the IMF to the pursuit of neoliberal policies within the context of stable liberal democratic governance (Jadresic and Zahler 2000). 'Good policies' coupled to 'sound political institutions' were seen as the substance of a second incarnation of the Chilean model. According to *The Economist* – a leading voice of neoliberal internationalism – Chile was once again the blueprint for the developing world to observe and replicate:

Not surprisingly, Chile has become the most studied country in Latin America. Visitors arrive from all over the world to see how they can emulate the Chilean transformation, and what they should be doing next. (*The Economist*, 13 November 1993)

Nonetheless, over the course of the 1990s, three successive elected governments drawn from the Concertación coalition of centre-left parties garnered attention for a brand of reformed neoliberalism that is suggested to give due attention to social issues. A significant increase in social expenditure and a more proactive role for the state in creating the social and institutional conditions for export-led development are the celebrated features of this revised neoliberal trajectory. In the context of growing international disillusionment with orthodox neoliberalism, these policy directions have led to a situation where Chile is viewed as a potential 'Third Way' option for Latin America that stands between the old orthodoxy of doctrinaire neoliberalism and the trajectory of populist governments such as that of Hugo Chavez in Venezuela. This sentiment was reinforced by the election in 2000 of the Socialist Ricardo Lagos to the presidency and the subsequent widely publicised visits of Anthony Giddens, a principal architect of the 'Third Way' neoliberalism of Tony Blair's New Labour governments in Britain.

Along these lines, Warren Barton and Warwick Murray recently echoed the attitude propounded by the elected Concertación governments that Chile could potentially offer a new development paradigm for Latin America predicated on a reformed neoliberal template:

Policy makers and academics in Latin America and beyond are looking at the country – which has been the site of several economic and political 'experiments' in the past – to provide new ideas about effective models of post-authoritarian governance and development. (Barton and Murray 2002: 330)

At a time when the soundness of neoliberal policy prescription is being critiqued by even some of its prominent former advocates (see Stiglitz 2000) and in which the World Bank has acknowledged the need to 'widen the development agenda' to give fuller recognition to the social dimensions of development processes (Wolfensohn 1999), Chilean policies are once again viewed as globally important trendsetters.

KEY QUESTIONS AND THE ARGUMENT OF THE BOOK

The accession of Chilean neoliberalism to model status, including its subsequent reformulations, raises several important questions that relate directly to ongoing theoretical and practical concerns in debates over global development strategies. These problematics form the analytical core of this book. First, it is necessary to explicate the motivations that led Pinochet's authoritarian regime to break radically with mainstream expectations regarding sound policy and embrace the prescription of a small clique of heterodox economists whose ideas most contemporary observers believed were an antiquated throwback to an earlier and redundant era of capitalism. At a time when state interventionism to regulate a broad array of social relationships was widely accepted as the only route to stable economic growth, the argument that neoliberal policies of trade liberalisation and state retrenchment would be an effective tool for economic reinvigoration seemed profoundly suspicious.

To adequately explain this rupture, it is necessary to revisit the question of what neoliberal reform entails beyond the immediate level of policy change. In this respect, the book argues that neoliberalism is not simply a set of economic policies that offers an alternative method of macroeconomic management to its Keynesian-inspired predecessors by, for example, liberalising markets and restraining inflation through austere monetary policies. Although such policy shifts are an important aspect of neoliberalism, they do not adequately convey how neoliberal restructuring imparts a complex and deep-rooted process of social transformation. At the heart of the social theory underlying neoliberalism is a specific normative vision of the efficiency and rationality of a society that reproduces itself solely through the mechanism of freely interacting individuals making private exchanges that together constitute the market. Markets are seen as natural, efficient and equilibrating forms of social interaction that express the highest form of social rationality. On this basis, neoliberal political practice represents a project of vigorous social engineering that intends to make this vision a reality by eliminating social relationships that do not conform to the market model.

To achieve this goal requires a significant restructuring of social institutions. Social institutions can be described as durable systems of established and embedded social rules and conventions that structure social interactions (Hodgson 2001: 295). As such, social institutions inevitably constrain yet also enable certain forms of social activity. By rapidly restructuring the established institutional forms of state–society relations through which the state attempted to mediate the course of capitalist development, neoliberal reform proposes to assert more fully the regulatory discipline of market forces upon social actors. The essence of neoliberalism, therefore, is a fundamental attempt to restructure the relationships and institutions through which capitalist society is reproduced materially, politically and ideologically. Not only is this strategy estimated to lead to stronger economic performance, but also it is intended to fundamentally depoliticise society by reducing societal reproduction to a succession of private, individual and rational market interactions that the state can oversee in an apolitical and technocratic manner.

The appeal of neoliberal policies to the Chilean authoritarian regime in the mid-1970s, I argue, rested primarily on their promise to provide a far-reaching programme of social transformation that could resolve the underlying crisis of Chilean society in the post-Second World War period. This crisis was manifested in intractable social conflicts, repeated bouts of political paralysis, and recurring economic stagnation, all of which were dramatically evident in the ill-fated socialist government of Salvador Allende, 1970–73. Neoliberal restructuring, its advocates suggested, would not merely fix the symptoms of this malaise, but would obliterate the root causes that led Chilean society to repeated and debilitating social, political and economic crises. It was this greater vision of social transformation, moreover, that precipitated the global propagation of neoliberalism in the 1980s and 1990s.

Furthermore, and in contrast to the notion that neoliberalism involves a retreat of the state in the face of the market, I contend that neoliberalism is categorically a state-led project of social engineering that seeks to reformulate the institutional forms of state–society relations. In so doing, neoliberal restructuring strengthens social institutions that advance the disciplinary power of markets upon social actors while transforming or retrenching those that provided barriers to the latter. The overall effect of recasting social institutions is to alter the mechanics of power within societies and, in so doing, transform the very way that power is manifested and exercised within society. In particular, the extended commodification of social relations and the reinforcement of market discipline enhance the social power of money, therein paving the way for a concentration of power around the holders of money, specifically financiers. These trends have been explicit in both Chile since the mid-1970s (cf. chapters 3 and 6) and at a global level (Soederberg 2004; Nesvetailova 2005).

Second, the book examines the social implications of the neoliberal reforms in the Pinochet period – both before and after the debt crisis of 1982. It is argued that the most important consequences of neoliberal restructuring should not be seen in terms of relative economic performance – which, if calculated over the entire period of the dictatorship, were below historical averages – but rather the underlying changes in social relations. At issue is a fundamental change in power relations effected through the re-crafting of social institutions. The institutions in question include those through which the state planned and directed economic activities; those through which the relations between capital and labour within the enterprise and in the labour market are channelled and regulated; and the institutions through which the state mediated the social reproduction of individuals and households through provision of welfare services including education, healthcare, and social security. Far from merely technical changes to the economic organisation of society, these institutional transformations incur profound alterations in the relations between social classes with manifold implications for the distribution of resources, power and insecurity within society.

On this basis, the book moves to a more specific examination of the contradictions that permeate the neoliberal project and argues that the latter led to the defeat of the dictatorship and a subsequent process of refining neoliberalism that pre-empted features of the 'Third Way' trend popularised by Anthony Giddens in the context of Great Britain's New Labour (Giddens 1998). The latter, I argue, responds to but also reproduces in new and complex forms the contradictions inherent to neoliberal restructuring. To make this argument, a detailed investigation of the policy practices and consequences of the post-authoritarian Concertación governments is undertaken. While significant praise has been given to the Concertación's attempt to reformulate neoliberalism in a manner that combines economic efficiency with social justice, I suggest that the political strategies of the Concertación governments embody a paradoxical attempt to mediate the contradictions of neoliberalism without undermining the new institutional context established by neoliberal restructuring. As a consequence, the results of the Concertación's strategy have been profoundly uneven and far less beneficial for the majority of Chileans than the accompanying rhetoric suggests. Given the attempts to refine neoliberalism that are ongoing at an international level – notable not only in the changing emphasis of the World Bank's best-practice prescriptions but also, and more importantly, in the shift to centre-left governments throughout much of Latin America – a critical analysis of the Concertación's achievements has important global implications.

THE LAYOUT OF THE BOOK

The book is divided into nine chapters. Chapter 1 historicises the genesis of neoliberalism in Chile by offering an analysis of the crisis-prone history of national developmentalism and the culmination of these trends in the socialist government of Salvador Allende and the coup d'état of 11 September 1973. This historical context is crucial to provide an adequate explanation of the authoritarian regime's adoption of the neoliberal project. Chapter 2 then builds on this basis to offer an original interpretation of why the dictatorship moved to embrace neoliberalism as a solution to the perceived ills of Chilean society. In so doing, the chapter examines the theoretical underpinnings of neoliberal policy practice and the anticipated outcomes of the latter. These propositions are subsequently deconstructed and, in doing so, the chapter provides the analytical tools through which the contradictions of neoliberalism can be discerned. Chapters 3 and 4 analyse how neoliberal reform was initiated in Chile, including a focus on the intended and unintended consequences of its implementation. Chapter 3 focuses on the macroeconomic and labour policies of the Pinochet regime, and I introduce the notion of neoliberalism as a form of 'creative destruction' through which existing social institutions are obliterated in order to construct a new social order. By enforcing the discipline of global competition upon national social relations, neoliberal political practice aims at enforcing a systematic restructuring of the latter, resulting in new productive structures and a reformulation of the class relations that underscore them. Chapter 4 subsequently analyses the Pinochet regime's correlated remodelling of welfare institutions. It provides an account of the motivations behind the neoliberal restructuring of these institutions and supplements this general analysis with a focus on health, education and pension reforms.

Neoliberal restructuring did not, however, engender the results anticipated by its proponents, resulting in social contradictions that led to the fall of the dictatorship and a shift in policy emphasis. Chapters 5 through 8 move from the fall of the dictatorship in 1989 to the policies and outcomes of the first decade and a half of elected governments, all of which have been formed from the coalition of parties known as the 'Concertación'. Chapter 5 examines the social context in which the political strategies of the Concertación were formed and indicates how a conjuncture of political, institutional and material constraints led to the Concertación adopting a refined neoliberal approach they termed 'growth with equity'. The latter, it is argued, is a sophisticated political strategy that attempts to satisfy the government's political constituencies within the context of the deep class divisions and restrictive social institutions forged during the initial restructuring period. Chapters 6, 7 and 8 concretise this argument by analysing the Concertación's economic, labour and social policies respectively. In highlighting the contradictions inherent to this refined neoliberal strategy, the book's conclusion in chapter 9 analyses the nature of the global shift toward 'Third Way' neoliberalism and addresses its implications for more progressive strategies of social transformation in Latin America and elsewhere.

1
The Rise and Crisis of
National Developmentalism

Chilean neoliberalism emerged in a context of deep social crisis that had specific historical roots. The purpose of this chapter is to account for the nature of that crisis through an examination of capitalist development, class formation and institution building in Chile from the 1920s. As the following sections recount, processes of capitalist development in Chile from the nineteenth century caused repeated social strains as the crisis-prone trajectory of capital accumulation created poverty and insecurity among large sections of the Chilean population. In response to the political struggles that accompanied these trends, the Chilean state underwent a period of institutional expansion in order to attempt to mitigate the resulting social contradictions. Although this expansion of state–society institutions was intended to consolidate the relationships through which capitalist development in Chile was reproduced, within the crisis conditions of the 1960s and 1970s various social groups saw them not as the remedy to the problems of Chilean society but as the source of those very ills. It was within these specific historical conditions that neoliberalism, as a political project of radical institutional restructuring, could rise to prominence.

CAPITALIST DEVELOPMENT,
SOCIAL STRUCTURES AND THE CHILEAN STATE

As with the other Latin American countries that gained their independence in the early nineteenth century, Chilean social structures bore the heavy imprint of a colonial legacy. The principal social institutions forged during the colonial period were centred upon large landed estates known as *haciendas*. Concentrated primarily in the fertile central valleys, these operated through a perpetuation of seigniorial authority over the rural peasant class. Their owners formed an oligarchic ruling class in conjunction with merchant interests that controlled export commerce and this dominance was amply represented in the multi-party parliamentary political system through the roles of the National Party, which tended to represent hacienda owner interests, and the Liberal Party, which was more closely tied to commercial interests. During the course of the nineteenth century, however, the increasing integration of Chilean agricultural and mineral production into the British-dominated international economy stimulated an important transformation of Chilean social structures with far-reaching effects (Pregger-Roman 1983).

Two socio-economic trends were prevalent. First, commercial agriculture expanded around the production of wheat for export to markets in the US, Australia and other parts of Latin America. This trend gave impetus to the rise of an internationally orientated agrarian bourgeoisie whose interests repeatedly clashed with those of the traditional hacienda owners, resulting in a conflict that generated notable tensions within the ruling elite. Simultaneously, outside of the agrarian sphere, the export of nitrates and mineral exports began to develop rapidly in the north of the country. This lead to the creation of new regional elites drawn from mining entrepreneurs and a supporting financial and commercial class in port cities that were strongly connected to British trading interests. At a parliamentary level, the new Radical Party became the political vehicle for the interests of bankers, mine owners and the limited but expanding urban industrialists.

Alongside this transformation of the Chilean bourgeoisie and landed elite, deeper integration into world markets and the expansion of local economies fostered the emergence of a middle class – composed of professionals, engineers, lawyers and government functionaries – and an incipient proletarian class. The latter formed initially from the remnants of a floating labour force left over from earlier frontier wars. As employment expanded in the mines and the cities, however, the migration of a surplus rural population that abandoned the relations of domination on the haciendas for waged work swelled its numbers.

These socio-economic trends of the late nineteenth century became more pronounced in the early twentieth century. From the turn of the century into the 1920s there occurred a notable growth in both the nitrate and copper industries, but also in the number and size of indigenous consumer goods industries geared towards small but expanding local markets and occasionally export markets in neighbouring countries. These industries were owned by a combination of an embryonic domestic industrial bourgeoisie and foreign entrepreneurs, and depended greatly on foreign loans and technology. As Harold Blakemore (1993: 61) has detailed, the period saw:

[A] sizeable expansion of Chilean industry in terms of both the growth of establishments and their variety, and of the labour force to operate them. The food and drink processing industry, cement works, ceramics, sugar refining, clothing; leather products, wood and paper, chemicals, foundries, machine-shops and metalworking establishments all expanded considerably in this period and largely in private hands.

A necessary corollary to the expansion of the industrial sector, however, was the sustained growth of the urban working class. This occurred most rapidly in the mining and docking sectors but also within new industries and on commercial farms that relied upon day-labourers rather than a bonded peasantry. Conditions for this incipient working class were frequently terrible, with long hours of work and wages that barely supported household subsistence. Inflation frequently rose at a faster rate than wages and a series of studies conducted by the labour office between 1911 and 1925 estimated that workers spent 97 percent of their wages on basic necessities (DeShazo 1983: 62). Additionally, vicious trade cycles attributable to fluctuating global demand for nitrates, wheat and copper periodically caused the destruction of jobs and the lowering of wages, leading to rampant pauperisation. Such conditions were not accepted passively, as evidenced by the spontaneous outbreak of countrywide strikes in July 1890 that began with dockers in the northern port of Iquique but spread as far south as Santiago and Concepción (Roddick 1989). Moreover, the emergence of a proletariat removed from traditional forms of social domination that characterised the countryside constituted a potential political threat to the status quo. With immigration from Europe expanding the ranks of the working class and providing workers with experience of labour organisation garnered in Europe, labour movements developed rapidly (refer to Table 1.1). At the same time, radical political groups such as the Communist and Socialist parties grew in size and, despite their inability to overcome factionalism at the national level, they exerted a growing influence on the political system (cf. Monteón 1998: 190–204; Roddick 1989; Vitale 1990).

The implications of these changing class structures and political dynamics for Chilean society were considerable. The traditional landowning oligarchies suffered a marked decline in both economic standing and political power, particularly as pre-capitalist social relations in the hacienda system resulted in low agrarian productivity. The existing political status quo between landed classes and the expanding mining and industrial bourgeoisie was subsequently placed under great strain as new social forces emerged from the middle and working classes in the cities and northern mining areas. In place of the old compromise between landed elites and new bourgeoisie, there emerged a pressing requirement to incorporate the emerging social classes into the political system so as to diffuse class conflict while maintaining the conditions for capital accumulation. This necessity was driven home by the strengthening of Chilean working-class organisations that repeatedly clashed with employers over wage levels and conditions of work, while simultaneously pressuring the state for protection from the insecurity inherent to the economic cycles of capitalist development (DeShazo 1983).

Table 1.1   Urban Unionisation in Chile, 1932–73

Year	No. Unions	Union Members	Percent Unionised
1932	421	54,801	(n/d)
1940	629	91,940	18.7
1952	1,982	282,383	19.3
1960	1,892	272,141	14.3
1970	4,001	436,974	19.4
1973	5,632	704,499	30.5

(Data drawn from Roberts 1998b: 90)

This vulnerability of the working class to rapid immiseration was starkly manifested through the collapse of the nitrate industry in the early 1920s and the subsequent Great Depression at the end of the decade. During the latter period Western markets for other Chilean exports collapsed and imports were severely disrupted, which caused a new and unprecedented degree of economic dislocation and social conflict that lasted well into the 1930s. The ruptures stemming from these events, including a collapse in exports, state revenues, wages and a dramatic increase in unemployment, unleashed social and political struggles that led to significant changes in the form and functions of the Chilean state. On the one hand, state-supported industrialisation projects garnered support from both economic and political elites chastened by the country's overdependence on exports. On the other, social reforms and the growth of state interventionism to regulate the social reproduction of the working class were put forward as a necessary solution to escalating levels of pauperisation and the political pressures they engendered.

The first systematic labour legislation that provided institutionalised structures for collective bargaining was enacted in 1924 and consolidated with reforms in 1931, creating the first labour code in the Western Hemisphere (Morris 1966). Similarly, the constitution of 1925 put in place the legal conditions for the beginnings of a social security system. Conflicting political factions and a lack of material resources, however, repeatedly undermined implementation. The result was an era of intense political instability that led by the end of the 1930s to the beginning of an era of populism in which the balance of political power shifted towards those parties that could fashion a support base from a wide range of urban class interests (Borzutzky 2002: 19). Pedro Aguirre Cerda's Popular Front government (1938–41) was paradigmatic of this trend. His administration rapidly expanded state assistance to industry as a strategy to overcome the economic crisis by encouraging the development of dynamic productive forces in Chilean society. To achieve this, Cerda created a state development corporation entitled the Corporación de Fomento (Development Corporation, CORFO), which provided technical advice for developing industries and then subsidised them through the provision of cheap credit and foreign exchange provided by newly nationalised banks. Concurrently, the government began to protect domestic industries from foreign competition by establishing an elaborate system of tariffs and quotas that regulated the entry and cost of imported consumer goods.

Although this shift in the relationship between the Chilean state and society occurred as a reaction to the economic and political disjunctures of the 1920s and 1930s, it proved to be a key moment in the long-term institutionalisation of a national-developmentalist form of the state. The latter crystallised around the project of encouraging capital accumulation through domestic industrial expansion via the establishment of institutions such as CORFO and other forms of industrial support. This approach subsequently became known as 'import substitution industrialisation' (ISI) owing to its aim of replacing imported consumer items with domestically manufactured goods (cf. Kay 1989). Such was the emphasis on industrialisation that the subsequent president Antonio Ríos Morales, elected in 1942, quipped, 'to govern is to produce'. With state support for import substitution policies, industrial production increased by 9 percent annually during the war years, a trend abetted by the reduced availability of consumer imports from the US and Europe (Drake 1993: 115). Following the culmination of the war, import substitution became the standard development strategy across Latin America. Within the Cold War environment, the United States government and international organisations supported the major tenets of ISI as a way to promote capitalist development in the Third World. The World Bank, for example, gave its first ever developing country loan to Chile in 1948 and made a further nine loans in the following ten years, all orientated towards infrastructural projects to further regional industrialisation or primary commodity production.

Far from merely an economic strategy for industrialisation, however, import substitution industrialisation became articulated within a wider national-developmentalist strategy that sought to reshape a wide array of social relations through new state–society institutions. In response to escalating social tensions, the populist state attempted to regulate a growing range of social relations through interventionist methods that led to the establishment and subsequent expansion of new state institutions. Within the sphere of production, state institutions including the 1931 labour code and provisions for state-sanctioned collective bargaining were created to regulate the conflict between capital and labour over wages and the conditions of work within the enterprise. Concurrently, the state began to play a greater role in mediating consumption by subsidising staple consumption goods and developing welfare institutions that aided and regulated the reproduction of various strata of working class households (Fortín 1985; Drake 1993; Borzutzky 2002). Through these institutionalised forms of intervention, the state attempted to harness the working classes to capitalist development, check the growth of subversive ideologies, and provide the social and industrial calm necessary for sustained capital accumulation. Simultaneously, by supplementing the purchasing power of the middle and working classes, the state helped to consolidate outlets for domestically produced consumer goods and cheapen wages for industry.

The proliferation of institutions tied to the national-developmentalist state, however, proved unable to resolve the contradictions of Chilean capitalism. Rather, they tended to reproduce them in new and complex forms. First and foremost, the institutional forms of the state became intensely politicised. By mediating the level of wages through centrally indexed salaries, the state became directly involved in regulating the distributional conflict between capital and labour with the necessary corollary that the state became a locus for the struggles of the working class. For example, whereas the maintenance of industrial order had previously relied on the discipline exerted by labour markets in conditions of uncertain employment combined with the hierarchical exercise of power in the individual firm; the institutionalisation of collective bargaining and the active intervention of the state in this process created a new institutional framework through which the resolution of industrial conflict over wages and the conditions of labour became national political issues contested by the collective actors of national unions, employer associations and state bodies.

Outside of the realm of production, a wide range of social movements and interest groups pressured the state for material compromises and these repeatedly became manifested in the institutionalised form of social policies, such as the granting of social security to particular occupational strata. As a consequence, welfare institutions developed in a profoundly uneven manner as their consolidation greatly depended upon the relative ability of social movements to voice their demands. The assorted systems governing pensions, healthcare and education became notoriously fragmented as different sections of working classes, ranging from state bureaucrats to blue collar industrial workers, met with varied success in pressuring the state to grant or extend coverage to their specific occupational group. By the 1970s the social policy system, despite its heavy centralisation, constituted a legislative and bureaucratic labyrinth with hundreds of programmes and institutions (Mesa-Lago 1989: 109). Although a certain degree of universality was reached relative to other countries in the region – Huber (1996: 148) estimates that 70 percent of the working population had some form of state-sponsored social security and Titelman (2001: 266) suggests that 90 percent of the population had access to the health system – there were notorious inequalities in both coverage and provision of services. Notably, social groups who fell outside of the urban-industrial realm, such as peasants, rural workers and the urban 'marginal masses' working in the informal sector, received extremely partial – if any – coverage.

Not only did the relations of production and consumption become intensely politicised within this environment, they were also framed within the fluctuating dynamics of Chilean capital accumulation. Institutional compromises required significant material resources and this in turn depended on the sustained accumulation of capital through industrial dynamism and increased primary commodity exports. Although sometimes characterised as an inward-orientated development strategy, national developmentalism was reproduced through deep integration within global capital circuits. Mineral export revenues, especially copper, were critical for sustaining capital accumulation as foreign exchange revenues provided for oil and technological imports that serviced the domestic goods sector, while export taxes provided a significant and growing source of state income. With copper providing almost 75 percent of Chilean export-earnings in the post-war period, capital accumulation in Chile was consistently vulnerable to the vicissitudes of world market prices for this commodity, especially its relative price compared to oil. Moreover, with the United States becoming Chile's major export destination and largest source of technological and consumer imports in the post-war period, fluctuations in the US economy had major implications for Chile's balance of payments and other economic indicators (Frank 1969).

Capital accumulation in Chile – and with it the material basis for the populist state – therefore remained heavily dependent on the course of global accumulation in the post-war period. Economic downturns served to intensify the respective distributional claims of capital and labour upon the state while simultaneously limiting the resources available to make compromises. During periods of economic stagnation, capital sought to stifle the wage claims of workers and clamoured for increased state credit while workers expected the state to protect wages and provide greater social security in conditions of rising unemployment. Such crises were repeatedly marked by the state discarding its populist veneer and attempting to renew the conditions for accumulation by suppressing real wages and repressing union movements, the political parties of the left, and other social movements (cf. Roxborough et al. 1977: 36; Stallings 1978; Vitale 1990; Salazar and Pinto 1999). The second presidency of Carlos Ibanez (1952–58) was paradigmatic in this respect, with his claims of economic nationalism and a populism above politics soon dissipating into a new emphasis on mineral exports and harsh anti-inflationary measures that stifled industrial development, stimulated unemployment, and caused a decline in real wages (Drake 1993: 126).

The tensions inherent to the ISI mode of accumulation became particularly acute in the mid-1960s as the post-war boom that had underscored global capitalist expansion for two decades began to falter and new social struggles in both rural and urban realms gathered momentum. By the end of that decade, signs of crisis became increasingly apparent in the stagnation of the import-substitution project alongside escalating instances of social mobilisation. In the mid-1960s the price of copper began a slow but notable descent from the high levels of the early 1960s. Although copper exports continued to buoy macroeconomic indicators, they nonetheless provided a decreasing source of revenue for the state. Considerable cause for concern, however, was to be found in a persistent inflationary trend and a failure of dynamism in industrial sectors orientated towards the domestic market operating under the protection of high tariff walls (Stallings 1978; Fortín 1985). Domestic industrialists faced a limited market for their goods and paid high prices for importing the technology necessary to increase productivity or to move into the production of more complex goods. Simultaneously, the agrarian sphere appeared to be stagnating, owing to the pro-urban bias of ISI policies that sought to keep basic food prices low coupled to highly concentrated land ownership and the remnants of the hacienda system. As a share of GDP, agriculture fell from 14.9 percent to 10.1 percent between 1940 and 1960 (Fortín 1985: 205).

Within this context, the political environment underwent a significant transformation. The existing social and economic institutions established since the 1920s and integrated into the national-developmentalist state came under assault through escalating social conflicts and the crisis-prone course of capital accumulation. The traditional political parties struggled to contain an escalating movement for more radical social change manifested in the growing electoral support for the parties of the left. As a polarisation of the political landscape threatened to rupture the parliamentary system, a new political force emerged in the form of the Christian Democrat Party (CDP) that sought to re-establish the middle ground of Chilean politics through a social democratic solution to endemic social conflict and economic stagnation. In so doing, the CDP saw itself as providing a new answer to the quandaries of capitalist development within Chile, one that could successfully maintain the benefits of the latter while countering its unseemly consequences through new social reforms. Following a resounding victory in the 1964 elections by the CDP, their leader President Eduardo Frei acceded to the presidency and immediately sought to reinvigorate the national-developmentalist trajectory through a period of concerted institution building.

FREI'S 'REVOLUTION IN LIBERTY'

Greatly influenced by the works of French Catholic philosopher Jaques Maritain, Frei and the CDP set out a programme of reform that envisaged an expanded role for the state in regulating social reproduction. Within Christian Democrat political philosophy, the state was seen as a tool that could be used to integrate Chilean society in the face of divisive social struggles and economic stagnation (Borzutzky 2002). In this vein, the Frei administration responded to the political and economic manifestations of crisis by deepening both the ISI model of industrial support and the populist politics of social integration through a programme of industrial credits, infrastructural investments, the nationalisation of copper, agrarian reform and new social programmes. The programme was termed the 'Revolution in Liberty', and its intention was to provide a model of socially progressive reform within a 'neo-capitalist' or 'Third Way' model of development. Proceeding beyond merely deepening the ISI model, Frei's 'Revolution in Liberty' represented a shift towards an explicitly transformative populism wherein the state actively sought to incorporate new social actors into a societal project that it believed could ensure social stability and accelerate national development. This strategy raised the politicisation of Chilean society to a new level as it proactively mobilised marginalised groups and constructed channels of access to state institutions for these groups.

In the realm of economic policy, Frei labelled the CDP programme as 'neo-capitalist' to emphasise the combination of state intervention in key industries (particularly mining) with substantial foreign investment. In an attempt to facilitate capital accumulation the state followed a Keynesian-influenced expansionary policy, drawing heavily on foreign credit to finance increased intervention in Chilean social relations. The strategy was buoyed by considerable US financing through President Kennedy's 'Alliance for Progress' initiative that, in the wake of the Cuban Revolution of 1959, sought to stave off further revolutions in Latin America by promoting moderate social change. Chile under the Christian Democrats was the recipient of over US$1 billion of direct US aid, resulting in a higher aid per capita ratio than any other Latin American country (Angell 1993: 149).

A primary objective of the 'Revolution in Liberty' was to modernise the rural sphere, where the remnants of the hacienda system were viewed as an impediment to agricultural productivity and a source of significant social tension. Additionally, the monopolisation of land by the remnants of the hacienda-owning class constituted an obstruction to the development of a rural smallholder class that could supplement demand for domestically produced consumer goods. Agrarian reform was therefore viewed as an integral aspect of economic reinvigoration and social harmony. Frei's reform programme – aimed at expropriating land held on estates of over 80 hectares in size and redistributing them to the peasantry – was envisaged to have three positive effects. First, agricultural productivity and overall yields were expected to rise. Second, a new class of smallholders were expected to increase their consumption of domestically manufactured consumer products, thereby giving a boost to industry and the ISI project. Third, a new basis of political support for the reformist project could be harnessed in the countryside through the state-sponsored formation of peasant unions that were expected to pledge political allegiance to the CDP project (Kay 1978). Literacy programmes in the countryside were intended to make agrarian reform more effective by educating the rural population and raising their political consciousness, although they also were designed to secure a stronger political base amongst the peasantry for the Christian Democrats (Kirkendall 2004).

Over the six years of Frei's term, close to 12 percent of irrigated land was redistributed to about 20,000 peasant families who gained from the programme. While certainly a significant start, this total represented only one-fifth of Frei's stated goal and the new land recipients frequently suffered from a lack of resources, such as machinery, livestock and credit, to greatly increase land productivity. Although agricultural productivity did undergo a notable increase in this period, this stemmed primarily from large landholders increasing production to avoid losing land to the reforms (Kay 1978). Far from imparting social harmony into the countryside, the unfulfilled promises of agrarian reform, new rural inequalities and conflicts over various instances of implementation led to an increased politicisation of the countryside. This often resulted in progressively more antagonistic relations between rural social movements, landowners and the state, as manifested in a marked increase in strikes, grievance petitions and direct land seizures (cf. Petras and Zemelman 1972; Bossert 1980).

Alongside agrarian reform, new social programmes directed monetary subsidies, welfare services and literacy campaigns to marginalised groups, such as the rapidly expanding urban populations that inhabited shantytowns and subsisted through informal sector activities. The programmes were designed to incorporate these subaltern groups into the mainstream of Chilean society through the auspices of the state. Political incorporation into state institutions was intended to ensure their political support while simultaneously expanding their ability to consume domestically produced goods, therein providing another boost to the industrialisation drive. Similar to the outcome of agrarian reform, however, politicising these groups did not lead to a new stable constituency of support for Christian Democrat reforms, but rather contributed to a new and dynamic mobilisation of social movements in the cities that looked beyond the services offered by the state to a more fundamental and rapid transformation of their marginal existence.

Conversely, the mobilisation of these groups by the state also proved insufficient to counter-balance the political power of the established labour movements. Owing to the success of the latter in securing rising wages following a massive upsurge in strike activity in 1965–66, capital was faced with growing difficulties in maintaining profit rates (Stallings 1978: 105). Inflation began to rise significantly and business interests clamoured for an end to the mounting redistributive component of the Chilean political economy and a cap on wage increases. The failure of the economy to respond to Frei's expansionary initiatives meant that resources became increasingly restricted precisely at a moment when social mobilisation augmented pressure for greater material compromises. Under these constraints and amidst growing social polarisation, the Christian Democrats' political consensus ruptured and rapidly broke apart. Notably, support for the Socialist and Communist parties grew considerably, comprising over one-third of the electorate, while the bourgeoisie became increasingly confrontational towards the radical edge of Frei's reformist programme.

In spite of unbridled optimism at the start of his presidency Frei's strategy proved unable to surmount growing political fissures and economic stagnation. Extending social programmes to the urban subalterns and introducing agrarian reform in marginalised rural areas did not result in the long-term dynamism of either industrial or agrarian production as hoped, but did increase the politicisation of Chilean society and provided a further drain on the social surplus, heightening fiscal indebtedness. The regime responded in 1968 with a shift to the right, reducing social expenditure and employing the security forces to crack down on the more explicit forms of popular mobilisation (Stallings 1978: 113). However, the contradictions unleashed by the crisis led to the dissolution of Frei's political middle ground, with polarisation manifesting itself even within the ranks of the Christian Democrats. The left wing of the party began to champion more radical reforms as a way to overcome the structural impasse. As Radomiro Tomic, presidential candidate for the Christian Democrat Party, surmised, strong contradictions surfaced between the populist project of expanded social reforms and the underlying relations of capitalist development:

I am convinced that the failure of the 'revolution in liberty' was inevitable, essentially because of the contradiction between its programme for economic development based on and reinforcing the capitalist structure of the Chilean economy, and its programme for social development. The latter, mobilizing the people in defence of their interests, increased the many contradictions in Chilean society, particularly those related to the functioning of the capitalist economy in an underdeveloped country. (cited in Angell 1993: 147)

Such divisions became sharply manifested in the general elections of 1970. Socialist candidate Salvador Allende won a narrow victory with 36.6 percent of the vote, as compared to the Conservative candidate, former president Jorge Alessandri, who received 35.2. Despite fears that the Congress would block Allende from taking up the presidency, Allende's promises to work within established constitutional procedures and the fallout from the assassination of General René Schneider by right-wing military officers trying to destabilise the political process, facilitated the confirmation of Allende as president in a Congressional vote. Although the Allende's opponents used the narrow margin of his victory to question the political mandate of his programme, it should be noted that the Christian Democrat candidate Tomic also advocated a significant programme of social reforms in the 1970 election as a radical attempt to break the status quo. Together, Allende and Tomic's radical reform platforms garnered 64 percent of the vote, which represents a convincing mandate for deepening the reforms of the 'Revolution in Liberty' period.

THE ALLENDE REGIME AND THE CRISIS OF THE STATE

In spite of the political uncertainties marking his election, Allende and the coalition of parties that had supported his candidacy expected to progress with their envisaged 'democratic transition to socialism' by extending and deepening three ongoing processes within Chilean society. First, by nationalising key industrial sectors, the government intended to place the most important industrial and export industries under state ownership within a sector known as the Aréa de Propiedad Social (Social Property Area). Second, Frei's agrarian reform bill had begun to break up some of the large estates that concentrated land ownership and the Allende regime aimed to speed up this fragmented process and potentially increase the number of estates appropriate for redistribution. Third, Allende intended to expand and deepen the social welfare programmes established by Frei in order to redistribute public resources and construct stronger political linkages with urban and rural social movements. Greater health and education facilities were to be provided to the poorest sections of Chilean society who had largely been marginalised from previous social welfare institutions, and low-income housing was to be built on an amplified scale. More than just redistributive policies and economic nationalism, however, the Unidad Popular aimed at consolidating a fundamental power shift within Chilean society. As cited in the electoral manifesto, the ambition of the Allende programme was to establish an 'Estado Popular' ('State of the Masses') whereby the popular classes would take power into their own hands and exercise it effectively in order to meet their needs (Barton 2004: 82). This appeared as the culmination of the trends towards social politicisation ongoing since the 1920s.

The ability of the regime to deliver on its programme, however, was circumscribed within existing power relations and new social struggles. Significantly, although the Unidad Popular had won the election and formed a government, many areas of the state apparatus remained beyond their control, including the legislature, where Allende relied on the support of the Christian Democrats to pass legislation, the judiciary and the armed forces. These wide divisions within the state apparatus forced Allende to adopt a two-pronged strategy to realise the Unidad Popular agenda. First, the government looked to forge compromises with the CDP and key members of the armed forces over policy direction by emphasising gradualism, consensus and the democratic process. Allende's initial programme of nationalisation and increasing state intervention in distributional issues, therefore, represented a compromise project that addressed the need to balance divergent interests within the Unidad Popular coalition as well as laying the ground for collaboration with the Christian Democrat party in Congress. Many aspects of the Unidad Popular agenda, such as deepening the agrarian reform and expanding social programmes, represented a further development rather than a significant break with the trajectory of the post-war Chilean state. Moreover, these initiatives were widely accepted within the CDP. Accordingly, Allende's bill to nationalise the copper industry was passed unanimously through Congress and the extension of the agrarian reform was supported by the CDP as a logical extension of Frei's earlier efforts. Between 1971 and mid-1972 more than twice as many farms were expropriated under the agrarian reform process as in the entire Frei presidency (Barton 2004).

Other elements of the programme, however, promulgated sharp divisions in the Congress and within the Unidad Popular itself, where different coalition partners hotly disputed broad areas of policy practice. The most contentious item was the regime's desire to forge a Social Property Area comprised of key industrial sectors. Opposition to this project led to the regime's second major political strategy which involved the invocation of an old constitutional statute from 1932 that allowed the expropriation of strategically important firms by presidential decree if they were judged to be suffering from production, financing or labour difficulties. Through this mechanism the regime began to forge its Social Property Area, although a key problem resided in the ambiguous definition of 'strategically important' economic sectors. Divisions existed within the Unidad Popular over which industries should be nationalised, and these uncertainties only added to the political malaise of the business class. Organised opposition to the measures were mounted through the judicial system and the Public Finance institution, both of which were used to question the legality of the nationalisation of a wide range of firms.

Within this period, the politicisation of Chilean society ongoing throughout the populist period took a new and dramatic turn. While populism had encouraged the institutionalisation of social struggle and the reconciliation of competing demands through the institutional expansion of the state, the Allende period raised the possibility of a de-institutionalisation of social struggles through direct action by varied social movements, from peasants to workers, shantytown dwellers to white collar workers, industrialists to small business owners. Through these conflicts, the basic relations of capitalist society became intensely politicised and contested. At an immediate and explicit level, the institution of private property – the bedrock of capitalist social relations – came under siege through the government's Social Property Area and agrarian reform. At a more subtle level, however, the power relations that stem from ownership rights became challenged as an empowered labour movement sought to refashion the shop floor relations through which industries could operate. Similarly, with the Unidad Popular seeking to guarantee the consumption rights of the Chilean working classes through extra-market mechanisms such as mandated wage increases and increased social programmes, the very foundations of a capitalist society operating according to the exchange of privately-owned commodities were destabilised.

These initiatives garnered substantial popular support, particularly as the immediate impact of the Unidad Popular social programmes furnished many working-class Chileans with a notable improvement in living conditions. As Jonathan Barton (2004: 11) highlights, government social spending was over 50 percent higher in the Allende years as compared to the Frei presidency, with significant increases in health, education and housing expenditures. As a result, medical and dental attention and social security provision were greatly expanded, alongside large-scale housing projects and provision of materials and technical support for self-constructed units. Rent and housing payments were set at no more than 10 per cent of family income in order to ensure that housing remained affordable. Unsurprisingly, a wave of popular support enabled the Unidad Popular to increase its seat holdings in the municipal elections of April 1971.

In spite of these successes, however, the programme necessarily engendered medium-term economic disequilibria and vigorous political opposition from the bourgeosie. Founded upon price controls, general wage hikes and deficit spending, the demand-driven growth strategy initially served to increase production in domestic consumer industries. Nevertheless, the inflation rate also began an ominous rise and the government deficit grew at a rapid pace, eventually equalling 50 percent of the entire government budget in 1973. Concurrently, the nationalisation of key industries – particularly that of copper – at first provided the regime with a reasonably vibrant state sector. However, the tendency to respond to the growing number of industrial conflicts by nationalising the enterprises beset by conflict brought many smaller and less profitable industries into the state's purview. By 1973, companies within the state's Social Property Area represented 39 percent of GDP, as opposed to 14.2 percent in 1965 (Fernández Jilberto 2000: 105). Moreover, the political uncertainty surrounding the regime and the trend towards nationalisation made small and medium sized capitals located in the domestic consumption sector extremely reluctant to invest, even to cover the renewal of machinery necessary for the production process (Fortín 1985: 150).

The economic crisis also grew in intensity owing to the unrelenting attempts of the Chilean bourgeoisie and the US government to undermine the material foundations of the Unidad Popular project. They did this by cutting off production, investment and external markets, which amounted to a strategy of, in President Nixon's words, 'making the economy scream'. Through US pressure, the Allende regime had also been excluded from World Bank and IMF loans and the Nixon administration blocked the rescheduling of its foreign debts. Notwithstanding this aggression, however, it was evident that medium-term structural problems would arise owing to the schism between a political project that sought to redistribute power and wealth, and its articulation within capitalist social relations predicated on private property and the extraction of social surplus by the owners of capital in the form of profit. In sum, while Allende's government acted under the banner of moving towards a socialist future, the immediate effects of restructuring were to rely upon and deepen the state's economic role and expand redistributionist aspects within a capitalist framework. The upshot of these actions was to further undermine the basis for capital accumulation, prompting the unleashing of even greater crisis tendencies that were sharply manifested in growing inflationary pressures and intensified social struggles.

Ultimately, the Unidad Popular did not possess the political strength to overcome these acute fractures by deepening the reform programme to a point where Chilean social relations had been fundamentally transformed. Excessive centralisation of Unidad Popular political structures and the failure to build a more grassroots-driven movement contributed to these political weaknesses (Harnecker 2003). Strikes broke out in Santiago in the winter of 1972, led by small and medium business owners who were threatened by rising wages and inflation. Other right-wing groups pursued a more violent paramilitary strategy of destabilisation. In response, a groundswell of community and workers' organisations mobilised in defence of the regime, particularly when military intervention began to look more likely in late 1972. As Lois Hecht Oppenheim (1999: 81) has argued:

The degree of participation in the rallies was also a sign of how the crisis had become generalised to society. The institutions of the state were incapable of resolving the political crisis; instead, the conflict was being played out in the streets.

Although in 1973 the Allende government prepared to moderate some of its reforms, other elements of the state-system began to mobilise in a contrary fashion. The bourgeoisie and allies perceived, in Guillermo O'Donnell's (1979: 295) words, 'a great threat to the survival of the basic capitalist parameters of society' and applied increasing pressure upon the armed forces to restore order. In so doing, they wished to re-confine state actions within the limits of capitalist social relations and therein reaffirm the basis for renewed capital accumulation. Notably, in the months leading up to the coup d'état, power within the armed forces gravitated towards the anti-Allende pole and those opposed to military intervention were ejected from their positions (cf. Collier and Sater 2004: 357). With the crisis of accumulation deepening and the US government openly supporting the growing anti-Allende forces, the military emerged from the barracks on 11 September 1973 and unleashed a bloody yet successful coup d'état during which Allende was killed. This violent ending of the Allende period brought a half century of national developmentalism to a close and ushered in a new and uncertain era.

SUMMARY

This chapter has charted how the contradictions of capitalist development in Chile that manifested themselves so severely in the depression of the 1920s and 1930s resulted in the emergence of a populist state within the aegis of a national-developmentalist political strategy. The period of 'national developmentalism' was characterised by growing state intervention to engineer changes in social structures and to further the construction of an industrial base that was intended to facilitate a transition to modernity, as judged by the mass-consumption industrial societies of the capitalist core. Within it, established political parties sought to alleviate social conflicts by mediating the demands of varied social movements and interest groups by incorporating their social and political demands through the formation of new state institutions, including welfare and labour institutions. Two extremely important outcomes of this process were the rapid expansion of the state apparatus and the growing politicisation of Chilean society. Far from securing a harmonious transition to modern nationhood, however, national developmentalism served to politicise the contradictions of capitalist development within the framework of an expanding state apparatus. Conflicts over the direction of state intervention and tensions between the reproduction of capital within Chile and its integration into global capitalism repeatedly generated moments of crisis within the Chilean development project. These trends peaked in the late 1960s and early 1970s with the Frei government's failed 'Revolution in Liberty' and the Allende government's attempted 'Democratic Transition to Socialism'. The military coup of September 1973 put a bloody end to the Allende regime yet left the new authoritarian regime desperately searching for a method to resolve the ongoing crisis of Chilean society.

2

'Chicago to the Rescue' –
The Emergence of Neoliberalism in Chile

The crisis of the Allende period shattered any remaining illusions of a linear and peaceful movement towards national development. In spite of the structuralist vision that modernisation was achievable through growing state intervention in economy and society, the project ran into the dual barriers of stagnation in key branches of production and escalating class-based struggles that politicised the fundamental relations of capitalist development. For many on the left, the limits to a socialist strategy that viewed the seizure of the capitalist state as its primary goal had been manifested. Although the Allende government had used state institutions to raise wages, nationalise industries, redistribute land and introduce new social programmes, the end result was not a democratic transition to socialism but the outbreak of intense crisis and escalating political confrontation. Most perceptibly, in undermining the conditions for the expanded reproduction of capital, the state clashed against the conditions of its own existence. Decreasing revenues and escalating intra-state conflicts occurred precisely at the moment when increased state expenditures and internal cohesion were necessary.

As the crisis deepened, the control of the coercive apparatus exercised by military leaders committed to reversing the trajectory towards a deepened, and potentially socialist, national-developmentalist trajectory proved decisive. For these actors – and the Chilean political right in general – the dramatic escalation of social conflict was perceived to have undermined some of the basic parameters of capitalist society. On the one hand, it was recognised that the mounting politicisation of Chilean society and the social mobilisation it gave rise to served to unite economic and political struggles as social movements adopted a more explicit class-based character and levied direct material demands upon the state. Rather than pursuing the goals of material reproduction through private and individualised exchanges within the capitalist economy, social movements pursued collective political activities that looked beyond market institutions to ensure their social reproduction. In this context, the boundaries between economic and political life that are fundamental to capitalist social relations seemed to be crumbling. Furthermore, the rule of law, with private property its most sacred tenet, was shaken through state expropriation of a growing number of industries and the deepened agrarian reform process. These accelerating tendencies generated an increasingly frantic call for the re-establishment of the rule of law, the upholding of property rights and a renewed respect for a sharp separation between economics and politics.

Under these increasingly polarised circumstances, the existing divisions within the state apparatus continued to widen, culminating in the coup d'état of 11 September 1973. On seizing power, the authoritarian regime sought to reassert as rapidly as possible the conditions for social pacification and sustained capital accumulation. Although their expertise in the means of coercion would prove to be an important tool, the new state managers soon realised that suppressing militancy and activism by repressing labour and social movements might not be sufficient to achieve their broader goals. With those on the right blaming the political process itself for the ills of the country (Borzutzky 2002: 156), the authoritarian regime viewed society as needing to be purged not only of the politicians responsible for the crisis, but of the very politicisation that seemed to be imbued in existing social institutions. A more profound process of social transformation therefore appeared necessary, one that could profoundly reorganise the prevailing social relationships institutionalised within Chilean society and put an end to the cycles of conflict and crisis. This aim was stated explicitly by the authoritarian regime, which proclaimed in a 'Declaration of Principles' in 1974 that it wanted to give Chile 'a new institutional basis ... to rebuild the country morally, institutionally and materially'. Moreover, it sought to initiate 'a new phase in the nation's destiny, opening the way for new generations of Chileans that had been schooled in virtuous civic habits' (cited in Taylor 1998).

Quite how it could achieve these goals, however, the authoritarian regime was uncertain. This indecision intensified in the context of a mounting economic crisis that aggravated the state's already precarious fiscal position. Although it was unafraid to exercise its expertise in the means of coercion, repressing social movements and the simple cessation of the formal political process would not accomplish the degree of long-term social transformation that the regime desired. A more fundamental renovation of social institutions would be necessary: one that could reassert a renewed separation of politics and economics by atomising the collective subjectivities forged in the previous decades, reasserting the rule of law and the primacy of private property, and by removing the state as the primary target of social mobilisation. The Pinochet dictatorship, however, did not seize the reins of government with a pre-established plan and lacked a strategy of sufficient sophistication to achieve these aims beyond short-term repression. Rather, its policy formation would necessarily prove to be reactive, changing course in response to new manifestations of economic and political crisis.

Short-term political stability was, nonetheless, expressly important for the regime and its first actions were aimed at solving the immediate political crisis through a policy of fierce repression that served to annihilate the political forces that had challenged the foundations of Chilean capitalism. Violence and persecution were justified by the Pinochet regime as merely the adequate tactics in a war to save the Chilean fatherland from a foreign-influenced Marxist menace. Under the pretext of ensuring 'national security', the regime initiated a period of human insecurity during which over 3,000 people were 'disappeared', and tens of thousands of activists were jailed, tortured or exiled. The repression was at its most intense in the immediate post-coup years, yet it remained present throughout the duration of the regime, with the period 1984–88 alone being marked by 163 political murders, 446 cases of torture and 1,927 political arrests, all committed with legal impunity (Petras and Leiva 1994: 124).

The primary achievement of repression was the decapitation of organised labour, the destruction of autonomous and politically active social movements, and the general suppression of political opposition including the established political parties. Together, the assault on organised labour, social movements and political parties enforced a relative stabilisation of the political climate and created the political pacification under which painful economic adjustment measures and the dramatic reshaping of established social institutions could be commenced. The violence and repression from which Chilean neoliberalism was born drew only partial condemnation from the United States government, which encouraged the anti-socialist character of the coup. Similarly, violent political oppression did not dissuade international organisations such as the World Bank from re-establishing a close relationship with the Chilean state. The World Bank made seven loans for infrastructural projects in the three years following the coup, rising to a total of 30 over the entire period of the dictatorship.

THE MATERIALISATION OF THE NEOLIBERAL PROJECT IN CHILE

Although unrestrained state coercion liquidated opposition and cultivated a political climate in which profound social restructuring was possible, the early years of the Pinochet regime were characterised by notable uncertainty over policy direction. Such ambiguities were reflected in divisions within the military junta and schisms within the Chilean bourgeoisie, of which many fractions, such as leading industrialists, were strongly wedded to the continuation of structuralist policies of industrial support (cf. Winn 2004a). These class-based interests, while clearly expecting the authoritarian regime to assert a new discipline upon workers within the factories and social movements outside, envisaged a return to a normalised trajectory of national developmentalism. Outside of the copper industry, other minor export sectors, and a handful of economic groups rooted in the financial sector, the Chilean bourgeoisie was materially wedded to a mode of capital accumulation in which state institutions played a significant role in protecting domestic industry, facilitating loans and credit and supporting domestic demand for goods through social policy initiatives. Neoliberal policies of state austerity and rapid liberalisation – which would inevitably cause mass bankruptcies in major industrial sectors – were therefore neither expected nor desired by the majority of the Chilean bourgeoisie, which espoused the necessity for the established Keynesian-inspired state intervention to overcome the present economic crisis. In simplified terms, Keynes had advocated that governments induced an increase in the supply of money to promote both investment and consumption:

The wisest course is to advance on both fronts at once ... to promote investments and at the same time, to promote consumption, not merely to the level which, with the existing propensity to consume, would correspond to the increased investment, but to a higher level still. (Keynes, from *The General Theory*, cited in Neary and Taylor 1998)

Deficit-financed government expenditures were intended to stimulate investment and consumption, leading in theory to a virtuous circle in which an expansion of economic activity would overcome the downward turn of the business cycle and provide increased resources through taxation for the state to cover its original deficit. The Chilean industrial bourgeoisie therefore expected an expansion of government credit through the nationalised banking system and new protectionist measures that could, at least temporarily, reduce competitive pressures from foreign producers.

Given these strong class interests and the hegemony of conventional Keynesian-influenced economic theory at both national and global levels, it could be perceived as counter-intuitive that over the course of its first two crisis-stricken years the authoritarian regime was drawn towards a heterodox strategy presented by a small group of Chilean economists that ran counter to all such expectations. This influential clique of economists working at the Catholic University in Santiago – who became known as the 'Chicago Boys' owing to their training by Chicago School economists – were avid propagators of the neoclassical critique of Keynesianism developed at Chicago and of the neoliberal policy prescription justified by the former. Mainstream economists and most politicians, however, tended to regard them as extremist proponents of a doctrine that history had already proved false in the experience of the 1920s nitrate crisis and Great Depression. Further, as indicated above, the Chilean bourgeoisie rooted in industrial production saw their prescriptions as a direct challenge to their survival.

To explain the disjuncture between expectation and practice in the early years of the dictatorship, it is necessary to understand the rise and reproduction of neoliberalism in terms of, firstly, the severity of the crisis that afflicted Chilean society and, secondly, the contention of neoliberal ideology to be able to address that crisis not merely at the surface level of economic disequilibria but also at the constitutive level of social relations. In the following sections, I demonstrate how the neoclassical roots of neoliberal policy practice provide more than simply an alternative economic doctrine. Rather, they build from a particular normative theory of social interaction and, from this base, offer a multifaceted political strategy that proclaims to refashion social relations in a way that will depoliticise and reinvigorate society by imposing self-regulating market institutions as the essential organising principle of social life.

FROM NEOCLASSICISM TO NEOLIBERALISM

The political practices of neoliberalism find their theoretical legitimation in the neoclassical tradition of economics, which represents a development and reassertion of the approach generated within the marginalist revision of economic thought that arose in the 1870s. In the eyes of its proponents, the marginalist revolution set economics on a rigorous scientific basis by providing a theory of price determination that is predicated on the subjective actions of individuals. In so doing, marginalism rejected the theories of value and their concurrent attention to class relations that had preoccupied classical political economy (Clarke 1991a). At the core of the marginalist revolution was the founding premise that capitalist society can be analysed as an agglomeration of pre-formed individuals, each of whom acts rationally according to the criteria of maximising her own satisfaction by exchanging privately owned goods. In this model, the modern individual is conceptualised as a private owner of property who is able to trade her commodities under conditions of equality, reciprocity and freedom in order to improve the subjectively measured value of her goods, which is referred to as utility. Neoclassicism then proceeds to use this abstraction in order to model a social universe composed of freely exchanging individuals whose private activities are coordinated by a market mechanism that arises spontaneously from the rationality and freedom of the actors involved. Within this construct, there is little room for any factors beyond the rational individual pursuit of self-interest through exchange activities. As John Brohman (1995: 297) has critiqued:

People are reduced to isolated creatures of the marketplace, devoid of history, cultural traditions, political opinions and social relationships beyond simple market exchanges. The conventional assumption is that non-market relations and institutions – the broader environments within which economies operate – are universal, unchanging, and have no significant impact on economic activities.

Not only are private exchanges viewed as the natural and therefore transhistorical quality of humanity – enshrined in Adam Smith's dictum of man's natural propensity to truck, barter and trade – they are also seen to serve the common good through the harmonising mechanism of the market. As Milton Friedman articulates, the basis of neoclassicism is the 'elementary proposition that both parties to an economic transaction benefit from it, provided the transaction is bilaterally voluntary and informed' (Friedman 1962: 55). The immediate appearance of exchange, therefore, is a rational encounter between two individuals seeking to maximise the utility of the possessions they hold in relation to their personal material needs and desires. If the exchange does not serve the self-interest of both parties, then it will not take place. Exchange is therefore a rational occurrence that reconciles the scarcity of goods with diverging tastes, desires and wants.

Neoclassicism takes the formal rationality of an abstract individual exchange and generalises it to the level of the capitalist society as a whole, within which the market appears as a spontaneous coordinating mechanism that aligns the atomised pursuit of self-interest by individuals possessing different goods into a socially optimal whole. As emphasised by the Austrian tradition (Hayek 1973), rational individuals will make economic decisions based on the information codified in the form of prices. Prices in turn represent the agglomeration of individual evaluations concerning the relative utility of finite goods. Predicated on the simple rational decisions of economic actors, this process is expected to generate the optimal distribution of society's resources as capital is invested in the areas of highest productivity as these offer the highest returns. Money, the instrument of exchange and account, functions simply as a rational device to expedite a system of exchanges. It serves as the social oil to facilitate the rationality of the system. As such, the stability of money itself is necessary for the sound communication of information to and between market actors in the form of prices. If these conditions are in place, the market is seen as an optimising and equilibrating institution.

The emphasis on exchange as the fundamental relationship of rational society is reflected in the neoclassical representation of production. The latter is comprehended as a technical exercise of combining through market exchanges the necessary factors of production (capital, land, labour) in order to create final products with greater marginal utility. This represents a judgement on behalf of the individual to defer immediate consumption by deploying capital in order to produce goods with greater utility. The production process, moreover, rewards the individual possessors of each factor of production according to the relative value of their contribution and the overall utility of the final product. In effect, this excludes the possibility of a direct relationship between profits, wages and rent – and therein between the classes of capitalists, workers and landowners – as each is derived from 'natural' laws governing the value of commodities (Kay 1975: 4). The value of the wage, for example, reflects the relative marginal productivity of labour in a particular task as a portion of the final utility of the good produced. The latter, in turn, merely reflects the aggregation of individual evaluations of the marginal utility of a particular item. The relationship between the owners of capital and the working class, therefore, is seen merely as a series of equivalent and equal exchanges between individual commodity owners, a factor to which we return below.

Two expressly important further propositions are built on these assumptions. First, given that the endless nature of human needs and desires must be reconciled with the finite provision of material goods (the condition of scarcity), the institution of private property that provides the legal basis for appropriation of scarce resources by the private individual is derived as the rational manifestation of a need to restrict potential conflict and anarchy. The sanctity of private property not only sustains the system of exchange, and therefore facilitates social rationality, but also upholds the relationship between contribution and reward that promotes the entrepreneurship integral to a dynamic economy. Ensuring the exercise of property rights – and the soundness of the contracting system that permits the exchange of property – therefore is the fundamental task of the state, and neoliberal political practice consequently seeks to retrench or remove state institutions that weaken the sanctity of private property and strengthen those that fortify it.

Second, if the market is presumed to be rational and lead naturally to the optimal distribution of resources, any distortion of market transactions by extra-market forces, such as government policy, collective interest groups or private monopolies, are deemed to infringe on overall efficiency. The latter are conceived as artificial and illegitimate impediments upon a condition in which individual rationality and freedom is maximised to the benefit of the common good. In particular, despite their proclaimed intention to serve the common good, state actors suffer from, at best, limited knowledge and foresight that undermines their ability to make efficient decisions. At worst they are prone to influence by special interests, rent seeking, and decision-making based on short-term political gain. As a result state actions will inevitably tend towards irrationality and the resulting compromised market signals will lead economic agents to make further sub-optimal decisions, therein escalating the cycle of inefficiency and interrupting the self-equilibrating tendency that would otherwise prevail. As such, state intervention threatens to rupture the formal rationality of the market imposed by the price mechanism. In consequence, neoliberal policy practice indicates the need for governments to provide a stable framework for market transactions and should refrain from interventions that would alter market outcomes. Whereas Keynesian-influenced theories of demand management encouraged governments to build state institutions that proactively regulate consumption and investment in order to maximise demand within the economy, neoliberals suggest that such actions distort natural market prices leading to sub-optimal investment decisions and a drop in overall economic output. Moreover, by breaking the nexus of effort to reward that the market is seen to promote, state interventions that subvert market forces create a dependency of actors on the state's discretionary and politically motivated decisions rather than on the neutral, efficient and harmonising mechanism of the market.

THE ECONOMICS OF NOWHERE AND THE POLITICS OF CHILE

As a host of economic sociologists, heterodox economists and others have pointed out, the restrictive initial assumptions of neoclassical economics – including, but not limited to, the notion of the utility-maximising individual, and the assumptions of full information and perfect competition – undermine its ability to explain actually-existing capitalist society. Accordingly, Geoffrey Hodgson (1999) has termed it the 'economics of nowhere' and others have labelled it as 'autistic' owing to its inability to engage with society beyond the confines of formalistic models (Fullbrook 2005). The strength of neoclassical economics for policymakers, however, was not its analytical precision, but rather the political implications of its projections. As Simon Clarke (1991a) reminds us, the intention of the marginalist revolution in establishing economics on foundations akin to the natural sciences was not to provide a rigorous account of actually-existing economic institutions. Rather, it was to offer an ideal type with which society could be judged according to scientifically grounded ideas of rationality and efficiency. This explicit normative dimension, wrapped in the trappings of a formalistic and 'value-free' science of economics, lies at the heart of neoclassicism and is directly juxtaposed into the core of the neoliberal project. Far from being deterred by the gap between abstract models and existing social processes, neoliberals use the divergence of ideal type and reality to justify reforms that are envisioned to make reality more closely approximate the ideal type. At its essential core, neoliberalism is an ambitious project of social engineering that attempts to restructure social institutions in order to coerce reality into the axioms of human interaction projected by neoclassical economics. The scale and ambition of this project should not be doubted. To invert the proverb, because Muhammad would not go to the mountain, the mountain had to be brought to him.

In this vein, Margaret Thatcher's oft-cited quip that 'there is no such thing as society, [just] individual men and women and families' is best understood not as an analysis of actually-existing social relations, for in which case it would be patently false, but a statement of aims. It was the ideological front for a radical strategy of social restructuring, one that sought to obliterate existing institutionalised forms of social relations that sanctioned collective and extra-market forms of social interaction and replace them with a society that conformed to the methodological individualism integral to neoclassical theory. Given that actually-existing society did not represent neoclassical ideals, neoclassicism provided a seemingly scientific basis for reforming social institutions to meet those ideals. Society could be harmonised – and crisis tendencies extinguished – by forcibly restraining social aspirations within the seemingly objective limits of marketised social relations. So long as individuals submit to the play of market forces mediated through monetary relations, the neoclassical argument contends, the optimal conditions for capital accumulation will predominate to the benefit of the individual and common good. Neoliberalism is a programme of drastic social engineering aimed to ensure society corresponds to such a scenario.

According to the reformers, accomplishing the latter involves the removal of institutional constraints that prevent society operating in the manner of the abstract models of neoclassical economics. Social institutions are durable systems of established and embedded social rules and conventions that structure social interactions (Hodgson 2001: 295). In so doing, social institutions inevitably constrain yet also enable certain forms of social activity and thereby structure the social terrain upon which some social interactions are possible while others are restricted. In the context of the Chilean crisis, the constraints to creating a more fully market-driven society were diagnosed as residing primarily in the institutionalised forms of state–society relations that, first, embedded the social power of collective social actors to levy demands upon the state – including labour unions, social movements and other interest groups; and, second, that shielded some social actors from the regulatory disciplines of the market. The latter institutions included the systematic economic interventions associated with national developmentalism, such as industrial policies and tariffs, but also labour and welfare institutions that mediated the exposure of individuals and households to market forces. Further, these two aspects were not unrelated but were mutually reinforcing, with collective actors pressing for institutional expansion that resulted in an expanded basis for further collective action.

A process of far-reaching institutional change was envisaged not only to remove these distorting factors but also simultaneously eradicate the institutional foundations upon which collective social actors had formed and acted. Based on the methodological individualism of the neoclassical tradition, all collective subjects are seen as special interest groups that inhibit rational individual decisions based on utility maximisation. In this respect, judging institutional configurations on the basis of neoclassical economics 'generally leads to the conclusion that the only institutions we should have are those – such as property rights and the rule of law – which enforce the roles of competition and exit, and hence limit the role of bonding or groups' (Storper 2005). In the name of the neutrality and rationality of the market, neoliberalism sanctions a concerted assault on all institutions that sanction the instigation of collective social action. In so doing, neoliberalism considers its prescription for institutional restructuring to result in the formal liberation of the individual from society through the elimination of institutional aberrations that have withheld the highest state of individual rationality and utility maximisation.

The appeal of this project for the authoritarian regime was not only that it offered a concrete programme of reforms to tackle the economic crisis, but also these same measures appeared able to realise a systematic depoliticisation of Chilean society and therefore resolve the political and social dimensions of crisis. By breaking up institutionalised patterns of social interaction that both facilitated the formation of collective social actors and systematically mediated market outcomes through state interventions, neoliberalism sought to coerce society into the methodological individualism that it championed as rational and efficient. The thorough reform of institutional structures was envisaged to destroy existing social institutions – such as industrial policies, welfare systems and labour institutions – which had become entrenched sites of political conflict between collective social actors. In contrast, new institutions would compel actors to align their expectations and actions to the seemingly neutral and objective movement of market forces. Instead of the interest-driven and inefficient mediation of the state, neoliberals claimed, market interactions were apolitical, rational and led to mutually positive outcomes, therein providing the basis for a new and prosperous route to development.

As a consequence, restructuring would permit the reduction of the political process into a largely technocratic science. Rather than relying on the discretional power of state managers to regulate various social relationships – a power that would be constantly subject to arbitrary and unceasing social pressures – the neoliberal project envisaged profound institutional transformation through which state and society together would be forced to limit individual and collective actions within the parameters set by rational market forces. Government could be turned into 'governance', the facilitation of market processes through building strong institutions that enforce the 'rules of the game' to compel all actors to work within the structures of a market economy. Simultaneously, the autonomy and isolation of technocrats who can assess policy choices on neutral efficiency criteria must also be safeguarded. The science of economics was proclaimed to offer a neutral and value-free method of calculating the efficiency of the social institutions through which individuals can achieve their ends. Such was the resolute faith of Chilean neoliberals in their comprehension of society that, in an interview with *The Economist* in 1980, leading neoliberal reformer José Piñera stated that:

The laws of economic science merely unearth and reveal objective aspects of reality, a reality which cannot be ignored because it is known that to act against nature is counter-productive and self-deceiving. (cited in Valdés 1995: 31)

Within the dramatic conditions of a seemingly intractable economic crisis, this larger project of social transformation attracted the authoritarian state managers because it promised an immediate strategy through which to begin implementing their desired reconstruction of Chilean society. Withdrawing the state from historically developed and institutionalised roles – such as price controls, wage agreements, welfare policies, industrial policy – and reinserting the primacy of the market was argued to offer not only a solution to the economic manifestation of crisis by controlling inflation and restructuring the productive apparatus, but also a mechanism of societal depoliticisation by obliterating the circumstances in which politics had become a means for attaining social and economic ends. At one and the same time, therefore, neoliberalism seemed to offer a solution to the existing economic crisis and the means to eradicate the configuration of social relations that had driven the country repeatedly toward crisis over the previous half-decade.

Neoliberal political practice is therefore categorically not 'economic' in nature, but represents an attempt to restructure the basic social relations through which society reproduces itself on a day-to-day, year-to-year basis. It was this duality of purpose, rather than the unproven functionality of its economic remedies, that underscored the eventual embrace of neoliberal policy prescription by the Chilean authoritarian regime. Indeed, despite the vigorous claims of the Chicago Boys, neoliberal economic policies were initially rebuffed by the regime and there existed considerable doubt that these throwback ideas to an earlier stage of capitalism could be effective. It was only when more gradualist measures failed to resolve the deepening crisis that the authoritarian regime began to listen more directly to this group of economists who professed to be able not only to mitigate the surface manifestations of economic crisis but to eradicate its social roots.

THE STATE AND NEOLIBERALISM

To achieve the degree of transformation implicit in neoliberal restructuring necessitated the armouring of social reform with the zealous application of coercive repression to overcome opposition on the streets, in the factories, and from within the state apparatus itself. The early neoliberal reformers were explicit that authoritarianism was an essential prerequisite to their project as the strong hand of the state was necessary to bestow the political space in which rational reforms that adversely affected entrenched interests could be implemented. The project to turn government into a technocratic process driven by the objective projections of economic science would inevitably be fiercely resisted by those who were wedded to the social, political and economic institutions that such a strategy would destroy. These included the industrial bourgeoisie, the labour movements and the large sections of the working classes who benefited from socialised provision of welfare. To circumvent such opposition, the Chicago Boys adamantly prescribed that the democracy of the post-war period needed to be temporarily suspended so that a new market democracy could be created in which a strong state would fashion the institutional conditions for a new social order. As Pablo Baraona, Minister for the Economy between 1976 and 1979, stated:

The new democracy ... will have to be authoritarian, in the sense that the rules needed for the system's stability cannot be subjected to political processes

... [and] technocratised, in the sense that political bodies should not decide technical issues but restrict themselves to evaluating results, leaving to the technocracy the responsibility of using logical procedures for resolving problems or offering alternative solutions. (cited in Vergara 1985)

Politics was to be reconstituted as a depoliticised and technocratic exercise of responding to economic 'facts' – such as inflation rates, balance of payments, capital account fluctuations – in accordance with the theoretical dictates of neoclassical economics. This was most evident in the monetarist emphasis on 'sound monetary policy' to ensure the tendency of the unimpeded market to reach equilibrium, which placed the maintenance of price stability above all other economic and social considerations. On this basis, the singular proactive function of the state is to help enforce market discipline upon society and its own institutional bodies alike in the name of the common good. This implies an important role for a strong state in disciplining both state and society to adhere to the process and outcomes of marketised social relations and, particularly, the preservation of fiscal responsibility through balanced budgets (World Bank 1997; cf. Bonefeld 2005). It was in this respect that Karl Polanyi (2001: 140), who examined an earlier period of market liberalism, observed that: 'the road to the free market was opened and kept open by an enormous increase in continuous, centrally organized, and controlled interventionism'.

As the above implies, the commonly propounded notion that neoliberalism entails a retreat of the state is entirely erroneous. It results from a perspective that views the state and market as opposed forms of social organisation, rather than two moments of the wider conjuncture of capitalist social relations (Müller and Neusüss 1975; Holloway and Picciotto 1977; Clarke 1988; Bonefeld 2000). While neoclassicism views the market as a spontaneous or ad-hoc phenomenon emerging from the haphazard interactions of free individuals, economic sociologists have emphasised how all markets require systematic organisation and regulation in order to function in a sustained manner (Sayer 1995). Put differently, markets are a deeply institutionalised form of social interaction, and in capitalism this institutionalisation rests upon multiple and prolonged state activities. Neoliberal social engineering therefore restructures state–society relations not in order to weaken the state but rather to strengthen those state institutions that create and reinforce the disciplinary power of markets while minimising those that can undermine such discipline. The neoliberal state is therefore by no means a weak state and, of necessity, it must constantly intervene across a range of social relations in order to reproduce the conditions for a market-orientated society. As Geoffrey Hodgson (1999: 82) succinctly elaborates: 'The creation and maintenance of private property rights and functioning market institutions require the sustained intervention of the state to constrain or eject economic forms and institutions that are antagonistic to private ownership and the market system. "Free" markets have to be preserved by an activist and efficient state.'

As the following chapters elaborate in detail, state institutions that uphold the regulatory power of markets are made more robust through neoliberal restructuring. This includes those institutions associated with property rights and contracting, such as the judiciary and taxation system, and also those that uphold the social power of money within capitalist society, most evident in the creation of an independent central bank with a mandate to pursue monetary stability in isolation from all political considerations (see also Burnham 2000; Campbell and Pedersen 2001; Saad-Filho 2005). Simultaneously, the forms of retrenchment that are frequently associated with the retreat of the state – such as privatisation of state-owned enterprises and of state-provided social services – serve to strengthen state institutions that uphold market regulation by disembedding the state system from functions that previously enmeshed it within political struggles in diverse social ambits. The latter range from labour institutions that entangled the state in conflicts over production; economic institutions that involved the state in influencing the pattern of investment and the relative prosperity of various economic sectors; through to welfare state institutions that engaged the state in directly regulating the social reproduction of individuals, households and social classes.

Even within the bosom of authoritarianism, however, a systematic programme of social transformation could be neither a short-term project nor a smooth process of implementing predetermined policies. As the following chapters detail, neoliberal restructuring in Chile would be unevenly implemented as the authoritarian regime reacted to unforeseen consequences and political struggles. Pointedly, the disjuncture between the 'economics of nowhere' and Chilean society would prove to be intractable: not because of a lack of determination to impose the social restructuring project, but rather because of critical flaws in the social theory upon which it is based. Before proceeding to examine how the authoritarian regime embarked on its ambitious project of social engineering in a more concrete fashion, it is useful to consider the failings of neoclassical economics as a basis on which to comprehend the contradictions of the political project of neoliberalism. This is not merely an academic question, for the incongruities of the neoclassical vision of society are manifest in the conflict-ridden and crisis-prone trajectory of neoliberal social restructuring.

CAPITALISM AND THE IRRATIONALITIES OF NEOLIBERALISM

Unfortunately for the neoliberal utopians – but more so for the Chilean population subjected to their grandiose project of social engineering – the vision they pursued was unrealisable owing to the implausibility of the assumptions from which neoclassical theories of the market begin. As highlighted above, the idealised market of freely interacting, utility maximising individuals is itself dependent upon a whole range of social institutions that do not and cannot operate according to market principles. In this manner, the central weakness of neoclassical economics is that it considers the act of exchange in isolation from the social relations in which it is necessarily embedded. This is most strikingly demonstrated in the way that neoclassical economics views the maximisation of utility in conditions of scarce resources as an unchanging and invariable question across history that allows the same methodological principles to be applied equally to Robinson Crusoe's desert island as to contemporary capitalist society. Inevitably, such an approach is unable to comprehend the specificities of capitalist (or any other) social relations and the historically evolving institutional forms in which they are embedded (Hodgson 2001).

A systematic critique of neoclassical perspectives is beyond the purview of this chapter (see Weeks 1989; Clarke 1991a; DeMartino 2000). Nonetheless, it is useful to highlight several key contradictions inherent to capitalist social relations that are either ignored or misconstrued within the neoclassical tradition. This is expressly important because such contradictions emerge as ghosts in the neoliberal machine, repeatedly injecting tension and conflict into the trajectory of restructuring in Chile. To understand the disjuncture between the neoclassical theory of society and actually-existing capitalist social relations, the following section engages Marx's account of how the formal rationality of market exchanges are embedded within a substantively irrational mode of social production (Marx

1973; Marx 1976; cf. Weeks 1981; Clarke 1988; Postone 1993). Marx's analysis – supplemented with insights from branches of heterodox political economy and economic sociology – sheds light on four systematic yet contradictory social phenomena that are central to an understanding of the nature and consequences of neoliberalism. First, contrary to a vision of money as the rational tool of exchange, Marx highlighted the dominating social power of money; second, in lieu of the equal market interactions between individuals, Marx emphasised the conflictual relations between social classes in which exchange is embedded; third, in contradistinction to asserting a harmonious market mechanism serving the common good, Marx analysed the systematic insecuritisation of social reproduction for a majority of individuals and households; and, fouth, in contrast to the vision of the market tending towards equilibrium, Marx sought to explain the inherent tendency toward destructive crises.

At the core of Marx's analysis is his critique of Adam Smith's ([1776] 1991) proposed 'self-evident truth' that consumption is the purpose of production in capitalism, an assumption that remains axiomatic within the neoclassical tradition. In contrast to Smith, Marx argued that within capitalist social relations it is 'self-evident' that the production of material goods is orientated not to consumption needs but to the creation and appropriation of profit. As a result, far from being a technical device to liberate individuals in the pursuit of self-determined desires, the capitalist marketplace stands within a framework of social production in which social needs are subordinated to the accumulation of capital. The consequences of the subordination of exchange to the overarching framework of capitalist social relations are manifold. In contrast to the neoclassical approach, the rationality of exchange and money cannot be judged in abstraction from the social relations in which they are embedded.

As Simon Clarke (1990) has argued, the neoclassical theory of the market is a theory of a social institution that does not exist. Capitalist society is not simply an agglomeration of freely interacting rational individuals who exchange goods in conditions of equivalence to pursue self-determined ends. Rather, it is a class society constituted by socially determined actors operating within the context of social relations that evaluate individual actions based on their contribution to the accumulation of capital. On the one hand, the owners of capital are obliged through the pressures of competition to secure an amount of monetary profit adequate to secure their reproduction as a capitalist. On the other, workers – who enjoy no independent access to the means of subsistence – are obliged to sell their capacity to labour ('labour-power') for money in order to acquire temporarily the goods for subsistence and avoid immiseration. Under such conditions, far from acting as a simple means of exchange, money becomes an autonomous social power that facilitates not the freedom of the individual from society, but acts as a social mediation that compels individuals to align their existence within the parameters of the expanded reproduction of capital. The capitalist who is unable to meet the demands of the market by exchanging goods for money, faces bankruptcy. Similarly, the worker who is unable to find a purchaser for her labour-power faces immiseration.

More than this, however, money acts as a materialised form of social power by providing those who possess concentrated supplies to enjoy its alchemic powers by turning money into more money. At essence, this involves purchasing the commodified labour-power of the working class and appropriating the surplus created by putting such labour to work (Neary and Taylor 1998). Capitalist social relations are therefore not the accidental relationships of free and equal individuals exchanging goods but are the socially reproduced relationships between classes. Class, in this usage, refers not to social stratification through income levels, skill sets, or group identity, as in the sociological tradition, but to the question of ownership or non-ownership of the means of production, therein capturing a fundamental structural differentiation of the capitalist social division of labour (Sayer 1995). Clearly, this understanding of class operates at a high level of abstraction, yet it recognises a fundamental social relationship on the basis of which other more complex and nuanced processes and structures arise or, indeed, are circumscribed. I am not suggesting that class is the primary locus of identification for individuals or that class positions necessarily lead to forms of class-consciousness and mobilisation. Classes are stratified in numerous manners consistent with the more specific position of individuals within the processes of production and circulation, and according to a variety of other social divisions including ethnicity and gender. However, at the same time, that the class relationship is not always recognised by its protagonists does not mean that it does not exist, that it does not structure the social universe of capitalism, and that it isn't a central explanatory concept for analysing the dynamics of contemporary capitalist societies.

Such concerns become evident when the neoclassical emphasis on individual exchange is rejected and class relations in the sphere of production are considered. As Ben Fine (2001b: 30) highlights, in the abode of production 'capital and labour directly confront one another over how much work will be done, with what quality and intensity, and subject to what wages and conditions'. At stake is the ability of the capitalist to compel the worker to produce a set of commodities whose value is greater than that of the wage and therein ensure the achievement of profit through the appropriation of surplus labour. Production is therefore a site of power and repeated conflicts, in which the competitive dynamics of capitalism ensure that capitalists must repeatedly seek ways through which to intensify labour, cut costs and improve productivity. Unsurprisingly, given that these power relations are heavily weighted on the side of the employer, workers have continually sought to organise collectively in order to redress the vulnerability they face individually, both in the labour market and within the labour process. Within neoclassical economics, however, these relationships are seen as natural and harmonious exchanges between individuals that lead to a prosperous equilibrium wherein each is rewarded according to the utility of the good they provide and in which profit is justified as the revenue equivalent to the utility of capital within production process. As such, beyond simply ignoring the historical specificities of capitalist society – which is not a universal and natural phenomenon but was constructed through the forcible and violent separation of peoples from the means of production in order to render them wage-labourers (Marx 1976; Polanyi 2001) – the methodological individualism of neoclassicism also renders it blind to capitalist society's most enduring divisions and conflicts.

The concentrated ownership of the means of production and the control over money in capitalist society is directly related to the social polarisation that afflicts capitalist societies nationally and on a global level. The social power inherent to capital and expressed through money drives the centralisation and concentration of wealth to historically unprecedented degrees. Put simply, those with capital use it to generate further capital, therein expanding their social power and future wealth-creating abilities. At the inverse end of the pole, those dependent on selling their labour to survive face the constant threat of immiseration owing to fluctuations in the accumulation of capital that can drive down wages or make labour redundant. Although in the neoclassical tradition, labour markets will equilibrate so that supply and demand for labour is equal, this assumes that the price of labour-power can fall as low as the market deems necessary (see chapter 7). As a result, the conditions for economic reproduction within capitalism do not necessarily ensure social reproduction. This insecuritisation of social reproduction puts complex strains on the gendered division of labour, in which not only the domestic work necessary for the reproduction of the household is primarily assigned to women, but the latter are also regularly faced with a double burden of seeking paid labour as a means to ensure household reproduction (Mies 1986; Acker 2004). On this basis, the tendency of segments of the working class to pressure the state to mediate such insecurities represents not the mobilisation of special interests that seek to distort the rationality of the market, but the response of those who seek respite from the irrationalities of capitalist social reproduction.

The final aspect of neoclassicism that needs to be challenged is the assumed tendency of the market to self-regulate at an equilibrium level, a theoretical proposition that sits awkwardly against the record of repeated and severe crises throughout the history of capitalism. Indeed, as not only Marxists but post-Keynesians and other heterodox economists have long argued, the existence of a tendency toward equilibrium can only exist in and through constant disequilibria (Katzner 2003). Capitalist production leads to constant imbalances between the production and consumption of commodities across time, and this stems from the social form of capitalism as a social division of labour between competing units of capital. As Simon Clarke (1994) has argued, the pressures stemming from competition force each individual unit of capital not to align their expectations and actions to the limit of the market so as to reconcile production and consumption, but to view the latter as a barrier to be overcome in the context of competitive struggle. Notwithstanding the ability to exercise monopoly powers or political influence, firms are repeatedly forced to increase productivity and the intensity of labour in order to lower the unit costs of their production to anticipate their competitors and retain profitability. The latter trends result not in the harmonisation of supply and demand but in the systematic extension of production without regard to the limits of the market.

Increased productivity by the individual capital further accentuates the competition in any particular branch of production, therein forcing other producers to match or better the new social standard for producing any particular commodity, either by advancing methods of production or increasing the exploitation of labour. As competitive pressures build further, this uneven development of capital holds the threat of crisis as the resulting overproduction of commodities leaves capitalists with goods that are not marketable at any satisfactory rate of profit. In the words of Clarke (1990: 461):

The very success of capitalists in improving the conditions for the realisation of surplus value – by creating new needs, opening up new markets, and forcing down wages, intensifying labour and revolutionising the forces of production – merely intensifies the tendency to the overaccumulation of capital, overproduction of commodities and the pressure of competition. Sooner or later the barrier of the market will reappear in the form of a limit; the threat always immanent in competition comes into the open as competitive pressure gives way to open crisis, and overproduction is moved through the devaluation of capital, destruction of productive capacity and the redundancy of labour.

In this way, while capitalism indeed develops the productive forces at a global level, this is an extremely uneven process that occurs at the cost of repeated crises and their socially destructive consequences. Crisis does not represent the human failings of irrational capitalists who have misjudged market signals, but rather the necessary outcome of a process in which social production is subordinated to the competitive pressures of capital accumulation. Within these dynamics, the credit system can temporarily suspend the limits of the market by providing loans to capitalists looking to invest in new technology or increase the scale of production. Simultaneously, however, the credit system can generalise the crisis to a social level through an over-extension of credit that transmits crisis throughout the banking system and into other branches of production (Itoh and Lapavitsas 1999). This tendency underscores the historical trend of crises in capitalism to manifest themselves most dramatically in the form of financial crisis, as shall be discussed in the Chilean case in the following chapter.

The outline of an alternative understanding of the dynamics of capitalist society has highlighted several key facets of capitalist society that are excluded from the neoclassical framework. In particular, the formal rationality of exchange, which is foundational to neoclassical economic theory and the political practices of neoliberalism, is rendered problematic within the framework of a substantively irrational mode of social production. Within capitalist social relations, the subordination of social production to the accumulation of capital introduces a number of contradictory tendencies including sustained conflict between capitalists and workers, the polarisation of wealth and the insecuritisation of the working class, and the tendency towards repeated crises that are resolvable only through the destruction of capital and livelihoods. Neoliberalism, as a political practice, promises to return capitalist society to a more 'natural' state in which social institutions that artificially restrain the rational tendencies of the market are removed. However, in spite of its professed ability to create a rational and universally prosperous society, the following chapters contend that the irrational tendencies intrinsic to capitalist society have become increasingly clear within the context of 30 years of neoliberal restructuring within Chile. The following chapters chart this trajectory. As indicated above, the neoliberal prescription necessitated a dramatic transformation of prevailing economic and labour institutions and this is the focus of chapter 3 which follows. Rapid changes to existing economic policies and established institutions were made in a coercive manner in order to impose a fundamental shift in the productive structure and class relations of Chilean society upon which further social restructuring could be implemented in the following years. Concurrently, the prescription also involved an extensive reshaping of the social institutions in which market relations are embedded. To this end, chapter 4 examines the extension of reforms to the welfare institutions that had, since the populist period, become important mechanisms in regulating the reproduction of Chilean society.

SUMMARY

This chapter argued that the adoption of neoliberalism by the authoritarian regime in Chile was – at the time – a counter-intuitive occurrence given the prevalent Keynesian economic orthodoxies of the day and the strong class interests that were invested in the existing, national-developmentalist form of capital accumulation. To explain this paradox, the chapter argued that it is important to look beyond neoliberalism as a set of economic policies to analyse the fundamental restructuring of social relations that it envisages and the depoliticising tendencies that it entails. As such, the adoption of neoliberal policies represented a bold attempt to obliterate many of the social institutions established over the previous half-century of national developmentalism and which were blamed for the insidious politicisation of social relations. The attractiveness of neoliberalism was its professed ability to reshape Chilean society in a manner that would fundamentally depoliticise social life by strengthening the regulatory role of markets. In the context of dramatic social crisis, it was this wider impact of neoliberal restructuring, rather than its much-questioned economic functionality, that ultimately lay behind its adoption by the Pinochet regime. Nonetheless, the neoclassical comprehension of the market upon which the professed rationality of neoliberalism is justified is profoundly questionable, with worrying consequences for the practical impact of neoliberal policies.

3
Neoliberalism and 'Creative Destruction', 1973–89

Through a campaign of sustained repression in the first years of the dictatorship, the authoritarian regime successfully extinguished the immediate expressions of political crisis that had afflicted Chilean society since the late 1960s. Nonetheless, the economic crisis was not resolved through the gradualist measures of the regime's first economic team and would elicit increasingly heterodox solutions that went beyond established methods of crisis management (Körner 1986). In spite of their unorthodoxy, the previous chapter argued that the authoritarian regime was drawn towards the implementation of neoliberal policies owing to their professed ability to transform existing social institutions in a manner that would extinguish the economic and political dimensions of the crisis. The current chapter examines how the neoliberal reformers lay the basis for this dramatic social transformation through a strategy of 'creative destruction' whereby macroeconomic policies were deployed in a coercive manner to engineer a period of abrupt recession. Through this strategy, existing productive structures and the social relations that underpinned them would be obliterated, paving the way for new institutional forms. In their place, it was envisaged, would arise a new society ordered according to the abstract disciplines of market forces and which would be characterised by depoliticised social relations and bountiful economic growth. The chapter proceeds to demonstrate how such expectations were badly misconstrued, leading to a new and deeper crisis and a further and more intense period of social restructuring.

FROM GRADUALIST POLICY TO 'CREATIVE DESTRUCTION', 1973–75

Notwithstanding the severity of the imbalances inherited from the Allende period and ongoing international economic instability, the initial economic teams of the military regime maintained a gradualist approach to macroeconomic management that moved cautiously away from the deepened structuralist approach of the two previous governments and reduced state expenditures in all areas except for the military. Crisis was attributed to the expansion of consumptive state expenditure and to wage hikes that undermined the profitability of capitalist enterprises while reinforcing market distortions. Under the guise of removing these distortions, the authoritarian regime lowered the price and wage controls implemented in the Frei and Allende periods. Simultaneously, import tariffs were selectively reduced and social expenditure was cut by over 20 percent (Torche 2000: 557), which impacted gravely on the quality and distribution of services such as education, health and the value of pensions. However, this tempered austerity programme merely sought to stabilise the macroeconomic variables, while the overall development strategy retained the primary characteristics forged over the previous half-century of national developmentalism, including the strongly institutionalised relationships between state, capital and labour predicted on centrally moderated wage increases, state supports for industrial sectors and substantial state ownership of industry.

The gradualist strategy of 1973–74, however, ran into the barrier of mounting economic disequilibria. Continued triple digit inflation, the stagnation of profits and a significant fall in the value of copper on depressed global markets pressured the military regime to adopt a more radical approach. Under the increasingly centralised leadership of General Augusto Pinochet, who engaged in a strategy of concentrating political power around his personage, the authoritarian regime began to follow the prescription of a group of economists based primarily at the Universidad Católica in Santiago. These economists became known as the 'Chicago Boys' owing to their training in the department of economics at the University of Chicago through a US funded academic exchange programme operational since the mid-1950s. Moreover, they were fervent proponents of the neoclassical critique of Keynesian orthodoxy developed at that institution. Although marginalised from policymaking circles during the height of structuralist economics in the 1960s, they nonetheless gained stature during the Allende period by providing business interests and the Chilean right with an alternative economic and social platform (Valdés 1995).

The Chicago Boys' ardent belief in orthodox monetarist formulas of price stability as the cure for the country's economic ills was matched by their unequivocal grasp of the wider implications of the societal transformation central to their project. They based their explanations of the current crisis on the statist and politicising tendencies of national developmentalism. In referring to the Allende period, leading Chicago Boy Sergio de Castro stated that: 'A detailed analysis of that three-year administration leads us to conclude that economic policies prevailing at the time were not actually modified, but rather that existing policies were merely applied more intensely. This led to the full development of a crisis that had been brewing for half a century' (cited in Valdés 1995: 59). In espousing the macroeconomic policies of monetarism tied to a wider concept of the depoliticising tendencies of neoliberal social restructuring, they established a clear and coherent plan for setting Chilean capitalism back on its feet through a dramatic reformulation of the institutionalised relationships between state and society.

Despite their gradual incorporation into the authoritarian regime's economic policy unit from mid-1974, the authoritarian state managers initially shied from implementing the full shock therapy called for by the Chicago Boys owing to the anticipation of economic recession, social destabilisation and protest from across the social spectrum. The opponents of such a course included significant segments of the industrial bourgeoisie, which feared any significant reduction of protective tariffs. At this historical juncture, long before neoliberalism had assumed the global hegemonic mantle that it presently enjoys, Keynesian assumptions regarding the necessity of institutionalised state intervention to mitigate crisis tendencies were prevalent and the idea of a retrenchment of state activity seemed bizarre and suspect. Indeed, the leading positions within the regime's economic team were initially offered to economists associated with the Christian Democrat Party who were well versed in structuralist thought. The relentless nature of the crisis, however, indicated that the gradualist techniques of stabilisation were inadequate to counter the surface manifestations of economic crisis, still less address their deeper social foundations. Moreover, the growing power of a small but significant fraction of the Chilean capitalist class with a heavy concentration of liquid assets that could increasingly reorientate production towards international markets provided a small but powerful group within the bourgeoisie that were supportive of a more radical strategy (Fortín 1985).

In 1975 Sergio de Castro was appointed to the key position of Minister of the Hacienda, a role equivalent to the Chancellor of the Exchequer in Britain, and other members of the group assumed central positions. Convinced by the monetarist doctrine that the stability of prices is the most fundamental element of any successful market economy, this new policy elite immediately sought to tackle the rampant inflation that was driving up prices at the rate of over 300 percent per year. Given their neoclassical analysis, the Chicago Boys were unconcerned that raising interest rates and stabilising prices at market rates would lead to the collapse of many industries and a massive increase in unemployment. Provoking a recession, they believed, was a necessary move in order to obliterate enterprises that were inefficient and that relied upon state institutions such as tariffs and state credit in order to survive. Further, these measures would aid in a process of redeploying both capital and labour from these sectors into new, export orientated and globally competitive areas of the economy. The Chicago Boys therefore welcomed a phase of *creative destruction* through which the basis of a new society could be forged out of the ashes of the old.

The usage of 'creative destruction' in this context contrasts with Schumpeter's 1942 employment of the term, by which he referred to the inherent tendency of capitalism to fashion destructive periods of competition that lead to new periods of growth (Schumpeter 1975). Here it refers to a conscious strategy of state-led social engineering that seeks to destroy the institutional forms in which the social relationships through which society reproduces itself are embedded. By manipulating economic policies in a coercive manner to destroy established institutions and productive structures, the particular form of social relations that underscored them could be quickly dissolved and eventually reformed in a new and – according to the dictates of neoliberal theory – rational, efficient and depoliticised manner. In particular, Chilean neoliberalism sought to destroy and rebuild the institutions through which economic activity was planned and directed; through which industrial relations were channelled; and through which the social reproduction of individuals and households was regulated. Despite the rhetoric of being a market-driven strategy, the neoliberal programme of creative destruction rests on systematic state interventions that seek simultaneously to reshape social institutions while mediating the political and social tensions that arise from this restructuring. It is worth highlighting once again the analysis of Karl Polanyi who emphasised how an enormous and continuous application of state intervention is necessary to establish and reproduce the conditions for a society regulated through market institutions (Polanyi 2001: 140).

THE IMPACT OF CREATIVE DESTRUCTION

As the battering ram for a period of intense social restructuring, the full fury of a severe austerity programme was unleashed in 1975. Remaining price controls were abolished, wages were left to deteriorate under hyper-inflationary conditions, formerly protected markets were rapidly liberalised, a dramatic reduction was made to public expenditures, and a mass shedding of jobs was introduced throughout the public sector. Together these measures precipitated a profound contraction of demand, spelling the demise of many small and medium firms in the consumer goods and service sectors, leading to a deep recession with per capita GDP contracting by a dramatic 14.4 percent. The destructive side of the Chicago Boys' equation was evident and Chile underwent a process of rapid de-industrialisation. The manufacturing sector, whose advancement was the staple of structuralist development strategy, declined to such an extent that production did not recover to its 1972 level until 1987 (Agosín 2000: 107). Unemployment climbed above 15 percent (refer to Figure 3.1) and real wages collapsed. The share of wages in the national product declined from 52.2 percent in 1972 to 36.7 percent in 1989 (ICFTU 1997), a transition from one of the highest in Latin America to one of the lowest (Petras and Leiva 1994: 26). These dramatic increases in the size of the reserve labour army and the rate of exploitation constituted fundamental pillars in the long-term recovery of Chilean capitalism.

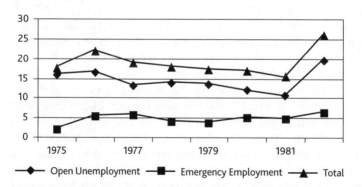

(Data drawn from Mizala and Romaguera 2001: 214)

Figure 3.1   Unemployment, 1975–82
(percentage of economically active population)

By prompting the mass destruction of fixed capital within key industrial sectors, the regime's austerity programme of 1975 immediately thrust a significant proportion of the labour force into unemployment. This was the first step in a comprehensive reformulation of the social division of labour within Chile and of the class relationships that underscored it. Even by the regime's generous understanding of what constitutes employment (cf. Díaz 1993: 1), over 15 percent of the workforce was unemployed by 1975 and many more were drastically underemployed. Notably, the Chilean state itself was both the author of and a major target for this dramatic decomposition of the Chilean labour force. In 1974, before the mass-privatisations that would follow in the late 1970s and mid-1980s, the state controlled 20 of the largest 25 Chilean companies, including the largest ten (Ritter 1992: 13). Consequently, public sector employment accounted for an extensive component of total employment, some 870,000 out of a total workforce of slightly fewer than 3 million in 1973 (Coloma and Rojas 2000: 519). However, in the years 1974 and 1975 the state implemented uncompromising measures to reduce the fiscal deficit and to raise the profitability of state-controlled industries. One-third of public employees lost their jobs, meaning that some 265,000 public sector employees were forced into the ranks of the unemployed (Larraín and Vergara 2000: 76). An expulsion of labour of this magnitude would have been politically inconceivable without the centralisation and prolific application of the means of coercion by the authoritarian regime. Public sector unions were among the strongest in Chile and faced intense repression in the post-1973 era and a ban on all local union activity. Concurrently, the sheer rapidity of the downsizing of the public sphere would also serve to damage the long-term strength of these unions, represented in a decrease in unionisation levels across the sector.

State industries, however, were not alone in pursuing drastic restructuring that precipitated the mass ejection of labourers from industry. With both public and private owned firms thrown into profound crisis, many of the branches of production that had been steadily growing since the introduction of national developmentalist institutions of industrial support in the 1930s underwent severe contraction. This trend was accentuated by the steady reduction of tariffs by the Pinochet regime between 1974 and the early 1980s, which permitted uncompromising foreign competition to enter into formerly protected domestic markets. Chilean manufacturers whose productivity stood below that of international competition were faced with cheaper imported products and a dramatic intensification of the crisis. The necessary outcome of this process was the destruction of fixed capital, rapid de-industrialisation, and the large-scale expulsion of labour from key industrial sectors where firms either folded or introduced new forms of mechanisation that reduced the need for employees. In total, over one-quarter of the industrial sector workforce was jettisoned into the ranks of the unemployed between 1974 and 1981 (Foxley 1986: 40–1). This dramatic expulsion exerted a tremendous downward pressure on wages and greatly increased discipline within the workplace owing to the threat of dismissal.

The effects of crisis and the mass expulsion of labour into the reserve army upon the working class were further shaped through the continued intervention of the state in the production and distributional relations between capital and labour. Importantly, the use of repression to restrict all union activity and impose a moratorium on striking and collective bargaining facilitated the political conditions under which the collapse in real wages could take place. By freezing wages in conditions of rampant inflation, the regime facilitated an immediate massive deterioration in their value. This provoked not only a reversal of the wage increases of the Allende period but, by 1975, a drastic lowering of real wages to 62 percent of their 1970 level (Mizala and Romaguera 2001: 214). Nonetheless, owing to the evaporation of a domestic consumer base and the threat of political destabilisation that this trend posed, the regime was unwilling to permit the complete immiseration of the working class. Hence, rather than permit the continuing collapse of real wages in conditions of an over-abundance of un- and under-employed workers, in 1975 the regime reinstated an indexed wage policy that would control the distributive conflict between labour and capital from 1976 to 1979. Within this framework, those who had been able to retain employment in the formal sector experienced a slow but steady recovery of real wages. Nonetheless, the raises were sufficiently moderate and built on such a low base, that they were largely accepted by the business sector (refer to Table 3.1). Indeed, the regime's complicity in deliberately undervaluing the consumer price index – so as to under-emphasise the base rate of inflation upon which wage rises were calculated – stunted the recovering trend by about 15 percent (Cortazár 1997: 241).

Through the destruction of industries, mass unemployment and a collapse in wages, the destructive aspect of the regime's austerity policies was plainly manifest. Although the austerity package did not restore an immediate macroeconomic equilibrium as intended – with inflation initially remaining above expected levels (cf. Fortín 1985) – it nonetheless succeeded in rupturing the existing social and economic fabric of Chilean society and therein establishing the basis for a wider transformation of social relations along the lines of the consolidating neoliberal consensus within the military regime. Whether or not this transformation would provide the basis for dramatic economic development with capital and labour moving into internationally competitive economic sectors was yet to be seen, although further reforms were viewed as integral to this process. As such, the chapter presently turns to the key neoliberal policies of capital and current account liberalisation.

Table 3.1   Real Wage Index, 1970–82

Year	1970	1972	1974	1976	1978	1980	1982
Index	100	126.6	64.1	65.4	75.1	88.5	96.1

(Data drawn from Fazio 2001a: 217)

ECONOMIC LIBERALISATION AND THE PRIMACY OF MONEY CAPITAL

Following the social transformation implicit in the 'creative destruction' of austerity policies, the next key aspect of the Chicago Boys' strategy was to enact a profound alteration in the relationship between domestic accumulation and global capital. The structuralist doctrine of national developmentalism, in its quest for domestic industrial expansion, sanctified a form of development in which the weaknesses of domestic production were to be overcome through state institutions. The latter sought to protect domestically located productive capitals by means of tariff barriers and to take a leading role in stimulating investment through a variety of institutionalised measures, ranging from tax relief and subsidised loans to direct ownership. The neoliberal solution was more radical. The Chicago Boys' analysis of the stagnation and crisis of the Chilean economy centred around the rigidities that had developed within the economy owing to the inefficient deployment and limited mobility of capital. They related the latter to the stasis of capital in relatively ossified productive forms that entailed not only sizeable outlays on fixed capital but also an inflexible relation with the labour-force governed by the historically developed institutions of the state. Hence, the essence of the neoliberal solution was a shift in state policy in order to prioritise capital in its money-form rather than capital as production. An emphasis on liquidity was expected to enable capital to overcome existing barriers to valorisation by escaping currently unprofitable engagements and concentrating in those sectors that offered more lucrative returns. Capital in mobile money-form, it was envisaged, would be able to seek a new and profitable deployment, freed from established spatial and political constraints. Concurrently, labour would also transfer into these areas of production as new jobs were created, leading to a new and efficient social division of labour within Chile.

This new dominance of capital in money-form was forged through the Pinochet regime's deregulation of both trade and finance. The implications were felt across Chilean society as liberalisation went hand in hand with a profound reorganisation of the social relations of production. In the financial sphere, alongside privatising banks and freeing internal interest rates, the regime removed restrictions and provided incentives for foreign capital to flow into domestic enterprises and financial markets. High interest rates were expected to curb the inflationary spiral and attract inflows of foreign capital, although one serious consequence was a rapid overvaluation of the peso. Additionally, from 1977 the regime enabled domestic banks to borrow directly from international financial markets. This allowed domestic banks to borrow at international rates and re-lend domestically at hugely inflated levels, making an extremely high rate of profit and therein helping consolidate the increasingly important position of the financial sector (Fortín 1985; Soederberg 2002).

Table 3.2 Distribution of Payments to Capital by Main Sectors

Years	Agriculture (%)	Industry (%)	Trade (%)	Banking (%)
1960–70	10.5	30.0	22.4	1.0
1981	7.3	20.9	27.8	18.0

(Data drawn from Fortín 1985: 186)

Concurrent to these changes in the financial sector, capital account liberalisation allowed large economic groups that had access to international finance to use this credit to purchase or establish industries in the new export sectors and also to procure state industries that the regime privatised at greatly subsidised prices. As such, this period witnessed a large-scale concentration and centralisation of capital, expressed in the emergence of large economic conglomerates known as the 'grupos económicos' (economic groups) (cf. Fazio 2000; also Martínez and Díaz 1996). The latter were rooted in the financial sector and used access to liquid capital to construct vast yet constantly changing portfolios of investments. Alongside the re-entry of foreign firms into the mining sector, this concentration of capital led to the domination of all key sectors of the Chilean economy by a handful of domestic economic groups and multinationals. Far from creating a competitive market economy in the model of neoclassical economics, the necessary result of the liberalisation measures was to aid the concentration of capital in the hands of a small number of giant conglomerates that could transfer resources internally in a manner far removed from the neoliberal emphasis on market forces.

Table 3.3   Concentration in the Export Sector by 1988

Industry	Number of Large Firms	Industry Share
Mining	7	97.1
Agriculture	8	80.6
Forest Products	5	78.4
Fish Products	6	51.1
Food	6	67.3
Wine and Beverage	2	70.2
Wood	7	78.6
Paper, Cellulose	2	90
Chemical Products	2	71.4

(Data drawn from Petras and Leiva 1994: 36)

These tendencies were also reinforced through the liberalisation of trade. By June 1979 the maximum tariff had been reduced to just 10 percent and this further encouraged the reorientation of capital away from the production of consumption goods for domestic markets and towards the newly emergent export industries, particularly primary produce such as fruit, fish, wine, lumber and metals. Intrinsic to this process was a partial recomposition of the Chilean labour force. Ejected from the crisis-stricken industrial and state sectors, labour was only partially reabsorbed by the informal sector, the export processing industries and the service sector. The cumulative effect of these processes was that between 1970 and 1978 secondary employment in general – comprising employment in the manufacturing, construction and utilities sectors – decreased from 37.8 percent of total employment to 24.4 percent (Díaz 1997: 167). Although the primary export sectors of the Chilean economy began to slowly increase their dollar importance in Chilean production – with, for example, exports of lumber and fishmeal increasing by over 40 percent between 1974 and 1981 (Agosín 2000: 16) – these sectors did not constitute labour-intensive branches of production and therein could not offer a significant outlet for the reserve labour army.

Within this context, both unemployment and underemployment remained at extremely high levels, with unemployment reaching 16.6 percent of the labour force in 1976 and a further 5.3 percent of the labour force reliant on state emergency employment programmes. For comparison, the average unemployment rate during the post-war era was 6 percent (Hojman and Ramsden 1993: 108). In addition to the physical repression supplied by the security apparatus, the disciplinary effects of mass unemployment upon those who retained employment had major ramifications for the power of working class movements. The prospect of losing one's job was a threat of immediate immiseration in the context of mass unemployment, therein reinforcing the coercive power of employers vis-à-vis their workforces. Furthermore, the state emergency employment schemes constituted a highly authoritarian manner of regulating those who had been pushed outside of the discipline of the capitalist wage relation. Initially incorporating fewer than 2 percent of the working population in 1975, the programmes quickly expanded to cover around 5 percent of the economically active population for the remainder of the decade as the Pinochet regime's creative destruction perpetuated the extreme levels of unemployment. Described by observers as 'the ultimate humiliation of the worker' (Graham 1991: 17), enrolees were set to work on manual labour tasks, often linked to building infrastructure for the armed forces and the business sector, and earned around one-third of the minimum wage (Fortín 1985: 182).

Simultaneous to these changes in the urban realm, social relationships in the countryside underwent dramatic state-engineered transformation. By reversing the land reform process, the regime transferred terrain away from the recipient peasantry, who retained only 31.1 percent of land grants, and either sold it to emerging large-scale agro-capitalist enterprises (33.8 percent) or returned it to former landlords (28.4 percent) (Ritter 1992: 13; also cf. Green 1995). Moreover, given the inability of those who retained their land grants to farm at a profit after the removal of agrarian tariffs and subsidies, many peasants were forced to sell their plots. As Marcus Kurtz has detailed, only 6.5 percent of land sales were to another reform parcel holder. The rest returned via sale to landlords or, more commonly, the new agro-businesses resulting in a substantial concentration of land in agro-capitalist hands that formed part of the new economic conglomerates (Kurtz 1999: 281). By the end of this counter-reform, only 5 percent of Chile's peasantry had managed to secure a holding. Reversing the agrarian reform process in this manner served to increase urban migratory processes, thereby escalating the century-long trend towards the growth of the cities and the further expansion of the urban reserve labour army (Riesco 1999).

To the extent that the labour force was incorporated within new forms of employment, it found limited opportunities in the tertiary sector through the expansion of commerce and services. Alejandro Foxley attributed half of the jobs formed in the recovery period of the late 1970s to these two sectors (Foxley 1986: 42), leading to a situation in which tertiary sector jobs accounted for 64 percent of employment by the early 1980s, as opposed to 46 percent in 1973 (Díaz 1993: 14). However, tertiary employment during this period has been shown to be largely spurious in nature, thereby functioning as a refuge from open unemployment for a portion of the reserve labour army. Specifically, the expansion of employment in the tertiary sector was centred on a growth in small informal commerce, various private sector services, and public services provided through the large-scale emergency work programmes initiated and expanded by the regime (Martínez and Díaz 1996: 120).

INSTITUTIONALISING CLASS RELATIONS

The Chicago Boys had promised that the painful effects of their creative destruction would soon be resolved within the context of a newly efficient and dynamic economic foundation for society. By the late 1970s, there seemed to be some basis to their claims. On the one hand, monetarist policies had reduced inflation, and substantial flows of foreign investment seemed to be pushing the economy into a period of boom. In this respect, GDP growth levels of above 8 percent at the end of the decade were proclaimed to be evidence of an 'economic miracle', notwithstanding that in 1979 per capita GDP remained only 95.5 percent of the 1971 figure (Fortín 1985: 156). Underlying this surge in economic activity was the entry of over US$6.5 million of foreign credit from international financial markets between 1975 and 1979 – a sum equal to five years of copper exports (Soederberg 2002). The influx of foreign capital was hailed as proof of the soundness of the Chilean reform process and, in spite of its fragile social basis, the late 1970s saw the global propagation of the myth of a Chilean miracle by the advocates of neoliberalism in US academia and international institutions such as the IMF.

Buoyed by such praise, the authoritarian regime proceeded into a new phase of the neoliberal project of social transformation. Almost all areas of the administration were colonised by neoliberal-orientated technocrats and they began to extend the reforms into further areas of social life, initially through a fundamental remodelling of labour institutions. Within the context of an upsurge in worker militancy and significant pressure from international workers' groups such as the International Labour Office (ILO) and the International Confederation of Free Trade Unions (ORIT), the regime recognised that re-institutionalising the relations between state, capital and organised labour in a manner that undermined collective action could help to restrain the spontaneous militancy of the labour movement and reinforce the new balance of social forces within Chilean society. Concurrently, with laws passed in both 1978 and 1980, the regime introduced the 'Plan Laboral' (Labour Plan), a new code to regulate industrial relations that, within the parameters of a framework that institutionalised the new power balance between capital and labour, formalised new legal structures governing the individual and collective rights of workers.

The Plan Laboral came into effect from 1979 and was modified consistently until the mid-1980s as the regime attempted to counter certain unanticipated implications and worker strategies that restricted the operation of the labour code as envisaged (Barrera and Valenzuela 1986: 253–9; Cortazár 1997: 242–2; Mizala and Romaguera 2001: 205–7; Winn 2004b: 38–43). Following six years of generalised labour repression and coercive economic policies that left the previous mode of industrial relations in a state of limbo, the code represented a defining moment in the institutionalisation of a new relationship between state, capital and labour. The Plan Laboral reinstated the right to unionise for the first time since the regime's suspension of union activity in 1973 although several important exclusions were made, most significantly the prohibition of unionisation of public servants and temporary workers. Such exclusions forbade, respectively, the formation of unions in what had been previously a pro-Allende stronghold (public servants such as teachers), and also in one of the new dynamic poles of the export sector (fruit exports). Simultaneously the laws eliminated all existing forms of compulsory unionisation while encouraging the creation of multiple, competing unions within each firm to fragment intra-firm organisations.

Collective bargaining was re-established only at the level of the individual firm, thereby ending sectoral and national forms of negotiation, and was restricted to solely the issue of wages. Labour conditions and management were placed strictly outside of the parameters of collective bargaining and, therein, collective action. This served to consolidate authoritarianism within the workplace, allowing capital to flexibly manage the labour process without politically imposed restrictions. Equally, the regime curbed the right to strike by confining all strikes to a maximum limit of 60 days and entitling firms to hire replacement, non-unionised labour during that period. All striking workers were entitled to return to work on an individual basis under the conditions of the last offer made by employers after 30 days of a strike and, should a strike involve more than 50 percent of the workforce, employers could implement a lockout. If agreement had not been reached by 60 days, workers were expected to accept the last offer made by employers or be considered as resigned from employment.

Finally, firms were permitted to fire workers without reason in order to give the firm flexibility over the size of its labour force in reaction to changing market conditions, but also to root out suspected subversive individuals when needed. One month's pay for each year of service was the stipulated compensation, although the regime imposed a maximum recognition of five years' service, therein greatly increasing the insecurity of workers in the absence of any generalised unemployment insurance. Simultaneously, amplifying the insecurity of employment provided employers with one further weapon in an impressive arsenal with which to enforce worker discipline. Within the context of unprecedented levels of unemployment resulting from the 1975 restructuring and which peaked again in the 1982–83 recession, power relations within the ambit of the firm had swung firmly in the favour of capital (see Stillerman 2004 for a comprehensive account of labour relations and the transformation of work in the Madeco copper processing plant in this period). Utilising the new labour institutions aided employers to engineer a steep decline in wages while increasing both the intensity of work and the length of the working day, all of which contributed to the eventual recovery of

Chilean capitalism in the 1980s by transforming the social relations of production. However, this was achieved at a steep social cost of insecuritisation, impoverishment and an escalation of the intensity of work.

The Plan Laboral therefore comprised an integral part of the dictatorship's strategy of re-institutionalising a new balance of class forces within Chilean society, and therein attempting to obliterate the institutionalised pattern of productive relations forged since the mid-1920s by imposing more sharply the disciplinary power of labour markets and reinforcing the power of capital over labour-power. By undermining the ability to intervene collectively in the formation of wages and work conditions, the state sought to remove collectively imposed restrictions upon the treatment of labourers as commodities. On the one hand, the regime established the basis upon which the wage question would no longer be the purview of national politics but would be determined through individualised exchanges in the market. To the extent that collective bargaining could proceed, it was limited to the level of the individual firm and was to occur through an institutionalised process decisively stacked in the favour of capital. On the other hand, the new code also weakened the power of labour to impose regulations concerning the uses of labour within the firm, therein increasing the control of employers over the labour process. Factors ranging from the length and intensity of the working day to the various tasks required of workers abruptly became out of the limits of collective bargaining.

The importance of the authoritarian state in fostering the political conditions for an intensified exploitation of labour cannot be overstated. Refashioning labour institutions greatly abetted the wider restructuring of capital in the neoliberal period by restricting the ability of workers to influence labour market outcomes or conditions within the enterprise. The dictatorship's reformulation of labour institutions into an anti-collectivist mould that consolidated the power of employers over the nature, tenure and remuneration of work would be one of the most enduring legacies of the Pinochet period. Not only would it remain the touchstone of industrial relations for the rest of the dictatorship but would become the site of major struggle in the post-authoritarian period as various working-class movements challenged the regressive nature of this institutionalised form of labour relations.

FROM MIRACLE TO CRISIS AND THE
COLLAPSE OF ORTHODOX MONETARISM

The regime attracted significant international acclaim for its 'miracle' policies that had seemingly opened a new period of rapid economic growth by the late 1970s. However, far from solving the problems of Chilean capitalist development, the ongoing patterns of social transformation and the prioritisation of capital in its money form quickly proved to be a significant factor in the build up to an even greater crisis. Although new forms of integration into the global chains of finance and commodity circulation certainly brought substantial reward to the large economic conglomerates that were able to partake in rentier activities and the production of primary exports, Chile's balance of trade rapidly worsened in the late 1970s as the growth of imports far exceeded that of exports. The steady overvaluation of the Chilean peso bolstered this process by cheapening the price of imports and further undermined the profitability of domestically located productive capital. In turn this accentuated the ejection of labour from domestic production as enterprises continued to collapse or introduce labour-saving technology in an attempt to regain competitiveness. Indicatively, the inability of restructured capital to profitably incorporate labour within the production process is one sign of the fictitious nature of the 'economic miracle' of the late 1970s.

With industrial production in decline, much of the investment associated with this boom was ploughed into unproductive and short-term ventures. Instead of freeing capital to re-establish the exploitation of Chilean labour on a new and profitable footing, many capitalists took advantage of the institutional context to avoid any relationship with labour at all. A speculative bubble quickly built up around sectors such as real estate while, in order to compete against the unhindered entry of foreign consumer goods, surviving domestic industries borrowed heavily at high interest rates in an unsuccessful attempt to regain their market position by improving production technologies. The expansion of credit seemed able to contain the contradictions of capital accumulation but only at the cost of mounting levels of debt and an extreme vulnerability to fluctuations in interest rates.

Such pressures were felt even beyond the traditional industrial sectors. As the sustained inflow of international capital caused the further appreciation of the peso vis-à-vis the dollar, even the dynamic new export industries began to experience wilting competitiveness and a contraction in profits (Ritter 1992: 17). To compound matters, the early 1980s witnessed a fall in simple commodity prices on the world market, high oil prices, and an unprecedented rise in international interest rates. The latter was caused – somewhat ironically – by the rapid introduction of monetarist policies similar to those of the Chicago Boys in the United States in late 1979. The interest rate hike placed even more strain on those capitals that had borrowed from international financial markets and increased the pressures upon the government's substantial external debt. Under these conditions short-term foreign investments in Chile were rapidly liquidated as investors fled. The debts of Chilean capitals soon became unmanageable and the Chilean economy plunged into deep recession. The crisis that the Pinochet regime believed it had resolved through its first attempt at creative destructive emerged again on an even greater scale.

RESPONDING TO THE DEBT CRISIS

When the full force of the debt crisis rocked Chile the military regime was in disarray and the Chicago Boys refused to make any decisive interventions under the naïve presumption that the markets would self-correct. However, as production fell by 16.7 percent, investment by over 40 percent, and official unemployment topped 26 percent, it became clear that the economy faced collapse without sustained state intervention. Facing such a profound crisis, the regime was propelled into action in direct contradiction of the neoliberal rhetoric of the self-regulating market. Intervention took three immediate forms: the takeover of collapsing firms by the state, the socialisation of US$7.7 billion of private external debt incurred by Chilean capitals, and the dramatic expansion of the emergency work programmes that offered less-than subsistence wages to a significant proportion of unemployed workers. Fiscal caution in implementing these latter programmes was largely jettisoned owing to the threat of political destabilisation that mass unemployment posed. At their height in 1983, the programmes entailed a state expenditure of around 1.5 percent of GDP and provided employment in 1983 to one-eighth of the economically active population (Raczynski and Romaguera 1995: 282).

It should be noted, however, that such a figure pales in comparison to the subsidies offered to capitals during this period. In the two years from 1982 to 1983 subsidies that included full takeovers, assumption of debts, subsidised dollars and debt renegotiation, amounted to 16.1 and 17.3 percent of GDP respectively (Larraín and Vergara 2000: 89). In desperation, the regime also signed a stand-by agreement with the IMF in 1983, followed by a structural adjustment loan from the World Bank in 1985. These settlements served to bolster the regime's commitment to neoliberal policies by making a renewed commitment to active social restructuring as the prerequisite for receiving financial assistance. In this vein, the regime not only committed to upholding the foreign debts of all state companies and major domestic debtors, but also to reverse the emergency import tariffs implemented in 1982, cut state expenditure, remove the final vestiges of wage indexing, and initiate another wave of privatisations.

Attempting to re-establish macroeconomic stability, however, did little to alleviate the immediate impact of crisis on the working class. The socialisation of the debts of the financial sector and the major economic groups did not impede capitals located in industrial sectors from once again either liquidating their operations or undergoing drastic rationalisation processes in an attempt to regain profitability. Consequently, the years 1982–83 represented the worst point of crisis as reflected in the massive destruction of fixed capital and a new wave of labour expulsion from production. This resulted in an additional expansion of the reserve army, contracting wages still further, and imposing a greater degree of immiseration. Employment in the secondary sector, as a percentage of total employment, dropped once more, from 24.4 percent in 1978 to 21.8 percent in 1986, with manufacturing falling from 19 percent to 15.6 percent (Díaz 1997: 167). As visible from Figure 3.2, unemployment reached new highs with open unemployment almost doubling to just under 20 percent in 1982, a figure that excludes the 6.5 percent of the labour force participating in the regime's emergency work programmes.

Within the institutional context of the new labour code, wages were subjected to full market discipline in conditions of a vastly expanded reserve labour army. The bulk of the immiseration process fell most heavily on the industrial working class. Poverty amongst households whose primary wage earner worked in industry and construction rose from 8 percent in 1971 to 47 percent by 1987 (León and Martínez 1998: 301). In this manner, poverty ceased to be a status prevalent only in the rural and urban marginal sections, but became a universalised phenomenon amongst the working class. Whereas employment in industry or construction had previously offered formalised and secure work conditions and relatively high

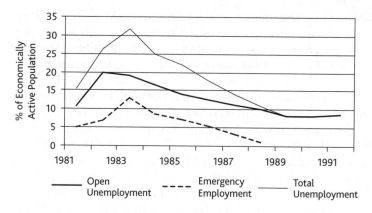

(Data drawn from Mizala and Romaguera 2001: 214)

Figure 3.2 Unemployment 1981–91

wages, crisis and restructuring obliterated these circumstances.
Likewise, for workers in the commercial and service sector, poverty
rates accelerated from 11 percent in 1971 to 42 percent in 1987 (León
and Martínez 1998: 302). Only the working class employed in mining
escaped the process of immiseration. In sum, from the 1982 crisis
until the close of the decade, just under one-half of the population
occupied a position below the poverty line, and therein was unable
to purchase the necessary goods for an adequate level of subsistence.
Notably, this new manifestation of crisis provided the conditions
under which real wages were subject to a second drastic decline.
Eventual economic recovery in the later 1980s would not translate
into rising wages but, on the contrary, a continued suppression of
wages marked the entire decade (Stallings 2001: 52).

Table 3.4 Real Wage Index, 1982–90 (1970 = 100)

Year	1980	1982	1984	1986	1988	1990	1992
Index	88.5	96.1	85.9	83.8	89.1	92.4	101.3

(Data drawn from Fazio 2001a: 217)

SECOND WAVE NEOLIBERALISM AND THE NEW 'ECONOMIC MIRACLE'

As a medium-term response to the crisis, the regime began to deepen
many of the existing reforms through amplified degrees of state

intervention and, therein, enhance and consolidate the processes of social transformation. The recognition that the state would have to play a greater role in fomenting the conditions for accumulation has often been labelled as a shift from orthodox monetarism to 'pragmatic neoliberalism' (Silva 1996; Ffrench-Davis 2002b). Dramatically increased state intervention translated into large expenditures, with average government spending as a proportion of GDP standing at 25.1 percent between 1983 and 1988, a figure 1.5 percent higher than in the 1967–72 populist period (Martínez and Díaz 1996: 66). Such expenditures, however, represented very different forms of intervention than those of the Frei and Allende governments. By socialising the debts of the private sector, moderately augmenting its activities in financial regulation, increasing its infrastructural investment, and selling public companies at below market rates, the state took a greater role in providing the supply-side conditions for capital accumulation. Specifically, by privatising large numbers of remaining public enterprises, the state further extricated itself from the politics of production, strengthened its own institutional coherence, and consolidated the modalities of private power within Chilean society (cf. Schamis 2002).

Following the economic debacle of the 1982–84 period, the regime and international advocates of its neoliberal policies proclaimed a second 'economic miracle' encompassing the period between 1985 and 1989. This miracle was announced on the back of sustained GDP growth rates, with an average rate of growth of 6.7 percent over this period, or 4.9 percent in per capita terms. This expansion was commonly credited to the reaffirmation of neoliberal ideals buffered with increased state activity to accelerate social restructuring. Economic expansion, however, must be understood in the context of a less miraculous combination of making up the massive idle capacity created by the severe drop in production during the recession period, added to the existence of a large labour reserve army and suppressed wages (Rosales 1998: 210). Moreover, economic activity was centred upon the further development of the 'new growth poles' in the Chilean export economy, a boom in the unproductive sector of the economy (services and finance), and high international prices for copper. These developments were significantly aided by the regime's 'debt for equity' swaps through which investors exchanged debt for ownership rights in both the export sector, particularly lumber, agro-export and fish processing, and in privatised companies such as the new private pension firms (Hannon and Gould 1987). In spite of this expansion, if the period 1982 to 1989 is taken as a whole economic performance is considerably less impressive with aggregate GDP growth being 2.6 percent annually, and per capita GDP growth at 0.9 percent (Stallings 2001). Notably, even in the expansionary phase of 1984–89, productivity remained stagnant (Campero 2004), indicating that the boom was predicated on the increased exploitation of labour rather than the introduction of new technology to improve productivity.

In addition to the reforms to welfare institutions addressed in the following chapter, two other pillars of the post-1982 policy approach can be discerned. First, the authoritarian regime began a concerted programme of removing obstacles to profitable investment and, particularly, aggressively promoted exports in order to raise foreign exchange for debt repayment. To start, this involved devaluing the Chilean peso, precipitating an 80 percent reduction in the real exchange rate by 1988 (Schurman 1996: 94). The intention was twofold, to boost the competitiveness of Chilean exports on the world market while improving the conditions for foreign investment in Chile. Exchange-rate manipulation, however, was only one of the means by which the state sought to fortify Chile as a profitable site for global capital investment. Other measures implemented to remove existing restraints on profitability included the further abolition of taxes on wealth and capital gains, and the withdrawal of restrictions on foreign profit remittances (Moguillansky 2001: 178). This new institutional environment benefited both foreign and indigenous capitals, a factor reinforced by amendments to law DL 600 that specifically guaranteed the equal treatment of foreign and domestic capital and gave numerous guarantees in terms of profit remittances and investor rights. By the mid-1980s, foreign direct investment began to flood into the Chilean export sectors, particularly the copper mining sector in which foreign companies reclaimed a position unseen since the early 1960s, a process that Hugo Fazio has analysed as the 'transnationalisation' of the Chilean economy (Fazio 2000). Conspicuously, however, the regime retained control of Codelco, the extremely profitable state-owned copper company that had been nationalised in the Allende period and which provided a major source of fiscal revenues of which 10 percent were channelled directly to the armed forces.

Second, the recomposition of capital in export-orientated productive sectors continued, with a deepening specialisation in agricultural and raw material exports. The state took a stronger role in promoting exports than orthodox neoclassical theory would allow, including providing tax rebates for exporters and waving duties on imports used to create exports. State industrial policy in this period involved facilitating a supply of credit to, and technological advancement within, the export sector and particularly to large producers working with economies of scale in the relatively infant agro-export sectors (Schurman 1996: 86; Kurtz 2001: 15–17; Ffrench-Davis 2002a: 166). By organising firms into networks of exporters and providing up to 50 percent financing for new export development initiatives, the state development agency CORFO played a notable role in the establishment of new export industries including agro-export, fish processing and chemical pulp factories (Perez-Aleman 2003; Phillips 2004: 200). The majority of economic expansion that occurred in the 1984–89 period was precisely in these new 'dynamic poles' of Chilean production. While in the 1960s the value of exports amounted to 13 percent of GDP, this had risen to 20.7 percent in the 1974–81 period and underwent a further large jump to 29.6 percent in the 1985–89 period (Stallings 2001: 46). The bulk of this expansion was performed under the aegis of the large economic groups who dominated the new-export sectors, although smaller capitals existed in some of the more peripheral activities that needed relatively little capital investment.

The emerging recovery and subsequent productive boom based on primary exports in the later 1980s slowly began to reincorporate the vastly expanded reserve labour army back into the waged labour force. This process was aided by a more flexible approach to trade liberalisation that jettisoned the uniform tariff rate and provided slightly more protection for some domestic industries, including non-export agriculture (Ffrench-Davis 2002a: 166). New forms of employment expanded in the unproductive sectors of the economy, with commerce and services rising as a percentage of employment in both formalised and informal forms. As a notable example of formal sector service extension, financial services rapidly expanded, growing from 2.4 percent of employment in 1970 to 4.8 percent in 1986 and 6.8 percent by 1994 (Díaz 1997: 166). Further, this re-absorption of workers was notable in the growth of urban labour forces involved in primary commodity production, specifically fruit picking, forestry, fishing and mining. While traditional forms of agriculture were declining, the growth of agro-industry created a large sector of urbanised workers involved in forestry and fruit picking, particularly in the Bío-Bío and central valley areas respectively.

Notably, as discussed in chapter 8, the jobs created in the new export industries have in many respects proved the most under-regulated and precarious, characterised by pervasive insecurity of tenure and poor working conditions.

It is perhaps unsurprising, therefore, that even with the intensification of the primary exports boom in the final years of the decade, in 1989 42.2 percent of the population lived in poverty, with 14.9 percent of the population existing in conditions of indigence (Schneider 1993: 30). Far from 'miracle policies' being able to account for a 'miracle economy', the social basis of capital accumulation lay in the deep-seated transformation of class relations coupled to a repositioning of Chile as a raw materials and primary produce export platform within the global economy. Significantly, the dramatic rise in the rate of exploitation through the lowering of wages and the increasing length and intensity of the working day was a fundamental aspect of the post-debt crisis restructuring, and provided the platform on which Chilean capitalism could regain its profitability. Re-institutionalising the social relations of production on this new footing, however, also required dramatic changes to state institutions that mediated consumption patterns in Chilean society. To this end, the following chapter examines the transformation of welfare institutions over the length of the Pinochet period.

SUMMARY

The neoliberal reformers who entered key positions in the authoritarian regime in 1975 sought to begin a major process of institutional restructuring that could put an end to the sustained economic and political crisis of Chilean society. Their strategy of 'creative destruction' attempted to impose this institutional shift by deploying coercive economic policies to engineer a recession of such intensity that it would obliterate the social and material basis of existing social relations. Together with the unplanned debacle of 1982, these periods of dramatic social upheaval prompted a profound recomposition of social relations in Chile, which the authoritarian regime subsequently sought to re-institutionalise. The new social basis of this society was the profound restructuring of the working classes, who were faced with shifting employment structures, decreasing wages and greatly intensified workloads. The latter trends were buttressed through the framework of reformed labour institutions that sought to solidify the new relations of power between social classes. The resulting social transformation was marked by a process of de-industrialisation in which industrial manufacturing underwent a period of capitalist rationalisation and concentration of ownership, with serious consequences for the sizeable number of workers who were ejected from these industries and forced into a reserve labour army. Conversely, the reforms led to the growing prominence of export-orientated branches of production that were integrated within global capital circuits and a heavy centralisation of assets, with the expansion of large economic conglomerates. A shift of this nature involved not only a re-emphasis on copper exports, which had played a central role in capital accumulation in Chile since the turn of the century, but also the development of new primary exports, such as lumber, fruit and fish products.

4
From Retrenchment to the 'Seven Modernisations' – The Great Transformation of Welfare Institutions

As chapter 1 elaborated, an extremely significant outcome of the national-developmentalist period in Chile was the establishment and expansion of welfare institutions – such as social assistance, health and education provision, and social security – through which the state mediated the social reproduction of various sections of the Chilean population. For the neoliberal reformers who rose to prominence within the authoritarian regime of Augusto Pinochet, however, these institutions were representative of the ills of Chilean society for two primary reasons. On the one hand, state interventions were seen to distort the operations of the market by insulating various social actors from market discipline and consequently creating inefficient economic outcomes. On the other, they were viewed as both source and outcome of the pervasive politicisation of Chilean society. Through mobilisation, special interest groups were understood to place political pressure on the state to attain material security rather than relying on private market interactions, therein subverting the rationality of the market. Consequent to these struggles, the state became increasingly overburdened, driven by short-term political motivations and – ultimately in the Allende period – a threat to the basic parameters of capitalist society.

The neoliberal technocrats within the authoritarian regime sought to recast welfare institutions in a manner that would remedy these ills and the current chapter charts this trajectory of reforms. It highlights the motivating ideology behind the neoliberal restructuring of welfare institutions and the contradictions inherent to it. Whereas the initial reforms between 1973 and 1978 were tentative, in 1979 the regime initiated a programme known as the 'Seven Modernisations' that constituted an ambitious project to restructure fundamentally the institutional forms of state–society relations. The title of this chapter deliberately evokes Karl Polanyi's work 'The Great Transformation' in order to emphasise not only the way in which the market order sought by neoliberals is only attainable through concerted social engineering strategies undertaken by the state, but also how market-led social regulation tends to undermine the conditions of its own existence. The illogics of neoliberal reforms are concretised in the case studies of the reforms implemented to the provision of education, healthcare and pensions that close the chapter.

RETRENCHMENT AND INITIAL REFORMS, 1973–78

Within the gradualist approach to policy that characterised the authoritarian regime's first two years, the intent of the economic team to address the state's fiscal deficit and to restore macroeconomic equilibrium by contracting consumer demand translated into a notable reduction of social expenditure. With few exceptions, existing welfare programmes were abolished, cut back or simply left to erode in circumstances of spiralling inflation. From 1975 onwards, further retrenchment of social expenditure constituted an integral component of the 'creative destruction' strategy. By withdrawing various subsidies that served to reduce the reproduction costs of the working class, the authoritarian regime reversed the expansion of welfare institutions that had resulted from over half a century of social struggles. State mechanisms to aid the reproduction of the household – through institutions such as subsidised consumption goods, housing provision, health services, income subsidies and social security – were reduced or abolished and the responsibility to attain these necessities were placed more fully on individuals through participation in the labour market.

Moreover, this retrenchment occurred alongside fiscal reforms that raised the level of taxes collected by increasingly regressive mechanisms. Not only did the state seek to finance existing expenditures, it also needed to cover comprehensive increases in the portion of state expenditure allocated to national defence and to service high levels of external debt incurred partially through an IMF stand-by agreement. Fiscal reform transpired in two stages. Immediate changes in 1973 sought to raise taxes on excise and property, increase upper-level income tax, and put into practice a more rigorous collection policy. The latter were changes that impacted primarily, if marginally, upon the upper and middle classes as the state looked for a rapid increase in revenues given the immediacy of the fiscal crisis. Nonetheless, the same initiative also abolished the tax on capital gains, a move that was consistent with the regime's attempt to promote renewed investment and which contributed towards the rapidly strengthening position of financial capital within Chilean society.

In 1975, however, these first reforms were supplemented by the introduction of a uniform 20 percent value-added tax (VAT) that replaced the former disjointed sales tax systems. With this move, which mirrored the rise of neoliberal technocrats within the regime, regressive forms of indirect taxation began to play a substantial and growing role in the consolidation of state finances. The new system was relatively successful in rapidly boosting state revenue, which grew from 20 percent of GDP in 1974 to over 24 percent in 1975 (Ritter 1992: 12). In the five years following the 1975 crisis, a substantial quantity of direct taxes was abolished, with others reduced. The latter initiative instigated a consistent decline of tax revenues as a percentage of GDP to below 20 percent by 1982 (Larraín and Vergara 2000: 80). Concurrently, VAT as a portion of revenue grew rapidly, increasing from 33.3 percent in 1974 to 49.1 percent in 1979 (Vergara 1986: 104–5). By transferring an increased proportion of the tax burden onto working-class households this movement shifted the responsibilities to contribute to state finances between social classes. As a consequence, the Chilean working class experienced heavier taxation on daily consumption items at the same time as the state greatly reduced its social expenditures.

Towards the end of the decade renewed economic growth eased pressures upon state finances and led to a slight reversal of expenditure retrenchment. By 1979 social expenditure had recovered from the immediate contraction of 1974–75 but remained at only 83 percent of the 1970 level in real terms (Torche 2000: 557). Retrenchment on this scale was manifested in marked decreases in the value of average pensions, hospital beds per person and per capita housing, health and education spending (Fortín 1985: 182; Huber 1996: 165). The most significant area of retrenchment was public housing, with spending cut by 60 percent in the year of 1975, and was further reduced to just 30 percent of the 1974 level by 1979, therein reversing the Frei and Allende government policies promoting public provision of housing and house-building materials. Healthcare also suffered large reductions, comprising a 40 percent decrease in state funding between 1974 and 1976 alone. Likewise, education expenditure was shrunk to 73 percent of its 1974 level by 1976, although it would subsequently recover, reaching 90 percent of the 1974 figure until further reductions in the early 1980s (data drawn from Torche 2000: 557).

The retrenchment of social expenditure achieved a dramatic reduction in the 'social wage' – that is, the amount of national income diverted to state-operated social programmes – at the same time that real wages declined sharply and unemployment expanded dramatically. As a consequence, a significant proportion of the Chilean population was forced to rely upon individual, familial and community-based survival strategies to supplement declining wages, faltering employment and reduced state support. Following the 1975 crisis, and again in the 1982–85 period, collective action, such as the formation of soup kitchens to address subsistence needs, shared accommodation to provide housing, group migration and the establishment of squatter settlements, helped to provide or subsidise social reproduction in the poorest neighbourhoods (cf. Oxhorn 1995: 87–9). The Chilean research group Programa de Economia del Trabajo estimated that by 1985 there existed 1,103 collective subsistence organisations directly involving some 110,000 people and sustaining many more (Oxhorn 1995: 86). Concurrently, mass unemployment forced increasing numbers of women and children to search for work in the informal sector in an attempt to spread income earning across the family. As such, this period saw a distinct transformation in the gendered division of labour in Chile, with a growing insecuritisation of traditional male paid work in industrial sectors, simultaneous to the entrance of increasing numbers of women into formal and informal sector employment (Tinsman 2004: 165–6).

Although familial and community based survival strategies became increasingly important to secure the reproduction of the household, the state retained a pivotal yet reformed role. Whereas the 'creative destruction' of austerity measures would eventually recreate the social foundations for renewed capital accumulation by driving down wages, increasing levels of exploitation and facilitating the movement of capital and labour into new economic sectors; this process simultaneously threatened to destroy its human foundations through the absolute immiseration of the Chilean working class. It is within these paradoxical conditions that the authoritarian state was forced to react. With widespread un- and under-employment, increasing pauperisation, and the emergent political organisation of community groups, the regime became concerned about the twin threats of social disintegration and mounting political opposition. Alongside the introduction of emergency employment programmes examined in the previous chapter, the regime responded by undertaking a reformulation of social assistance programmes in a manner that laid the foundations for a wider reshaping and depoliticisation of welfare provision in the remainder of the decade.

TARGETED SOCIAL PROGRAMMES

The dictatorship's initial reforms to welfare institutions were predicated on the introduction of social mapping techniques that differentiated the working class according to income and vulnerability. In so doing, the regime claimed that expenditure could be targeted towards the extreme poor in an objective, efficient and apolitical manner. Introducing technically defined criteria to judge which households deserved state support and which would be excluded, the regime sought to sustain the poorest sections of the working class in conditions of generalised pauperisation without politicising these relations. As such, the regime initiated a change in the institutional form of state–society linkages in order to regulate and depoliticise extreme poverty within the context of a general retrenchment of social expenditures and a reshaping of class relations. Although cautious in their initial application, these transformations in the institutions of state intervention in social reproduction would subsequently become one of the basic modes assumed by anti-poverty policy in Chile for the succeeding three decades, not to mention a hallmark of neoliberal social policy on a global level (cf. Sottoli 2000 and chapter 8).

The implementation of targeted subsidies played a key ideological function by enabling the Pinochet regime to declare it was acting to end extreme poverty and guarantee a greater degree of equality amongst Chileans even as the opposite trends were occurring. Targeted social programmes were not new to Chile and had been important tools for the distribution of resources and the social and political incorporation of marginalised groups in both the Frei and Allende regimes. In this respect it is worth emphasising that targeted social programmes are not exclusive to neoliberal social policy regimes, but can operate effectively within universalistic social policy regimes (Haagh 2002c). Under the dictatorship's reforms, however, targeting occurred alongside a retrenchment of universal social policies. Wherever possible, expenditures were to be directed solely towards the category of the 'deserving' poor as measured by technocratic techniques while other households were to rely on their own means – primarily through labour markets – to reproduce themselves. Creating welfare institutions of this nature lay in contrast to the politicised relations that underscored the period of national developmentalism in which institutions were formed and developed in an ad-hoc manner as mobilised interest groups and social movements pressured the state for material compromises.

By highlighting that the old forms of social protection and services had privileged certain sections of the middle and working classes while excluding others, the regime proclaimed that new assistance programmes would provide the means through which marginalised households could share the benefits of increased development. For example, family allowances based on the number of children per family were equalised across the board, thereby homogenising previous benefit differences between white-collar and blue-collar workers that had resulted from the varied ability of occupational groups to effectively impress demands upon the state in the post-war period (refer to chapter 2). Similarly, disability and unemployment benefits were standardised, countering the fragmentation of benefits that previously existed. Nonetheless, although the authoritarian regime was able to accomplish this standardisation, which previous governments had attempted and failed, this must be viewed in the context of a strong depreciation of the value of benefits. For example, by 1979 the above-mentioned family support payment had shrunk to almost half of its 1970 real value and the average pension was reduced by a quarter (Vergara 1986: 104).

Systematic social mapping techniques were a necessary tool for the new policies in order to measure and, thereby, distinguish the intended recipients. A new governmental body called ODEPLAN, the National Planning Office, was set up to accomplish this task and was managed by technocrats who championed the introduction of strongly focalised social expenditures. In creating a system to categorise the wellbeing of the Chilean working classes, however, the regime was faced with a dilemma. While, on the one hand, social mapping, categorisation and distinction were all essential to the implementation of highly targeted spending, the regime was also unwilling to give precise details on the fate of the Chilean population under the austerity measures. As a result, an idiosyncratic form of measuring poverty was created that abstracted away from the immediate effects of economic crisis, such as declining real incomes. So long as a household satisfied a small number of criteria – for example, owning a television was one criterion – it would be classified as above the poverty line and therein ineligible for state subsidies (Torche 2000: 547–8).

This method of measuring poverty and distinguishing between the poor and non-poor was applied at both local and national levels. Household surveys were collected by municipalities working under the direction of ODEPLAN and turned into a stratification index called the 'Ficha CAS'. The latter provided the basis on which subsidies were targeted at what appeared to be the 30 percent of the population in greatest need. At the national level, the same forms of measurement were used to give strongly underestimated accounts of poverty levels. Hence, when the 1982 national census results were employed to repeat the procedure, the regime triumphantly declared a drop in poverty from 21 percent of families in 1970 to 14 percent in 1982. Virtually all other surveys and poverty measuring techniques displayed strikingly different results, showing a considerable rise in both indigence and poverty. Carol Graham (1991: 5), for example, compiles data that shows a leap in the percentage of households living in indigence from 8.4 to 11.7 between 1969 and 1979. Likewise, for Graham, poverty increased from 20.1 percent of households to 25.3 percent over the same period.

Despite its inadequacies in the quantitative measurement of poverty, the new system was vigorously employed to aid the targeting of several branches of state social expenditure. For example, a national complementary feeding programme (PNAC) had existed since 1954, offering supplementary food to pregnant and nursing mothers, alongside their infants. In 1974 the regime abolished the universal dimension of the programme, and established criteria through ODEPLAN for those who were to receive continued nutritional subsidies. Although some 'leakage' did still occur, by 1985 approximately 50 percent of the benefits were directed towards those in the bottom three income deciles (Graham 1991: 9; Torche 2000: 558). Similarly, the National Association of Child Care Centres (JUNJI) programme offered food, day care and cash subsidy for poor families with children, and a school lunch programme targeted children under the age of six and pregnant or nursing mothers. Consequently, the maintenance of nutritional and child support programmes at the bottom end of the social spectrum played a leading part in maintaining and improving several social indicators, particularly child mortality, in conditions of generalised material immiseration. In terms of its primary aims, therefore, targeting originated as a technique for continuing to subsidise the poorest section of society in the context of generalised cutbacks in social expenditure and the coverage and value of family subsidies.

A more positive side effect of targeted social policy was its tendency to integrate some households and areas that had indeed been marginalised within the former systems. This was certainly the case in healthcare where free primary care was generalised to cover all pregnant women, children and infants and the extreme poor. Some of the latter had been excluded from the previous system despite its universal pretensions. Nonetheless, such beneficial aspects occurred alongside an arbitrary income cut-off that excluded those above the extreme poverty line from free care, and a substantial deterioration in the quantity and quality of all available services owing to budgetary austerity. At the same time, the regime's pronouncements that it would only offer assistance to those unable to take care of themselves placed a great deal of stigma upon those households and individuals that took recourse to them leading authors such as Carol Graham (1991: 11) to suggest that targeting 'often served to stigmatise and alienate the poor rather than to enhance their potential to participate in society'.

FROM SOCIAL ASSISTANCE TO THE 'SEVEN MODERNISATIONS'

The early reforms to social assistance strategies provided an initial restructuring of welfare institutions through which the state continued to support the poorest sections of Chilean society in a depoliticised form while simultaneously undertaking a generalised retrenchment of social expenditure. The general tenets of a far more radical transformation of welfare institutions, however, had been put forward prior to the overthrow of Allende by neoclassical economists working at the Universidad Católica de Chile. The latter created a blueprint in the late 1960s for a comprehensive restructuring project known as 'El Ladrillo' ('The Brick'). This document outlined a thorough reform of the institutions of welfare provision upon neoliberal lines that served to offer a radical break with the national-developmentalist character of state policy. Nonetheless, on assuming power the military junta refrained from implementing a restructuring package of this profundity – despite being convinced of the need for depoliticising reforms to social institutions – owing to a combination of structural and contingent factors. These included the drastic deepening of crisis caused by the macroeconomic restructuring and the existence of opposition within sections of the governing regime, national bourgeoisie, and professional associations (Castiglioni 2001).

By the late 1970s, however, the military regime had undergone a process of consolidation around the figure of Pinochet and many of those advocating a more gradualist approach to economic and social policy reform had been ejected from positions of power. Economic growth in the late 1970s, despite its tenuous nature, generated talk in both domestic and international policy circles of an 'economic miracle'. This led to a rise in the prestige of neoliberal macroeconomic management under the banner of 'the Chilean model' and resulted in the colonisation of most state departments by neoliberal technocrats. Concurrently, by 1980 the regime had also promulgated a new constitution and, through a plebiscite held in conditions of extensive intimidation and repression, granted itself a further eight years in power. Under these circumstances, the regime felt secure enough to unveil and initiate an extensive package of reforms that sought to advance the restructuring of Chilean social relations to a new level. With significant attention from the international policy community, Pinochet unveiled a series of dramatic institutional reforms that he termed the 'Seven Modernisations'. Like its contemporary, the 'Four Modernisations' strategy unveiled by Deng Xiaoping in China in 1979, the Seven Modernisations opened a period of concerted state intervention aimed at systematically refashioning the institutions through which Chilean society reproduced itself materially and socially. Whereas earlier reforms had reshaped state economic institutions, causing a dramatic shift in Chilean productive structures and class relations, the Seven Modernisations targeted the institutions governing labour relations, education, health and social security provision, judicial procedure, political decentralisation and agrarian reform.

NEOLIBERALISM AND WELFARE INSTITUTIONS – MOTIVATIONS AND THEORY

In essence, the 'Seven Modernisations' constituted an audacious programme to reconstruct comprehensively the institutional form of the state. The regime anticipated that a fundamental remodelling of the entire spectrum of welfare institutions could complement and consolidate the greater social transformation that it had begun in the mid-1970s. In this vein, there were three specific motivations for the post-1979 welfare restructuring. First, all initiatives aimed to redefine further the nature of state–society relations through individualisation, privatisation and decentralisation. As such, the reformulation focused on the explicit goal of frustrating the creation of collective social subjects through an atomisation of the populace and the removal of the centralised state apparatus as the primary target of social movements. Second, the regime sought to tailor the new measures so as to open further opportunities for profitable enterprise. Third, where possible, the forms of social policy were intended to dovetail with observable labour requirements of the new productive structures arising through restructuring. Addressing these points in turn it is possible to outline the major trends of the reformulation before examining their concrete development through an examination of health, pension and education policies in the following sections.

Through the Seven Modernisations, the dictatorship desired to transform welfare institutions in a manner that would achieve a fundamental recasting of the expectations and behaviour of individuals and families towards their means of social reproduction. Specifically, an overriding aim was to negate the historically developed forms of class struggle that characterised the previous 50 years and led to the sustained expansion of state welfare institutions. No longer would social services be conditioned on the mobilisation and articulation of various collective social subjects that levied demands on the central state apparatus. Rather, such relations were to be recomposed where possible as market relationships between individuals and firms. This atomisation of social relations was to be achieved through processes of decentralisation and privatisation that would transform the institutions that regulated social service provision. The reproduction of the household was to be divorced from socialised forms of provision and reconstituted as a private responsibility to be achieved through market integration supplemented with familial solidarity.

Historically-developed state institutions that regulated working-class reproduction, and particularly those forms that involved a shared responsibility between worker, state and employer, were deemed to be anachronistic, inefficient, and ultimately prejudicial to those they ought to help. In contrast, introducing the market into the sphere of welfare through privatisation of service provision was justified under the veneer of increasing the efficiency of service provision to the benefit of all welfare 'consumers'. The latter were now to be free to choose between those providers that offered the best services at the lowest prices. As such, the transformation of the institutions of social welfare was juxtaposed with a correlate ideological shift to an emphasis on the freedom of choice of the user. The market was presented as the realm of freedom and equality and, concurrently, the competition between service providers who would react to consumer choices was suggested to create an optimal allocation of resources throughout welfare provision. Although this neoliberal formulation of welfare reform could cloak itself in the rhetoric of individual choice being an innate and essential element of human liberty, it rarely concerned itself with the social circumstances within which individual choices are made (see Myers 2002).

In this manner, under the justification of removing the pernicious effects of state intervention and concurrently increasing the elements of user choice and competition, the regime encouraged private sector provision of key social services on a for-profit basis. This included a compulsory privatisation of pensions for new entrants to the labour market and the creation of dualised systems of health and education in which private enterprises would compete with each other and the state to provide services to paying customers. In many respects, this process offered a significant opportunity, subsidised by the state, for the emergent economic groups to increase their investment opportunities. Whereas the privatisation of the pension system offered the most lucrative profit-making opportunities, not least because it was protected by the guarantee of state intervention in the event of crisis, the prospect of providing profitable high-end medical care and private education also offered high returns. The nature of the privatisation processes was specifically crafted to offer investors the most profitable aspects of service provision while leaving the state to provide a general safety net for the majority of the population, a process that María Olivia Mönckeberg (2001) refers to as the 'pillaging' of the Chilean state by the economic conglomerates.

The necessary corollary of the privatising process would therefore be twofold. On the one hand, the rapid privatisation of a broad range of state services induced a concentration of service providers. These were primarily drawn from the large economic groups who, enjoying privileged access to finance, were the best placed to capitalise on the new opportunities for profitable investment. For example, the five large private health insurance companies, who in 2000 captured 74 percent of the market, have dominated the market since the reforms of 1980 (Barrientos 2002: 448). On the other, there would quickly emerge a pronounced stratification of the quantity and quality of services attainable in relation to the purchasing power of the individual. Unsurprisingly, privatised services would become the preserve of primarily the rich and upper middle classes, with the state maintaining a minimal form of intervention in the reproduction of the working class. Indeed, despite the rhetoric of efficient markets and freedom of choice, the dictatorship understood the very clear limits to which privatisation could be taken. In those cases where the state was required to retain an involvement in provision owing to the impossibility of reconciling service delivery with private sector profitability, processes of decentralisation were implemented in order to segment collective articulation into the localised realm of municipal governments that had been stacked with functionaries hand-picked by the Pinochet regime. Social service decentralisation was not only envisaged as a manner by which to fragment the subjectivities of service recipients, but also to disarticulate the national power of unions involved in the provision of services. For example, the powerful teachers' union had been a principal backer of the prior Allende regime yet received a further blow to its internal cohesion through the decentralisation of education provision to municipal levels alongside its partial privatisation.

Finally, following the shift from national developmentalism to an export-orientated model predicated on primary goods with little value added during the production process (i.e. copper, fruit, wine, fish products and lumber), the regime sought a qualitative change in social policy in order to forge a better articulation between welfare provision and production relations. As examined in chapter 2, one justification advanced by structuralist thought for the creation of relatively expansive social policies was that a redistribution of social wealth towards various strata of the working class would provide a significant boost to domestic consumption and therein help to bolster processes of national industrialisation. This direction was taken furthest in the Frei and Allende regimes, as discussed in chapter 1. For the authoritarian regime, however, the logic of implementing social policies to promote domestic demand for consumer goods collapsed owing to the concentration of capital in export-orientated branches of production. From the perspective of the export-orientated conglomerates, whose accumulation strategies had been exten-sively internationalised, expanding domestic consumption through expansive social policies was contrary to their interests. Many of the welfare institutions that had developed over the preceding four decades appeared not only as drains on social surplus, but also as barriers to the free functioning of labour markets, thereby restricting the flexible utilisation of labour across the economy. In contrast to the large economic groups, those capitals that retained a dependence on domestic consumption were generally medium and small producers (PYMEs) who, given their limited political strength and their more marginal role in the accumulation process, would continue to struggle ineffectually for measures to boost domestic consumption throughout the dictatorship period and beyond.

EDUCATION REFORMS

The military regime's reform decree of 1980 enacted a significant reformulation of Chilean education. With an explicit aim to reduce the role and expenditure of the state and supplant state provision with private sector involvement, the reform created a dualised public–private education system that remains the basis for education provision in Chile today. In referring to this dramatic transformation of the infrastructure of education, the former education minister Gonzalo Vial claimed in an interview that the government did not have an education policy per se, but rather an economic policy of education (Castiglioni 2001: 43). This remark, however, does not bear scrutiny as the regime determinately instigated a political remodelling of education through a purge of education institutions and the teachers' unions to remove those suspected of sympathies to the Allende regime. Surveillance of teaching practices by both police and informant networks consolidated this purge and, on a pedagogical level, the educational content of teaching and textbooks was altered to reflect the national security doctrine preached by the regime. Higher education was recast to promote studies functional to the new productive structures of Chilean society, whereas traditional arts and humanities studies were discouraged (Austin 1997).

On a structural level, however, the institutional and administrative format of Chilean education indeed provided the major focus for the reformers. Decentralisation was a central pillar of the reforms and responsibility for administering schools was rapidly passed down to the municipal level. By April of 1982 almost 85 percent of public schools had been transferred to the municipalities (Gaury 1998: 24). Municipalities could take two approaches. One option was to establish a municipal education administration department (DAEM) within the structures of local administration that would be staffed by municipal functionaries, regulated by normal municipal guidelines and with the departmental head being a teacher. The alternative was to follow a corporate model and privatise education administration through the establishment of a Corporación Municipal (Municipal

Corporation). The latter would run the organisational structure of local education as a privately operating entity (Beyer 2000). Despite the great faith placed in the transformation of public administration into private regulatory bodies, most municipalities chose to establish DAEMs owing to the greater ease of their establishment and also the reduced costs involved. Moreover, by 1988 the formation of any further Municipal Corporations was prohibited owing to a legal challenge that deemed the passing of public institutions into the bounds of private law as unconstitutional.

Alongside these changes to the administrative structures of education, the second part of the reform package involved a radical reformulation of the relationship between state and schools. Rather than continue funding schools directly, the regime proclaimed that a demand-side approach would encourage greater efficiency. Similar to Milton Friedman's celebrated voucher system, resources were no longer provided directly to schools. Rather, the state funded them indirectly by assigning resources to the students. Thereby, schools would receive financial support based on the number of students that they could attract, imparting a strict competition ethic into the education system. If schools were unable to compete in this new marketplace environment, they would be allowed to fail and face dissolution. Moreover, this decentralisation of financial responsibility in education, alongside healthcare, has placed an extensive financial burden on municipal governments resulting in widespread indebtedness (Raczynski 2000: 127).

The decentralisation process was supplemented by permitting private, profit-orientated institutions to establish primary and secondary education schools that would also compete for student enrolment, and therein receive public funds for each student. Run by private sector companies on a for-profit basis, these private yet state-subsidised schools would expand to cover about 30 percent of student enrolment. In spite of this process of opening education to private sector involvement and the introduction of a competition ethic between educational institutions, the state nonetheless remained the fundamental financial guarantor of education, albeit in a modified form. Over 60 percent of school enrolment remained in government hands, and a further 30 percent was privately operated yet funded through the state voucher system (Raczynski and Romaguera 1995: 212). It would actually be under the post-dictatorship governments of the Concertación, as detailed in chapter 8, that these initial reforms would be extended and a greater privatising trend undertaken.

By the end of the 1980s the successive quantitative retrenchments in primary and secondary education imparted more serious effects than the qualitative changes. The sharpest cuts in the education budget occurred immediately following the rise of the dictatorship, with a 25 percent reduction between 1974 and 1976. Spending then rose again, recovering to 90 percent of the 1974 total by 1979 (Torche 2000: 557). However, after 1981 the rest of the decade was marked by an acute downward trend, with a further cutback of 25 percent between 1982 and 1990. This was directly reflected in the diminishing value of the per-student subsidy that the government paid to educational institutions, as indicated in Figure 4.1. The implications were felt across the education system, most notably in the impoverishment of school resources and the decline of teacher wages, particularly those in the poorer municipalities serving the poorest sections of society (Raczynski 1999: 138–9). In 1990 the minimum salaries of teachers were more than 50 percent lower than in 1980 (Raczynski and Romaguera 1995: 294).

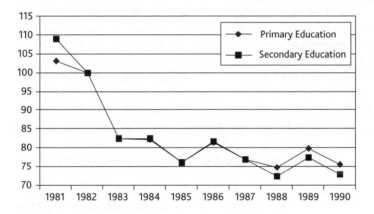

(Elaborated from data in Beyer 2000: 668)

Figure 4.1   Value of State Education Subsidy (1982 = 100)

In the realm of higher education the decreases in funding were even greater and the subsequent disparities along class and income lines were more fundamental. Under the 1981 General Law of Universities, the regime pursued a policy of privatisation that would diminish drastically the state funding of higher education. Resources destined for higher education underwent a 40 percent reduction between

1981 and 1990 (Beyer 2000: 668). The reform ended summarily all pretences of a free university system and promoted the establishment of small private higher education institutions. In the verdict of Robert Austin, such reforms transformed higher education into an entity of the capitalist marketplace, promoted entrepreneurial profit-minded investment and remodelled the content of post-secondary education to consolidate the reorganised productive structures of the economy (Austin 1997).

In sum, providing a high quality mass education was not a priority of the regime. Given the emerging productive structure based upon primary resource exports with little value added and whose international competitiveness rested in no small measure on the employment of cheap labour, there was little demand for a workforce with universally high levels of educational achievement. Where more sophisticated skill sets were needed, the state-led transformation of higher education increased the burden of advanced training on the individual household or enterprise. A basic, if declining, level of primary and secondary education would be provided for the working class, and the opportunities for a better grade of basic education or the possibility of undertaking further education, and therein occupying a more privileged position within labour markets, would fall to those with the income to purchase it. Concurrently, the political dimensions of the reform centred around the fragmentation of social mobilisation over the material aspects of education provision through decentralisation processes, particularly to delimit the strength and oppositional nature of the national teachers' union.

HEALTHCARE – THE CREATION OF A DUALISED SYSTEM

The reform of healthcare provision was founded upon a similar set of ideological principles to that of education. Once again, decentralisation and partial privatisation were guiding elements of the reform. However, the latter would be implemented to a further degree than in education, thereby institutionalising a dualised system that more closely linked the quality of healthcare to household incomes. Prior to 1973 the health system was comprised of a state funded yet often under-resourced National Health Service existing alongside a private fee-for-service system, with the former providing the bulk of services. Doctors would commonly work part-time for the state sector and part-time in private clinics. In the 1974–80 period the dictatorship generally left this system unchanged in its fundamentals concurrent to stringently reducing public health expenditures. Notably, by 1979 per capita health expenditure had dropped to 64 percent of its 1974 level (Torche 2000: 557), thereby intensifying acutely the failures of the existing system. Raczynski and Romaguera (1995: 294) indicate that the cuts were manifested in a lack of infrastructural investment alongside falling wages for health workers, factors that, alongside the new reforms, would lead the public system to a crisis point in the late 1980s.

Introduced in 1981, the new institutional framework was predicated on several key changes. The most important was the establishment of obligatory private health insurance payments for all workers. Under the new system individuals were required to pay 4 percent of their earnings for health insurance, although this sum rose to 7 percent after further reforms in 1987. In the spirit of optimising personal choice and increasing the role of the private sector, contributors are presented with the choice of either paying into the public health system (Fondo Nacional de Salud, FONASA) or to one of the private health funds (Institutos de Salud Previsional, ISAPRE). These private health funds generally do not employ a permanent medical staff but rather operate as health insurance brokers who contract doctors and relevant medical apparatus as needed while providing hotel-standard facilities for patients receiving care (Hiscock and Hojman 1997: 359). They are universally regarded as offering far superior healthcare services. However, to belong to an ISAPRE an individual or family has to be able to cover the specific premiums charged by the fund. The latter are based on an individual risk analysis of each prospective entrant according to considerations of age and gender and are far higher than the contributions required for membership of the public system. The result was that the ISAPREs presented an exclusionary system with, in 1990, only 16 percent of the population being members (Titelman 2001: 271).

Alternatively, the public system – FONASA – operates according to a system whereby services are financed through the mandatory contributions alongside subsidies from the public treasury. On undergoing any form of medical attention users are means tested and charged a co-payment relative to their income level for the particular treatment received. During the 1980s the quality of care within the public system was considered to be very low. In view of the significant cuts in social spending by the dictatorship, a pronounced decline in the quality of public health services was not surprising. Between 1974 and 1979 and again between 1980 and 1989 the regime reduced per capita health expenditure by one-third. This meant that by 1990 per capita public health expenditure had fallen to under half of its 1974 level in real terms (Torche 2000: 557, 567). In 1990 healthcare staff were vastly underpaid, overworked and the standard and availability of medical equipment had drastically deteriorated. A decline of this nature did not go uncontested within the public system. In 1984–85 several regional medical associations publicly derided the state of the healthcare system (Raczynski and Romaguera 1995: 294). Protests of this nature, however, were unable to precipitate an increase in public expenditure devoted to the health system.

Central to these problems is the strong structural bias against the state system that is inherent to the dualised institutional form of healthcare provision. Entrance into the ISAPRE system, structured upon class, gender and age lines, is clearly discriminatory. Older women and men, and particularly women who fall in the age range deemed statistically probable to become pregnant, are faced with prohibitively increased premiums or, in some cases, are simply rejected by the ISAPREs. Contrarily, middle age high-income (and low-risk) males are prime ISAPRE material. As a result, despite incorporating only a minority of the population into private healthcare, those that were incorporated were those most able to pay the elevated fees. Therefore, in 1990 ISAPREs collected just under 57 percent of the total value of contributions despite providing care for only 16 percent of the population (Castiglioni 2001: 43). On this basis, the profit-making private health funds are able to siphon off the population statistically less likely to need health services alongside the greater part of mandatory contributions, while the state sector with less resources must provide for the majority of the population, including those sections most likely to require sustained health services. To compound this situation, observers note that many members of the ISAPRE system used the public health system for most non-serious medical treatment in order to protect their 'no-claim bonuses'. A household survey conducted in 1992 suggested that ISAPRE members used the public system to treat 30 percent of preventive medicine issues, 39 percent of hospitalisations and 69 percent of medical emergencies (Barrientos 2002: 449). Also, many of the lower-income entrants to the ISAPRE system enjoy only coverage for particular ailments and once again must revert to the public system for the more costly forms of medical attention (Cid Pedraza 2001: 5). As such, the public system operated as a pressure valve that absorbed many costs of the private system and therein served to augment the profitability of that sector with a detrimental impact on overall efficiency.

Although such extreme structural biases may seem irrational outcomes, they are the entirely logical result of the neoliberal dualisation of health provision. These problems, however, did not stop the World Bank in 1990 from enthusiastically labelling the Chilean reforms as a particularly worthy model for the developing world to follow (World Bank 1990: 85). In contrast to such acclaim, the Chilean experience indicates that, contrary to its proclaimed benefits in terms of efficient private sector involvement, downsizing of state action and an increasing freedom of choice for users, dualisation served to prejudice the healthcare of the majority of the population and place an increasing burden on the state in order that the more privileged classes may indeed enjoy the benefits of high quality healthcare. As detailed in chapter 8, these problems inherent to the neoliberal dualisation of healthcare have hindered the ability of the post-authoritarian governments to ameliorate services through sustained expenditure increases.

THE PRIVATISATION OF PENSIONS

The dictatorship's radical reform of the pension system, designed by leading Chilean neoliberal José Piñera, has been intensely applauded by neoliberal advocates. Likewise, the World Bank has used a slightly altered version of the Chilean reforms as a best-practice model for global propagation since 1994 (Mesa-Lago 2002). Piñera attributed the faults of the previous system to the 'basic error of a collectivist conception of human beings and of society that inspired the old system' (cited in Acuña and Iglesias 2000: 439). Predicated on a radical individualism, the system that he designed to take its place is often cited as a model of social security reform *par excellence*. The reform entailed a rapid privatisation of the pension system with workers obligated to place a requisite 13 percent of their monthly salaries in an individual account with a private pension fund of their choice. The latter, known as an Associación de Fondos de Pension (AFP, Pension Fund Association), proceed to collect a 2 percent administration charge and then invest the remainder in a regulated fashion, with investments predominantly directed towards domestic bonds and equities. Future pensions are therein tied to the performance of the investments made by the AFP.

When the reform was introduced in 1981 all future entrants to the labour force were mandated to move into the new system and those in dependent employment were strongly encouraged to switch. The self-employed, alternatively, could choose whether or not to participate, whereas those with sizeable contributions already made and who saw a potential diminution of their prospective pension under the new system were allowed to remain within the state system. Nevertheless, the vast majority of workers by choice or compulsion joined the new system with the result that it encompassed half the active labour force by 1990 (Acuña and Iglesias 2000: 456). At the lower end of the spectrum, those unable or unwilling to participate in the new scheme are guaranteed a state support pension that is intended to act as a safety net ensuring that all Chileans receive some form of coverage.

By breaking up the former system founded upon respective contributions from state, employer and employee, and replacing it with a new relationship between individual and private pension company, the reform aimed to free firms from the burden of social security provision and, simultaneously, increase the flexibility of the labour market. The economists behind the Pinochet regime justified their policy on the neoclassical principle that unemployment levels would remain exaggerated while market distortions inflated the market value of wages (Mesa-Lago 2002: 1313). Until wages had properly adjusted following the removal of the various forms of state intervention, serious disequilibria would remain in the labour market thereby hindering the achievement of an optimal distribution of labour. In removing social security provision from the ambit of the firm and institutionalising it as a relationship between individual and private company, the reform aimed to enable firms to hire and fire workers without considerations of pension stipends and, therein, remove one of the distorting factors acting upon the price of labour. Concurrently, capital would be able to operate without the bureaucratic element of pension provision, the latter remaining an issue of individual responsibility vis-à-vis the private pension company irrespective of the manner of employment. Accordingly, pension reform was viewed as one further step towards an unfettered labour market that would operate without political restrictions on the purchase and release of the commodity labour power. As Louise Haagh (2002b) indicates, between the late 1960s and mid-1990s, the burden of social security provision upon firms fell from 40 percent of non-wage costs to just 3 percent.

Likewise, reform represented one further aspect of the regime's strategy of depoliticisation. By removing the issue of pensions from the ambit of the state to be administered in an ostensibly impartial and technical manner by private companies, the reform attempted a depoliticisation of the pensions issue. The state would become a minimal actor, serving only to regulate the investment profiles of the AFPs to avoid unnecessary risk, finance the minimum pension safety net, and, ultimately, act as a guarantor of last resort for the system if necessary. As the state would no longer be responsible for the level of pension benefits, the reforms removed collectivised responsibility for the social reproduction of those in old age. In fact, the future value of pensions would rest to a large degree on the performance of Chilean stocks and bonds – an actuality that has been perversely incorporated into the discourse of Chilean capitalists to justify maintaining low taxes on corporate profits. The coalitions of pensions beneficiaries, on the other hand, faced a process of political disarticulation as the resolution of the levels of benefits was jettisoned from the hands of state-managers and deposited in the realm of private financial actors and the level of savings of the individual. In the place of the provision of collective security by the state, Chileans were encouraged to embrace the ideology of an 'ownership society', in which even the most humble of workers would own a stake in the future of the country (cf. Schamis 2002).

The practical effects of this dramatic reform of social security were manifold and, given that the implications of this reform became more explicit in the 1990s, are examined in more detail in chapter 8. At this point, however, it is sufficient to conclude by highlighting two significant factors. First, the AFP system involved a qualitative change from a system operated – however unevenly – on the principle of a guaranteed benefit underscored by the state to a defined-contribution system with pensions directly representing the accumulated salary of the worker. While such a transition from a socialised to a privatised system has undoubtedly benefited a minority with stable and highly remunerated employment who are able to make frequent and significant contributions to their fund, it has proved decisively deficient in its coverage of the majority Chileans in tenuous, low-paid and informal work (see chapter 8).

Second, the privatisation of the pension system involved a large transfer of resources from the public sphere to the private sphere. While the shift from public to private pensions was partially justified under the pretence of removing the fiscal burden upon the state, the cost of transferring pensions into the private sector has actually been considerable. Between 1981 and 1998 it cost some US$41,000 million, which is equivalent to 5.7 percent of GDP per year (Paiva and Riesco 2001). Moreover, by incorporating worker's savings for retirement into private financial funds, the privatisation of the pension system involved a significant transfer of resources into the private sector where – channelled through the large economic conglomerates – it aided the processes of concentration and centralisation of capital. This transfer of resources meant that by 1991 the emergent AFPs controlled funds accounting for more than 34.5 per cent of GDP. A substantial portion of this money (28 percent) was reinvested directly in Chilean equity through the medium of the major Chilean financial groups, providing liquidity for the economic conglomerates to advance their control over productive assets within the Chilean economy. The heavily concentrated control over financial resources cast further shadows on the regime's rhetoric of pension reform leading to a pluralist 'ownership society'.

SUMMARY

This chapter has highlighted how the transformation of welfare institutions is situated within the context of the Pinochet regime's wider attempt to reformulate the relations between state and society. It constituted a key moment in a project to individualise, atomise and depoliticise Chilean society that had been envisaged by neoclassical thinkers prior to the coup d'état and unevenly implemented by the authoritarian regime since the mid-1970s. Initial reforms sought to retrench social expenditures simultaneous to technocratising the criteria used to judge whether households merited social assistance. As such, the regime attempted to direct social expenditures towards the most impoverished Chileans in a seemingly neutral and depoliticised way. However, this occurred within the broader parameters of a wide-scale retrenchment of social expenditure and a regressive reshaping of tax systems. The reforms initiated within the 'Seven Modernisations' of 1979–82 took the reform of welfare institutions to a new level. Where possible, market mechanisms were introduced to service provision in order to recast socialised provision into atomised and apolitical relationships between individuals and private service providers. These reforms, however, have proved to be replete with contradictions owing to the inability of a substantial number of impoverished Chileans to participate in profit-driven service provision. As a consequence, dual systems of private and public provision remained in all key service areas, with acute structural tensions between the two.

5

Towards a Third Way? Power and Politics in Post-Dictatorship Chile

This chapter examines the circumstances that led to the political breakdown of the Pinochet dictatorship and the rise of the post-dictatorship coalition government known as the Concertación. Although the election of the Concertación was widely expected to precipitate a radical break with the policy direction of the dictatorship period, most observers have highlighted notable policy continuities, particularly in macroeconomic management and labour policies. At the same time, altered political discourses and new initiatives in the area of social policy, have led to the recognition that the Concertación period has marked a new moment in Chilean neoliberalism. Proponents have suggested that the Concertación approach represents a progression toward a 'Third Way' strategy that stands between neoliberalism and social democracy by retaining the neoliberal emphasis on market-driven economic dynamism yet recognising that market failures require repeated state interventions. Nonetheless, in spite of these changes, there has been a relentless unease within Chilean society and amongst the coalition parties that progress in addressing the social contradictions of the Pinochet era has been muted.

To help explicate and explain the causes and areas of both policy convergence and rupture between the dictatorship and Concertación, the current chapter examines the nature of the dictatorship's defeat and the institutional and material basis of the incoming Concertación coalition government. On the one hand, the Concertación faced substantial pressures from its popular base to address the contradictions of the restructuring period manifested in ubiquitous insecurity and impoverishment imposed through low wages, disciplinary labour markets and welfare retrenchment. On the other, three principal constraints on the Concertación's political practice restricted the Concertación's response: first, the balance of social forces in Chile in the post-dictatorship period; second, the institutional form of the post-dictatorship state; and, third, constraints imposed by the trajectory of capital accumulation in Chile following two decades of neoliberal restructuring. Such factors, it is argued, have led to the development of what can be termed 'politics within limits' manifested in the Concertación's 'growth with equity' programme. The latter represents a sophisticated political strategy that seeks simultaneously to mediate the contradictions of neoliberal capitalist development while reproducing the core institutions. As such, it is representative of many of the trends of 'Third Way' neoliberalism at a global level. Moreover, it is a strategy replete with contradictions and the present chapter highlights its underlying fault lines before the following chapters elaborate more specific instances.

POLITICAL PROTEST AND THE DEFEAT OF THE DICTATORSHIP

The cataclysmic drop in social conditions following the 1982 crisis debacle fuelled existing political discontent throughout Chilean society which had to that point been partially controlled through repression. The contradictions of neoliberal restructuring became brutally manifested in exacerbated levels of poverty and inequality and the society-wide insecurity created by the destruction of protective institutions such as labour regulations and many welfare policies. The neoliberal ideal of a harmonious society of private individuals relating to each other through market exchanges evaporated as collective organisations formed to meet local needs and to protest against the dictatorship's project. Organised resistance was given an immediate impetus by the labour movement, driven by the copper workers, which had been seeking ways to protest the repressive hue of the regime's labour code since its implementation in 1979. Although the dictatorship's reforms were intended to instil a long-term individualisation and fragmentation of labour relationships, the initial result was a politicisation of the workplace given that established labour movements resisted the imposition of new power structures between workers and employers (cf. Winn 2004c). However, fearful of the state repression that had been levelled against strikes in the preceding years, the labour movement decided to call for generalised street protests as an alternative form of struggle that would avoid recriminations in the sphere of production and possibly generate a large enough movement to dampen the prospect of coercive suppression by the military.

This strategy proved relatively successful. In spite of the spectre of violent repression, numerous highly visible public protests occurred in most major cities, therein helping to forge tentative links between the labour movement and other opposition forces. Nonetheless, the early protests remained sporadic, driven by an eclectic mixture of labour groups and social movements, including shantytown dwellers (*pobladores*) and clandestine political organisations. As argued by Alejandro Fernández, the mobilisations did not constitute a single centralised movement, but were the point of convergence of several sectoral mobilisations with different degrees of organisation, spontaneity and combativeness (Fernández Jilberto 1993). It was only with the dislocation caused by the 1982 recession, added to the emergence and consolidation of contending oppositional leaderships, that a sustained protest movement emerged with added vigour between 1983 and 1985. The neoliberal belief that dramatic state-led restructuring could eradicate the impetus for collective forms of social mobilisation through the creation of institutions that promoted private market relationships proved spectacularly misplaced.

The first of a new and larger wave of protest erupted in May 1983 and regular demonstrations subsequently became a constant feature of the political panorama until the defeat of the dictatorship at the close of the decade. Although the labour movement and the urban poor remained the primary social base of the protest movement, opposition transcended class lines to include sections of the middle classes and bourgeoisie (De la Maza 1999: 378; also cf. Salman 1994; Oxhorn 1995; Roberts 1998a). The latter had largely been locked out of decision-making processes since the mid-1970s, a situation deemed intolerable when combined with the heavy losses incurred during the debt-crisis period (Silva 1996). Moreover, the emergence of armed opposition, inspired by the Nicaraguan Sandinista Revolution of 1979, increased the sense of an escalating political crisis within Chile and worried the United States government. The unsuccessful assassination attempt on Pinochet in September 1986 was both the highpoint of the armed resistance, but also the confirmation of its wider political failure.

In the years following 1985, the intensity of the protests began to wane and Pinochet once again appeared to be more secure in his position. Within the opposition, a more consolidated directorship of the anti-dictatorship movement began to coalesce around a group of moderate politicians connected to the old political parties and organised within the protective auspices of the Catholic Church. This led to the emergence of a political opposition cadre in 1984 called the Alianza Democrática (Democratic Alliance). The Alianza Democrática was able to prosper over other political groupings, particularly the more radical Movimiento Democrático Popular (Popular Democratic Movement), owing to its willingness to insert itself into authoritarian political structures, endorse liberal capitalism, and to court business and international support. Its two primary constituent forces, the old Christian Democrat and Socialist parties, had both undergone processes of reconstruction within the political environment of the dictatorship. Each placed the resurrection of a formal democratic state at the centre of their political practice and by the late 1980s both parties had announced strong support for an export-orientated development policy predicated on neoliberal macroeconomic management (Roberts 1998b: 163).

Ideological renovation was most profound in the Socialist Party and contributed to a deep rupture amongst the parties and movements of the left. On the one hand, the dominant tendency within the party came to the conclusion that, with certain modifications, neoliberal macroeconomic management was fundamentally sound and needed to be retained to maintain the stability and dynamism of the Chilean economy. On the other, the party reinvented socialism as a process of institutional change aimed at attaining and deepening democracy through the provision of greater civil and social rights within the framework of liberal capitalism (Petras and Leiva 1994). In short, there needed to occur a process of rebuilding social institutions that promoted equality of opportunity within existing economic structures. This shift facilitated the common cause of the Socialists with the Christian Democrats and provided the ideological framework for the moderate wing of the opposition to the dictatorship. In contrast, the Communist Party and smaller radical groups remained committed to an insurrectionary counter dictatorship line, more radical visions of social transformation and the reversal of the neoliberal social restructuring.

Against this background, the Alianza Democrática began to focus its political strategy on the institutional openings present in the dictatorship's constitutional amendments of 1980 (Fernández Jilberto 1993). The latter, promulgated at a moment when the insecure political foundations of the dictatorship pressured the regime to consolidate its institutional basis, provided a constitutional provision for a referendum in 1988 that offered a choice between a further eight years of Pinochet's 'protected democracy' or a return to civilian rule. With the United States government of Ronald Reagan moving from a position of resolute support for Pinochet to an emphasis on 'democracy promotion', there was mounting international pressure for the regime to comply with the referendum process that it had established. Moreover, the US encouraged the regime to guarantee some media access to the opposition and to allow international observers to validate voting practices (cf. Robinson 1996).

Approaching the date of the plebiscite the regime arrogantly yet sincerely believed that a comprehensive victory would reinforce its legitimacy by displaying wide popular backing for the project of subordinating society to the discipline of the marketplace. Its campaign emphasised the social order and economic growth that characterised the second half of the 1980s, and contrasted this to the anarchical situation at the fall of the Allende regime, which it suggested would re-emerge if the dictatorship's 'protected democracy' was removed (Paley 2001: 120). The regime, however, placed too much faith not only in its control of the media but also, more generally, in the ideological fortitude of its 'economic miracle' and the appeal of its proclaimed 'market democracy'. It therein greatly underestimated the strength of the opposition and, despite the major advantages of intimidation, public expenditure and media manipulation, the dictatorship was shocked to find itself voted out of power by a margin of 54 to 46 percent.

Although Pinochet was loathe to accept the result, important sections of both the armed forces and the business sector acquiesced to a transition to civilian government and this, alongside international pressure from international bodies including the US State Department, ensured that the referendum was respected. In 1989 national elections were held and resulted in a comfortable victory for a centre-left coalition led by the Christian Democrat and Socialist parties called the Concertación, the leaders of which had played major roles within the Alianza Democrática. Notwithstanding defeat at the plebiscite and in the subsequent election, the constitutional framework under which the referendum had taken place provided the regime with over a year's grace period in which to prepare for the transition. As the following section details, the dictatorship would use this period to reaffirm the shape of Chile's future institutional structure in a manner consistent with the overarching tenets of neoliberal social transformation.

DEMOCRATISATION AND THE LIMITS
TO THE POST-DICTATORSHIP STATE

As the climax of considerable political mobilisation, the fall of the Pinochet dictatorship in 1989 seemingly ushered in a new epoch for

Chilean politics. The social basis of the incoming Concertación regime was precisely the popular mobilisation that had emerged to combat the dictatorship and that had subsequently delivered a clear electoral victory to the coalition. Although there was widespread recognition of the limited character of the victory over the authoritarian state, expectations remained high that the first Concertación president, Patricio Aylwin, would harness popular social forces in a political movement directed against the perceived excesses of the dictatorship's authoritarian neoliberal technocracy. For their part, the Concertación leaders announced a prospective programme of labour law reform, tax code revisions, increased social expenditure, new social programmes, a review of human rights violations, and constitutional reform (Silva 2002: 344). Having focused on the removal of the Pinochet regime, it was now anticipated that political practice would at this time centre on democratising society and the state (Barton 2002: 367; Haagh 2002a).

In essence, this project established a liberal form of social democratisation as its primary goal through which the regime would rebuild social institutions through which civil and social rights could be extended to those marginalised within the restructuring process. At its most radical moments, the programme appeared to offer a fundamental reconstruction of labour and welfare institutions in order to reshape the prevailing trends of inequality in income and power that permeated Chilean society. Nevertheless, a combination of structural and contingent factors would decisively condition the Concertación's possibilities of action, leading to a situation in which the new regime would maintain and even deepen the pivotal tenets of the neoliberal social transformation undertaken in the dictatorship period while failing to deliver the expected degree of civil and social democratisation. To explain this disjuncture, the following sections examine three factors in turn: the institutional form of the post-authoritarian state; the balance of social forces; and the structural constraints of capital accumulation within the global context.

AUTHORITARIAN ENCLAVES AND THE
FORM OF THE POST-DICTATORSHIP STATE

In spite of the victory of the anti-dictatorship forces in the 1988 plebiscite, the military regime had not been overwhelmed by popular mobilisation. Rather, it suffered defeat within the parameters of a political framework that it had established in the 1980 constitution.

Crucially, this provided the constitutional grounds for the regime to retain provisional hold on all key aspects of institutional power during the transition period, which lasted until Pinochet formerly rescinded power on 10 March 1990. Bolstered by the constitutional provisions that allowed it to preside over the transition, the authoritarian regime enjoyed an extremely powerful position from which to influence the institutional form of the post-authoritarian state. In the period between the plebiscite defeat and the elections of 1989, the military regime and civilian representatives negotiated the constitutional framework for the transition of power. Within this process the outgoing authoritarian regime ensured, not least through the active promulgation of legislation that continued until the final day of the dictatorship, that there existed multiple institutional safeguards (known as 'authoritarian enclaves') to impose moderation upon the incoming elected government by strengthening state institutions that would act to maintain the status quo.

Of particular importance for the embedding of the neoliberal project was the creation of an independent Central Bank by the Pinochet regime in 1989. Following the dictatorship's referendum defeat, there existed considerable consternation amongst the business elite that an incoming elected government would not continue the monetary policies that underscored the export-orientated shift in the Chilean economy. Given that the status quo of macroeconomic policy greatly aided the large economic conglomerates that had consolidated over the Pinochet period, substantial pressure was placed on the outgoing dictatorship to insulate the Central Bank from the incoming elected government under the guise of safeguarding economic stability from the potential actions of politically motivated elected governments with a short-term mentality. Consequently, a law promulgated in 1989 made the Central Bank autonomous and legally insulated it from the influence of the Minister of the Hacienda. In place of control from the Hacienda, the bank was to be governed by a five-member board, each of whom would serve for a period of between two and ten years and could only be removed under a strictly defined set of circumstances. Furthermore, Senate approval would be a necessary prerequisite before appointing any new personnel. This shift did not represent a decrease in the power of the state, but rather a transfer of that power between state institutions. The aim was to 'depoliticise' macroeconomic management by removing it from the ambit of democratic politics and assigning it to an independent board of technocrats who would ensure continuity of the aims and mechanisms established in the Pinochet period.

Significant reforms also were made to political institutions and the judiciary to constrain further the Concertación's ability to challenge the status quo. These measures included the appointment of nine designated senators – including one from each branch of the armed forces and the national police – that would ensure that the political right enjoyed a majority in the Senate; the appointment of Pinochet as a lifelong senator and commander of the armed forces; and an electoral system that served to create an over-representation of the parties of the right (cf. Taylor 1998; Portales 2000; Siavelis 2000). These reforms were of singular importance in strengthening state institutions that fortified the social power of money and private property through which the class structure of Chilean society is reproduced. In so doing, the dictatorship sought to ensure that the Concertación could not directly challenge the institutional basis of neoliberal social transformation.

Such particularities of the post-transition state have therefore greatly abetted the reconciliation of the Concertación with a neoliberal trajectory by imposing political limits on the possibilities of government policy and also by serving as an expedient device by which the Concertación has been able to justify its moderation to the popular constituency. It is important to highlight, once again, that these institutional idiosyncrasies did not represent a weakening of the Chilean state. On the contrary, various elements of the state apparatus, such as the Central Bank and judiciary, have been strengthened and the state as a whole remains a pervasive force within Chilean society particularly by providing the institutional framework in which the disciplinary power of money and property operate. As such, the reforms consolidated the changing modalities of power within Chilean society and have undoubtedly frustrated the ability of the more radical sections within the governing coalition to pursue a more comprehensive process of re-democratisation. In this way, they have reinforced the Concertación's call for a politics within limits.

In spite of the importance of these reforms, the suggestion made most forcibly by James Petras and Fernando Leiva (1994) that the perseverance of authoritarian political structures coupled to the ideological 'betrayal' of the new state managers can account for policy continuities in the Concertación era, is an argument that cannot be sustained. As the decade progressed, many of the authoritarian political structures began to diminish in importance or, indeed, to operate in a manner that favoured the Concertación. Over time, the Concertación has been able to insert its own central bank officials and designated senators, and curtail other institutionalised expressions of the previous order. Concertación president Ricardo Lagos stated in 2001 that the newfound willingness of the political right to reform the political process derives from the constitution currently being 'on our side' (*Financial Times* 2001). However, this shift in the balance of power within the state has occurred without a significant change in policy trajectory. In contrast, while not downplaying the ability of authoritarian enclaves to influence the legislative process on several key issues, to explain more fully the Concertación's political practices it is necessary to highlight the wider material and social impacts of the restructuring of social institutions undertaken within the dictatorship period.

ORGANISED INTERESTS AND THE EXERCISE OF POWER

Following 15 years of neoliberal restructuring that specifically sought to transform social institutions in a manner that imposed the disciplinary power of market institutions to a greater degree, the balance of power between social classes remains extremely uneven. As a consequence of reinforcing the power of money as the primary regulatory force within Chilean society, neoliberal restructuring inevitably shifted social power into the hands of those who controlled capital and away from those with few resources and who are reliant on collective forms of mobilisation to influence their social environment. Of particular note are the structural weaknesses prevalent in both organised labour and other social movements. The latter weaknesses, born both through direct repression and the authoritarian regime's destruction of their institutional power bases, reduced the ability of these social actors to influence the politics of the Concertación.

Despite its important role in the initial anti-dictatorship movement of 1983–85, organised labour suffered almost two decades of systematic repression and social restructuring that profoundly debilitated its political capacities. At a grassroots level, the union movement had been impeded by the character of economic transformation coupled to the institutionalisation of anti-union practices enshrined by the authoritarian labour code (discussed in chapter 3). Owing to the processes of de-industrialisation and privatisation that were integral to neoliberal reform, the movement was left devoid of its traditional heartland in the industrial and public sectors and had to readjust to a more fractured membership. This entailed a corpus drawn from smaller and weaker unions that covered more diverse economic sectors. Simultaneously, the labour institutions established by the dictatorship's Plan Laboral promoted the fragmentation of the labour movement at the local level through the encouragement of multiple small unions within enterprises that represented different sectors of the workforce and through the disempowerment of labour bodies organised at sectoral or national levels. At the time of the democratic transition only 44.2 percent of unions belonged to the re-formed national labour federation (Central Unitaria de Trabajadores, CUT), therein reducing its national bargaining strength within the new political arena (Ruiz-Tagle 1993: 146).

At a national level, the political momentum of the anti-dictatorship movement had given rise to a union leadership drawn primarily from the Concertación parties, embedded in those political networks, and strongly in favour of the new regime's moderation. Indeed, the initial reaction of the CUT was one of complicity with the Concertación's extremely moderate political direction, accepting the strategy of economic liberalisation and cooperation with capital over production relations in return for a greater emphasis on investment in workers through training, education, health, pensions and job security. The leaders who presided over the transition period explicitly embraced a strategy that involved the suppression of labour's demands in order to help guarantee the stability of the democratic transition. Although mounting frustration with the outcomes generated by the post-transition compromise would gradually induce a radicalisation of the CUT and its eventual rupture with the politics of conciliation in the mid-1990s, the legacy of acute structural and institutional weaknesses compromised its ability to influence the Concertación. One of the most telling signs of the weakness of the labour movement over the 1990s was its inability to pressure the state into a more fundamental reform of the Labour Code, an issue discussed in detail in chapter 7.

Similarly, although multiple social movements played an important role in the struggle against the dictatorship, political oppression and the effects of extreme economic marginalisation perpetuated weaknesses and factionalism within these small groups. In terms of their political impetus, many threw their limited weight behind the Concertación's electoral movement in the mid-1980s and became less visible after the victory of the latter. As indicated in Philip Oxhorn's detailed study of popular movements in the anti-dictatorship struggle, most had set their aims on re-establishing the procedural guarantees that would both protect them from the routine violence of dictatorship and ensure a political process that was not immune from popular pressure (Oxhorn 1995: 171). However, once the unifying principle of the struggle for democracy had dissipated, most social movements either disappeared or retreated onto issue-specific and geographically localised campaigns.

This fragmentation of social movements both facilitated and was reinforced by a second trend that manifested itself as the decade progressed; namely, the transformation or displacement of social movements by foreign supported and generally apolitical NGOs. Remaining grassroots movements that sought to retain a politically independent nature have been considerably marginalised by this process. Where they have chosen to interact with the state, they have been commonly subordinated as instruments of state policy within the technocratised institutions of anti-poverty policy and have been unable to effect notable policy change above the level of implementing localised development projects (Paley 2001: 169). Alternatively, where they have avoided interaction, they have often been reduced to marginalisation and ineffectiveness (Foweraker 2001: 847). Power structures of this nature have been reinforced through the specific tenor of government welfare institutions, such as the FOSIS anti-poverty policy, analysed in chapter 8.

In contrast to labour and grassroots movements, the organised bodies of capital emerged strengthened from the authoritarian epoch and, in the post-transition period, have proven well structured, highly mobilised, and presciently aware of the political strength that stems from concentrated ownership of the means of production within an institutional setting that privileges financial power (Silva 1998). The Chilean bourgeoisie – and above all those in control of the large economic conglomerates – have enjoyed multiple channels through which to assert political pressure, including influence over major media sources. There are at least two tiers of organised business interests. In the first tier, a powerful overarching business union called the Confederación de Producción y Comercio (Conferation of Production and Commerce, CPC) represents the interest of big business at a national level. In the second tier, specific sectoral business unions represent capitals located in each branch of production. As well as these directly representative organisations, there has been a consistent representation of the interests of capital by the political parties of the right, and particularly through the close links forged between the CPC and the largest right-wing party, the Unión Democrática Independient (Independent Democratic Union, UDI). On this basis, Jorge Nef (2003: 22) has suggested that for the first time in Chilean history, 'the size, financing, organization, interlocking capacity, representation in official government agencies, control over the media, internationalization, and ability to determine the intellectual agendas of universities', has forged a hegemonic business class.

Given their organisational strength and numerous channels of influence, capitalist organisations have enjoyed an active and privileged relationship with the government throughout the Concertación period, and particularly under the administration of the Christian Democrat president Eduardo Frei Ruiz-Tagle (1994–2000). All important policy initiatives, including fiscal and labour reforms, were negotiated through a dialogue between the Concertación and the CPC and the opinions of business interests were widely propagated through their ownership of most national media outlets (Bresnahan 2003). Even the administration of Ricardo Lagos (2000–06) – who was viewed with wide suspicion by the Chilean bourgeoisie owing to his socialist roots – has maintained close consultation with business interests in the formulation of economic and financial policies. In this vein, the US State Department quickly attempted to reassure American investors in the credibility of Lagos' administration, claiming that: 'Lagos has put in place a top-notch economic team: his principal economic advisers are U.S.-trained and internationally acclaimed for their technical expertise, and they share Lagos' strong commitment to Chile's successful free-market economic model' (US State Department 2001: 10).

CAPITAL ACCUMULATION AND THE STATE

As the third element shaping the post-dictatorship political environment, it is expressly important to highlight that, regardless of the political leanings of particular state managers, there are strong systemic pressures upon the Chilean state to ensure the continued accumulation of capital by reinforcing or reconstructing existing social institutions. Within capitalist society, the very reproduction of society – including the state-system itself – hinges on the relatively smooth continuance of the capital accumulation as it is the manner by which capitalist societies reproduce their material and social foundations on a day-to-day basis. At an abstract level, this entails that the entire institutional structure of the state is pressured to facilitate the social conditions for capital accumulation – characterised by the systematic need for the owners of capital to expand its value through profit-making activities – and these pressures condition the possibilities and limits to the action of state managers and bodies.

This is not to put forward a crude functionalism wherein the state is bound to chart the optimal course for capital accumulation (a 'capital logic' approach). Undoubtedly, pressure to attempt to ensure capital accumulation at a social level is very real, as manifested not only in the direct – yet often conflicting – demands of specific capitalist interests but also, more generally, through the everyday movement of economic indicators such as the rate of profit, inflation and employment levels, tax revenues, and balance of payments and exchange rate fluctuations. These pressures can lead to various and frequently inconsistent courses of action put forward by state managers, leading to conflicts within and between various bodies of the state. As indicated in chapter 2, far from being a smooth and harmonious process, the accumulation of capital necessarily produces intense social conflicts and strains. On the one hand, the pressures to maintain profits repeatedly generate conflicts between capital and labour within the production process. On the other hand, capitalist society suffers from an intrinsic propensity to subordinate social and environmental needs to the dictates of profit appropriation. These tendencies ensure that capital accumulation gives rise to a multiplicity of social struggles including industrial strife, social movement activities, and pressure group politics. This basic contradiction – the tendency to subordinate all aspects of social life to the demands of capital accumulation – lies at the heart of capitalist society and is therefore imprinted onto the state, which must constantly aim to mediate these tensions while simultaneously reaffirming the conditions for capital accumulation that underscores the material reproduction of society.

Although much has been made of the tendencies of 'globalisation' to constrain the actions of states, this complex relationship between the state and capital accumulation was no less present in the national-developmentalist period, as chapter 1 discussed (cf. also Müller and Neusüss 1975; Holloway and Picciotto 1977; Radice 1984; Clarke 1991b). As such, the internationalisation of capital does not reduce state capacity, but rather changes the nature and forms of state actions. Since neoliberal restructuring necessarily created a substantial dependence of accumulation within Chile upon the global movement of money and commodities, subordination to the discipline of capital in the contemporary period is closely tied to reaffirming Chile's position within global capital circuits. To maintain economic growth, the validity of accumulation within Chile must constantly be reasserted vis-à-vis the competitive pressures imposed by the trajectory of global accumulation. The state is constantly involved in this process through a multiplicity of institutionalised forms through which it regulates the social relationships that underpin capital accumulation. For example, one of the principal forms by which the discipline of capital is exercised upon the actions of the contemporary Chilean state is through the constant necessity to retain flows of world money anchored within the Chilean financial system. Owing to the accelerated processes of integration with global capital circuits, sustained capital accumulation within Chile relies in no small measure upon the constant input of foreign capital, both as investment and as credit (foreign direct investment [FDI] and portfolio capital respectively). This constant influx of capital is necessary to service high-levels of private sector debt, finance new investments and to implement the technological advances necessary for sustained productivity increases to keep Chilean exports competitive on global markets. Concurrently, a significant decline in capital inflows or accelerated capital outflows threaten to plunge the Chilean economy into serious crisis, as was acutely realised in 1998 following the Asian financial crisis.

In this respect, the intrinsic mobility of capital in its money form generates further pressures upon the Chilean state to provide a stable and profitable investment environment and to reproduce the conditions for the comparative advantage of Chilean exports on global markets. The latter are constant considerations for the Concertación in the management of trade and exchange rates policies alongside its interventions in diverse social relations, including labour markets, production relations, education and training, and the financial system. In the contemporary global political economy, this concern with sustaining the conditions for capital accumulation implies a relative commitment to maintaining the social institutions fashioned by neoliberal restructuring and that are taxonomised in the publications of the IMF, World Bank, credit-rating agencies and other international financial actors. To be sure, however, the most vocal advocates of the neoliberal status quo are the large Chilean economic groups who are deeply integrated within global capital circuits.

Given that the political practices of neoliberalism sought to fashion social institutions that would uphold the viability of Chilean capitalist accumulation through precisely this subordination of both state and society to the discipline of capital as a global social relation, there is a strong material basis to the Concertación's dedication to the neoliberal project. To attempt to implement a significant break from this mode of capital accumulation would not be impossible, but it would require a rupture in the established patterns of capital accumulation with notable ramifications for medium-term economic stability and the direct antagonisation of established interests. While some within the Concertación's grassroots were keen for the coalition to attempt just such a rupture, the social and political conditions for such a radical course of action that would inevitably cause severe economic dislocations, including mass capital flight, did not exist in the early 1990s.

THE GROWTH WITH EQUITY STRATEGY – A CHILEAN 'THIRD WAY'?

Within these parameters, the Concertación's political mandate was initially grounded upon an appeal for the acceptance of politics within limits. In the context of the manifold political weaknesses that characterised organised labour and progressive social movements, the more conservative wing of the Concertación, rooted within the Christian Democrat Party, was able to assert its predominance within the coalition and adopt a heavily elitist (*'cupular'*) style of politics. The latter served to insulate the political cadre of the Concertación from direct engagement with more radical voices located in the grassroots of the coalition parties (Taylor 1998). All reform, argued the Concertación, would involve change within a fourfold conjuncture of limits: namely, the limits of the stability of the democratic transition, the limits of the sanctity of private property, the limits of fiscal prudence, and, ultimately, the limits of sustained capital accumulation. Consequently, in the months before formally coming to power the Concertación pledged to recognise the sanctity of private property, institutionalise the dictatorship's economic model, and make no dramatic changes to the country's social structures. Explicitly, it promised to exercise fiscal prudence and refrain from the populist excursions of past Christian Democrat and Socialist governments in order to maintain the pro-business climate of the Pinochet years, but also to avoid repoliticising issues that the dictatorship attempted to reduce to the realm of technocracy (Muñoz Gomá and Caledón 1996; Portales 2000). In spite of some differences highlighted in the following sections and chapters, the three successive post-dictatorship Concertación governments, headed by Patricio Aylwin 1990–94, Eduardo Frei Ruiz-Tagle 1994–2000 and Ricardo Lagos 2000–06 respectively, have constrained their political practice within the parameters of the social institutions forged by neoliberal restructuring.

This pledge to maintain a basic continuity with the neoliberal model, however, did not entail a carbon copy of Pinochet-style neoliberalism. Unlike the Pinochet regime, which relied upon the systematic deployment of coercion to fortify its position, the Concertación operates in a formally democratised state apparatus that, for all its authoritarian idiosyncrasies, necessitates the establishment and maintenance of a strong electoral base. Political struggle within the electoral arena would add a further mediating link between state and society, and the legitimacy of successive Concertación governments rested in no small part upon their pledge to strive for social justice within the neoliberal model. At one and the same time, the Concertación was pressured to respond to the contradictions of neoliberal restructuring even as it reproduced the fundamental parameters of the neoliberal project.

In response, while the Concertación has maintained neoliberal and technocratic solutions to socio-economic issues in an attempt to promote continued capital accumulation, this has occurred alongside an emphasis on building social institutions that correct market failures and promote social inclusion. The banner under which they christened this strategy was 'growth with equity', a designation chosen to emphasise the confidence in the free market, export-orientated strategy and its amalgamation with a more progressive social policy agenda that would compensate the strata of society marginalised by the dictatorship's restructuring programme. Hence, while remaining wedded to the primary economic and labour institutions crafted by the dictatorship, the Concertación ideologues argued that reconstructed welfare institutions could be used to correct market failures that restricted the benefits of economic growth from reaching all parts of the population and, in a less pronounced manner, to initiate a virtuous circle of increased human capital leading to sustainable and more equitable economic expansion.

The discourse of correcting market failures in order to reaffirm economic dynamism and social inclusion closely relates to new refinements to the neoliberal discourse at a global level. The Concertación's political programme – like that of Tony Blair's 'Third Way' in the United Kingdom – presents itself as assuming the middle ground between free-market capitalism and traditional social democracy, one that could combine the capitalist dynamism heralded by the political right, with the social justice craved by the left. Giddens' (2003) typology of an ideal Third Way project of reform closely resembles the rhetoric and policy practice of the Concertación governments:

[T]he restructuring of the state and government to make them more democratic and accountable; a shake-up in welfare systems to bring them more into line with the main risks people face today; emphasis on job creation coupled with labour market reform; a commitment to fiscal discipline; investment in public services but only where linked to reform; investment in human capital as crucial to success in the knowledge economy; the balancing of rights and responsibilities of citizens; and a multilateralist approach to globalisation and international relations.

The theoretical underpinnings of the Concertación's position rest upon the recognition of three broad areas of market failure that were ignored or suppressed in the more orthodox neoliberal approach (Vial 2000; Javier and Fuentes 2000). The practical effects of such weaknesses have underscored the constant revision of neoliberal theory and policy practice, including the World Bank's rapid rush to emphasise the importance of institutional structures on the basis of a partial incorporation of the insights of the new institutional economics within the mainstream neoclassical canon (World Bank 1997). The shift is also ably represented in the work and influence of Joseph Stiglitz and information-theoretic economics that attempts to theorise and justify the existence of non-market social institutions on the basis of individual responses to informational imperfections (Stiglitz 1998; see Fine 2001a).

At a general level, the approach highlights three areas of weakness within the orthodox neoliberal perspective. First, the approach recognises the presence of 'externalities', whereby 'rational' market outcomes produce harmful social effects such as pollution or monopoly control, and therefore require state intervention to regulate such occurrences. Second, market activities rest upon numerous social institutions outside of the market and may therefore be incomplete as judged against the market model used in neoclassical theory. For example, differences in the information possessed by actors can create sub-optimal market performance and therefore necessitate state intervention to create supporting institutions that improve market performance. Third, the unequal distribution of resources in society prevents all individuals from adequately and fairly participating in market activities, which can lead to a further form of market failure. State intervention can be deployed to correct some of these inequalities by providing public goods such as education, training, healthcare and other subsidies to raise the level of human capital in excluded groups.

Retaining the core institutions of the neoliberal project while providing correctives to these instances of market failure, it was argued, would provide the optimal route to overcoming the social contradictions of the Pinochet era without undermining economic dynamism. It is on this ideological basis, moreover, that the reformed neoliberalism of the Concertación has been a source of inspiration for the spirit and content of a refined neoliberalism emergent on a global level since the late 1980s and, subsequently, adopted and propagated by the World Bank and other development institutions during the 1990s. The discourse of the 'Chilean model' employed by international financial institutions would therefore undergo a process of metamorphosis in this period. Moving from a belligerent emphasis on the virtues of sound economic fundamentals as demonstrated by the Chilean experience, the stress shifted to new concerns with democratic procedure, building institutions and attaining a requisite level of social equity which could improve economic efficiency (cf. World Bank 1997; 2000; 2001; for critique, cf. Taylor 2004).

The argument of the current and following chapters, however, is that 'growth with equity' represents not an idealist endeavour to engineer a more just society, nor simply a technical corrective to flaws within neoliberal policymaking. Indeed, the ability of 'Third Way' policies to address social inequalities and market failures are quite limited, as detailed in the following chapters that examine various facets of the post-1990 Chilean political economy. Rather, 'growth with equity' represents a complex political strategy that emerged unevenly from the clash between popular pressure to mitigate the inequalities and insecurities associated with neoliberal restructuring and the constraints imposed by the vastly asymmetrical power relations that characterise post-dictatorship Chile. The contradictory heart of this strategy is manifested in the need to assure the expanded accumulation of capital by reaffirming the class relations forged in the dictatorship period, which in turn undermines the potential to reshape prevailing structures of production and distribution that would be necessary to create a more equitable society.

In these circumstances, the 'growth with equity' strategy soon developed into an attempt to allay pressure for more profound forms of social transformation by incorporating social aspirations of the working class into the realm of social policy. On the one hand, this strategy would maintain the social relations of production that underscored capital accumulation characterised by a sharp division between the consolidated power of capital and a 'flexibilised' labour force, as detailed in chapters 6 and 7. On the other, it offered a strategy of translating and containing political struggle into areas where the state anticipated the ability to exercise greater control. Increasing social expenditure and initiating new targeted social programmes therefore formed the mainstay of the government's social reconciliation strategy, whereby they pledged to seek consensual arrangements between major social groups including the organised bodies of business and labour over all key issues. Ultimately, the issue of labour reform provoked irreconcilable tensions between organised business and labour and, with the regime leaning to the side of business, it prefigured the ultimate demise of the attempted consensus-building strategy (Frank 2004). Nonetheless, the Concertación retained its pledge to divert more resources into social expenditure so as to ameliorate the sharp inequities produced by the two decades of restructuring. This intervention, they warned, would be both gradual and would have to remain set within the bounds of fiscal responsibility in order to maintain macroeconomic balances. Concertación ideologues were adamant that their new regime would not succumb to populist pressures (Weyland 1999). A 'responsible' social strategy of this nature was contrasted to the older forms of Chilean populism as it rigidly grounds the expansion of social expenditure within the constraints of firmly embedded neoliberal macroeconomic management and would be administered in a heavily technocratic manner.

To propose such an interpretation of 'growth with equity' is not to suggest a crude instrumentality in the Concertación's actions. On the contrary, the strategy emerged and evolved through the political struggles between various coalition factions within the circumscribed political and economic environment. From this perspective, therefore, 'growth with equity' constituted an evolving attempt to reconcile the tensions in the Concertación's political position as a coalition whose electoral support and grassroots activism was based upon a pledge to ameliorate the social conditions of the working class, with the three conditioning factors highlighted above: the material constraints of ensuring the expanded reproduction of capital in Chile, the institutional constraints of the post-transition state, and the strength of contending social forces. In this way, far from a pre-formed and static core of policies, the political doctrine of 'growth with equity' would undergo periods of turmoil and change during three phases that loosely correspond to the three successive presidencies.

The Aylwin presidency (1990–94) would mark the rapid ascription of limits to the 'growth with equity' strategy, as the outcome of struggles between the Concertación and the political forces of capital and the right undercut many of the more progressive aspects of the reform package. Aylwin himself coined the phrase 'justice within limits' to describe the inability of the government to hold the armed forces accountable for human rights abuses during the dictatorship, yet the saying had far wider connotations. Growing frustrations heightened ruptures and conflict within the Concertación coalition itself, particularly between its grassroots activists and its political cadres (Portales 2000). The remainder of the Aylwin period and the majority of the Frei Ruiz-Tagle administration (1994–2000) witnessed a consolidation of 'growth with equity' within the context of sustained economic expansion that temporarily eased social tensions by providing the conditions for expanded employment opportunities and increased wages. Nevertheless, the implosion of the economic boom in 1998 put an end to the fragile social and political peace that had, until that point, been tenuously maintained. Shortly before the culmination of the Frei Ruiz-Tagle administration in 1999, the Concertación encountered growing social and political tensions, which became manifested in escalating intra-coalition struggles and a moderate shift leftwards within the Concertación coalition prior to the 2000 elections. This move was reflected in the choice of Ricardo Lagos, a member of the Socialist Party, as the Concertación's presidential candidate for the 2000 elections, yet was not resolved by Lagos' appointment and continues to the present.

Indeed, the succeeding Lagos presidency (2000–06) has reacted in a patchwork and contradictory manner to the challenge of maintaining social discipline while simultaneously reinvigorating prevailing forms of capital accumulation. The end of the export boom and renewed political polarisation has placed the greatest strains yet on the Concertación and its Third Way paradigm of 'growth with equity'.

Such strains, despite being driven by the dynamics of social struggles, are not merely contingent, but rest upon the contradictions at the heart of social reproduction within capitalist social relations and their current articulation within the Chilean social formation. To elaborate this argument, the following three chapters analyse the major areas of the Chilean political economy during the period 1990–2003. This includes, in chapter 6, a focus on macroeconomic policies and the uneven effects of an export boom that occurred from 1990 to 1997 and which was followed by a period of recession and socio-economic dislocation at the turn of the millennium. Subsequently, chapter 7 focuses on labour relations and, specifically, the Concertación's attempts at reforming the existing labour code established by the Pinochet regime. Finally, chapter 8 indicates both the successes but also the limitations of the Concertación's approach to social policy which, as noted above, lay at the heart of their 'growth with equity' political discourse.

SUMMARY

The defeat of the dictatorship in the 1988 plebiscite put in motion a political process that ended in the election of a new government. The latter was formed from an alliance of the Christian Democrat, Socialist and other minor parties and was known as the Concertación. Despite hopes that this reintroduction of electoral democracy would lead to a pronounced reversal of neoliberal social transformation, the Concertación was quick to scale back such ambitions. This moderation reflected a threefold structure of constraints. First, the institutional form of the post-dictatorship state impeded the ability of the Concertación to implement significant policy changes owing to the perseverance of 'authoritarian enclaves'. Second, the balance of social forces within Chilean society reflected the dictatorship's explicit project to marginalise labour and social movements and to permit the fortification of organised business. Third, the Concertación faced the structural impediments inherent to capitalist society, which functions in and through the expanded reproduction of capital. Given that capital accumulation had been significantly reconfigured through the internationalisation of Chilean commodity chains, capital accumulation became strongly dependent on the reproduction of Chilean society within its neoliberal form. Within this conjuncture of constraints, the Concertación has gravitated towards an emphasis on the limits of politics. This strategy has involved an attempt to discipline both its own party apparatus and its social base so as to accept a liberal form of social democratisation predicated on strengthening welfare institutions while maintaining the basic parameters of neoliberal capitalism. Such an approach bears similarities to other forms of 'Third Way' neoliberalism and shares common tensions implicit to these strategies. The following three chapters explain in more detail how this policy orientation has unfolded in practice, and details some of the many contradictions it has engendered.

6
Production, Power and Exports – The Political Economy of Post-Dictatorship Chile

Chile's economy entered a period of dramatic boom between 1990 and 1997. Notwithstanding a significant recession in the years 1998–99, the average annual GDP growth rate over the decade as a whole was 6.3 percent, a level significantly higher than other Latin American countries and a striking improvement on the record of the Pinochet regime (Stallings 2001: 46). Both national and international proponents of neoliberalism, such as the IMF, have heralded this economic expansion as proof of the long-term virtue of Pinochet's restructuring programme and of the Concertación's adherence to the fundamental parameters of neoliberal macroeconomic strategy within a democratic framework (Aninat 2000; Barro 2000; Jadresic and Zahler 2000). On this basis, Chile is offered as a benchmark of good macroeconomic governance that other developing countries, in Latin America and beyond, should take note of (OECD 2003). Even authors who have recently become more critical of the neoliberal paradigm tend to see Chile as something of an exception (Stiglitz 2002). Much like the controversy over the East Asian 'model' of successful development (Burkett and Hart-Landsberg 2000; Berger 2004), Chile has become a touchstone in debates over the salience of neoliberalism as a development strategy. The purpose of this chapter, however, is not merely to analyse economic policy and performance during the Concertación period but also to assess the very terms of this debate.

To accomplish these aims it is pertinent to pose several key questions. First, the chapter addresses the extent to which Chilean macroeconomic trends were determined by the maintenance of standard neoliberal prescription in the 1990s. Neoliberal acolytes point to Chile as a success story for the implementation of neoliberal fundamentals and it is therefore important to indicate, first, the degree to which the Concertación governments have remained true to such principles and, second, to what extent these policy decisions have been determinate in creating economic expansion. As discussed in chapter 2, neoclassical economists tend to view economic growth simply as a result of creating a good policy environment that facilitates the invisible hand of the market to marshal resources in a socially optimal manner. This allows them to fashion a template of policy practice that they claim will bring success wherever it is implemented owing to the universal nature of its founding premises. The approach adopted here, however, differs greatly by highlighting the complex social and institutional underpinnings of capital accumulation and questioning the universalising assumptions of neoclassical economics. On this basis, the chapter indicates how Chilean macroeconomic performance is not reducible simply to the result of policy choices within a free market context but rather is: (1) predicated on the specific re-organisation of social relations fashioned through Pinochet's brutal restructuring programme, (2) dependent on continued and pervasive state interventions, (3) related to the exceptional natural resources that Chile uniquely possesses, and (4) reflective of contingent dynamics in global capitalism during the 1990s and 2000s. In so doing, the chapter highlights the power relations, such as the monopolistic power of the Chilean conglomerates, which also contribute to the accelerated character of capital accumulation in this period.

Building on this analysis, it is possible to question the extent to which the Chilean socio-economic trajectory in the 1990s and beyond represents a success story by moving beyond the narrow criteria of economic growth as measured by GDP and adopting a wider socio-economic perspective. Whereas economists tend to view GDP increase as the primary indicator of successful economic performance, the more holistic approach adopted here views the issues of social equity and economic and environmental sustainability as inseparable from good economic outcomes (cf. DeMartino 2000). Given that the social restructuring project undertaken within the Pinochet regime had important social and environmental implications – including dramatically increased inequality and poverty levels, reduced wage rates, increased intensity and precariousness of work and a new dependence on fickle global primary commodity markets – it is pertinent to consider whether the continuation of such trends in the Concertación period necessitates a re-evaluation of the virtues of the Chilean 'model'. By examining levels of inequality in terms of both income differentials and the power relations between oligopolistic sectors of the economy and smaller Chilean firms, the current chapter begins to answer this latter question. However, as the concerns raised extend well beyond the scope of economic policy, these issues continue to be addressed in the following chapters on labour and social policies.

NEOLIBERALISM AND ECONOMIC POLICY IN POST-DICTATORSHIP CHILE

The neoliberal prescription for economic policy is widely familiar and was analysed in chapters 2 and 3. Here we briefly overview the main economic policy areas in Chile that have attracted considerable attention from neoliberal advocates, namely: fiscal responsibility; trade liberalisation; capital account liberalisation; and continued privatisation of state owned enterprises and services. In the period 1990–97 the Concertación governments of Patricio Aylwin (1990–94) and Eduardo Frei Ruiz-Tagle (1994–2000) remained largely true to these neoliberal parameters of macroeconomic policy. Firstly, the Concertación placed significant emphasis on macroeconomic stability through fiscal discipline, exercised tight monetary control, and constrained exchange rate movements within a fixed band (Ffrench-Davis 2002b). Although the Concertación have championed this policy orientation, it was partially determined by the institutional restructuring of the authoritarian regime that created an independent central bank in 1989, therein insulating monetary policy from the Concertación's influence (see chapter 5). By running an average fiscal surplus of 1.5 percent from 1989, the Concertación went beyond merely balancing the budget and, in part, used this surplus to pay back the considerable public debt incurred by the Pinochet regime (Marshall 2003). Equally, domestic interest rates were kept high in order to attract inflows of foreign capital and mitigate any inflationary tendencies. Tight fiscality in this manner, alongside the imposition of market discipline on wages, brought inflation down to extremely low levels relative to historical trends. Between 1992 and 2001 the weighted average annual rate of inflation was maintained at 3.72 percent (Heritage Foundation 2003: 140). Those standing behind the Chilean development strategy have subsequently applauded the 'mature behaviour' of the Concertación regime for its pursuance of monetary conservatism and fiscal prudence rather than submitting to an 'irresponsible expansionist policy and being prisoners of economic populism' (Weyland 1999).

Second, and in spite of a long heritage of state-promoted industrialisation within the Christian Democrat and Socialist parties, the Concertación coalition has reaffirmed the Pinochet regime's emphasis on export-led growth through trade liberalisation and the internal reallocation of capital and labour that it promotes. The Concertación governments of Aylwin and Frei continued the liberalisation project by suppressing the exchange rate and by maintaining low import tariffs at 11 percent before, in 1999, beginning to reduce them to a flat rate of 7 percent by 2002 (Ffrench-Davis 2002b). Furthermore, all three Concertación governments pursued and completed the signing of bilateral and multilateral trade agreements, a process that served to make Chile the most liberalised country in Latin America in terms of the entry and exit of goods. Although differing in their precise terms, free trade agreements now cover relations with the NAFTA (North American Free Trade Agreement) countries, the MERCOSUR, Andean Pact and the European Union. Both of the post-1994 governments have pushed for full entry into the NAFTA and, although this aim remains currently unfulfilled, an agreement made in November of 2002 instituted a further bilateral trade pact between Chile and the United States (Stiglitz 2003). Concurrently, the Concertación has also attempted to actively mediate the downward pressures on the real exchange rate in order to benefit the exporting sector (Ffrench-Davis and Tapia 2001).

Third, the Concertación continued the process of privatisation initiated by the authoritarian regime. Unlike the latter, which provided a significant subsidy to capital by underselling public companies to selected economic groups, the Concertación operated a policy of open, competitive bidding. Over the course of the decade a combination of the privatisation of state-owned companies and the leasing out of state service provision to the private sector raised some US$2.5 billion in revenue (Aninat 2000: 2). The privatisation of water treatment, telecommunications, electricity, transport, and infrastructure creation and maintenance, are prime examples of the new trend. Proceeding beyond the privatisation of state owned productive enterprises and social services, the Concertación created new areas and forms of investment for domestic and foreign capitals, including techniques of semi-privatisation through concessionary and associational forms of public–private partnership (Hachette 2000: 125). Notably, partnership in this sense has been most explicit in opening new copper deposits to exploitation through joint extraction by the state copper industry and foreign companies.

Fourth, financial liberalisation had been largely completed by the Pinochet regime, which substantially opened Chile's capital account. Following the 1982 debacle, more stringent regulations of the banking system were introduced and the Concertación continued this trend (Held and Jimenez 2001). Nevertheless, in the Concertación's first years of government, the sizeable volume of foreign portfolio capital flowing into Chile led to an appreciating exchange rate and threatened the viability of Chilean exports. The Aylwin regime felt compelled to respond and implemented a minor control called a unremunerated reserve requirement (URR) on portfolio inflows. While the IMF disapproved of this intervention at the time of its implementation, suggesting that global financial markets would self-regulate, the Concertación administrations remained adamant that the control would limit financial speculation and therefore facilitate the greater goal of macroeconomic stability (Soederberg 2002). Although the implementation of a capital control ran against the grain of neoliberal free capital mobility, the IMF has since come to recognise the Chilean variant as potentially an important temporary tool to help achieve other macroeconomic management goals within an ongoing process of neoliberal reform and integration into global financial markets (Grabel 2003; Soederberg 2004: 111–14).

For many neoliberal advocates, the resolution of the three post-1990 Concertación governments to pursue this neoliberal macroeconomic policy approach – which, as analysed in chapter 5, emerged from within a conjuncture of power relations surrounding the transition to civilian rule – is the primary determinant of Chile's economic performance in the 1990s. Six years of unparalleled GDP growth rates between 1991 and 1997 seemed to validate the policy approach and led to the claim of Chile being a 'jaguar economy' (Oppenheim 1999) with its success predicated on adherence to the primary tenets of neoliberal development strategy.

Table 6.1 Chilean GDP Growth (%), 1990–99

	1990	1991	1992	1993	1994	1995	1996	1997	1998	1999
GDP	3.7	8.0	12.3	7.0	5.7	10.6	7.4	7.4	3.4	–1.1
GDP per capita	1.5	6.2	10.4	5.2	4.0	8.9	5.9	5.9	2.0	–2.4

(Data drawn from CEPAL 2001a: 492)

There are several major problems with this explanation, however, that are due largely to the manner by which neoclassical economics conceptualises the economy as a universal, natural and self-determining realm that will automatically generate optimal performance when allowed to operate freely in conditions of good governance. On this basis, credible policy choices and ensuring the 'rules of the game' are assumed a priori to lead to efficient economic growth by minimising external distortions on self-correcting markets (see chapter 2). The trouble with this approach is that, while policies and governance structures are important determinants of social outcomes, capitalist economies are not merely agglomerations of rational individuals but are composed of complex social relations in historically specific institutional structures. As Ilene Grabel (2000: 11) points out, absent from neoclassical accounts are 'considerations of class conflict, and the distribution of income, wealth and political power'. To accept the neoliberal explanation of the Chilean boom at face value would be to accept the superficial determinism inherent to that approach; namely, that all economies are constituted by rational individuals and operate according to universal principles of exchange and, therefore, relative performance can be attributed simply to the 'external' factors of policy approach and governance structures. The following sections elaborate an alternative analysis that historicises the Chilean export boom and indicates the power relations that underlie it, before highlighting three major contradictions that emerged from this trajectory.

THE SOCIAL DETERMINANTS OF THE CHILEAN EXPORT BOOM, 1990–97

To reject the neoliberal policy fetish, it is necessary to adopt an approach that focuses on the underlying social relations of capital accumulation and the complex institutional forms they assume. As chapters 3 and 4 demonstrated, the basis of renewed capital accumulation during the final years of the Pinochet period was a restructuring of two fundamental sets of social relations; first between classes within Chile resulting in a dramatic increase in the power of capital over labour; and second, a change in the relationship between Chilean capital and the world market, with Chile shifting resources away from industrialisation and towards primary commodity production. These restructuring processes eventually created the conditions for rapid capital accumulation predicated upon strong demand for Chilean exports, high levels of exploitation, social depoliticisation that marginalised opposition to the neoliberal agenda, and the centralisation of domestic capital into the hands of oligopolistic economic conglomerates with roots in the financial sector.

By subsequently ensuring that all actors subscribe to the established 'rules of the game', the Concertación has carefully maintained a particular balance of class power that was enshrined in the restructuring undertaken by the Pinochet regime. While capital became ever more concentrated through the formation of large Chilean economic conglomerates that exercised control over the new areas of economic dynamism through financial power, the Chilean working class saw the value of its labour-power plummet and was stripped of protective institutions. Wages declined precipitously during the restructuring period, and only recovered to their 1970 level in real terms in 1992 (Coloma and Rojas 2000). In effect, this meant a freeze on wage increases that lasted almost a quarter of a century, resulting in the decrease of wages as a share of national product from 52.2 percent in 1972 to 36.7 percent in 1989 (ICFTU 1997). Concurrently, in 1996, the Global Competitiveness Report and the International Labor Organisation found that Chileans work the longest hours in the world, averaging over 2,400 hours per year. These factors indicate the manner in which the class relation between capital and labour had been decisively shifted in the favour of capital, with highly delimited rights for labour to act collectively in defence of its interests. While these changing relations at the point of production are explored in detail in the following chapter, it is worth noting here that in spite of alterations to labour laws in the 1990s, organised labour had been weakened to such an extent that those workers involved in collective bargaining over the 1990s achieved average wage increases under the level of non-unionised workers (Campero 2004: 17).

Alongside the reshaping of power relations between capital and labour, the social terrain of post-dictatorship Chile is also characterised by hierarchical relations between the large economic conglomerates formed in the Pinochet period and firms in the competitive sector. By 1994, for example, some 7,300 companies of a total of 480,000 (less than 2 percent) accounted for 76 percent of all sales in Chile (Cademartori 2003). Furthermore, these market-dominating companies are in turn controlled through financial ownership by a combination of foreign interests and the two dozen large Chilean economic conglomerates that consolidated their power in the Pinochet period (Fazio 2000). These large conglomerates have been the primary beneficiaries of the Concertación's supposedly neutral macroeconomic policy. The policies of suppressing the exchange rate to promote exports while keeping interest rates high to maintain monetary stability greatly benefit those companies who have access to cheap sources of international credit. Simultaneously, they intensify the competitive pressures on those firms that produce for internal markets and have limited or no access to external credit. As Osvaldo Rosales (2000: 222) has critiqued:

While the political discourse might defend even-handed, non-discriminatory policies, the macroeconomy favors large companies that can acquire inexpensive foreign financing and punishes companies that export goods not associated with natural resources.

As a result, all the main export sectors, such as mining, fisheries, lumber and agro-export, exist in the form of oligopolistic markets characterised by the domination of a few large firms. Within these sectors, the market-dominating firms exercise considerable price-setting capabilities while simultaneously enjoying notable subsidies from the state such as tax rebates on imported technology and other reimbursements for export promotion (Gwynne and Kay 1997; Fazio 2000; Nef 2003). The latter subsidies amounted to US$148 million in 1995 (Javier and Fuentes 2000: 244). Far from passively operating according to the dictates of market forces, as neoclassical theory would theorise, these enterprises use their market power, financial capabilities, political influence and control over their workforces and subcontracted firms to shape significantly the environment in which they function.

In the newly privatised service sectors, for example, oligopolistic firms use their financial clout and political influence to shape the forms of public regulation that they are subjected to. Through the medium of public–private partnerships established to fashion regulatory codes, they attempt to guarantee the conditions for exceptionally high rates of return on investment. In an analysis of these firms, Eduardo Bitran and Pablo Serra (1998: 959) highlighted the monopolisation of several areas, such as pensions, long distance telephone services and power generation, and suggested that:

Regulation is increasingly turning into a bargaining process where the relative power and influence of different interest groups has a big effect on the outcome. This environment has led to the appearance of rent-seeking, as it becomes profitable to use resources cultivating influence in the hope of favorably affecting regulators' decisions. The outcome of this is a situation where regulated public utilities earn high returns on capital.

Within the productive sectors of the economy, such power relations are compounded by ability of the larger firms to displace costs and risks onto smaller firms further down the supply chain. These trends have been exacerbated by the vertical disintegration of many export-orientated firms who have reduced their permanent workforces by means of subcontracting practices. The latter facilitate an indirect relationship with labour through the mediation of small firms that are contracted for specific tasks or over short time periods. The flexibility provided by subcontracting allows the large firm to reduce expenses by forcing small firms to compete for short-term contracts that can be easily shed in periods of market instability. Power relations between the monopoly sector firms and the small and micro-enterprises, which provide the bulk of employment in Chile, therefore permit economic conglomerates to push many of the risks that stem from volatile global commodity markets onto the smaller players. The end result is to maintain the stability of profit margins by imposing insecurity onto smaller firms and their workforces (see chapter 7 and Escobar and López 1996).

Aside from acute asymmetries of power, also missing from neoliberal accounts of the Chilean 'free market miracle' is the active role of the state in fashioning this socio-economic environment. At one level, and in spite of the continuing reduction in the number of state-owned enterprises through privatisation, the most important company in Chile – CODELCO – remains publicly owned and operated, having been formed in the period of Frei and Allende's nationalisations. CODELCO is the largest copper producer in the world, holding 20 percent of known global copper reserves, operates with the greatest efficiency of all global copper companies, and exercises great influence over national and global copper prices. Taxation of CODELCO's oligopolistic profits has provided an important source of revenue that aided the creation of budget surpluses and social expenditure increases throughout the 1990s, which remain expressly important determinants of the Chilean political economy in the post-dictatorship period.

Beyond direct state ownership, it was highlighted above how the supposedly depoliticised and neutral economic policies specifically privileged the large export-orientated enterprises over all others. Similarly, government policy continues to help form networks and institutions in the export sector that promote technology sharing and group market power (Perez-Aleman 2000; Kurtz 2001; Cypher 2004). Far from policies of liberalisation and a pro-business environment automatically engendering a booming export sector, key industries from agro-export to fisheries and lumber benefited from the organising activities of state agencies such as CORFO and PROCHILE. As Perez-Aleman (2003: 796) indicates in the context of a study of the tomato paste processing industry, PROCHILE has played a fundamental role in coordinating firms to meet international product quality standards, as well as to improve production practices and develop new product lines. State institutions of this nature did not begin with the Concertación and do not represent a new policy shift, having been initiated in the late 1930s and retaining a reformed roll within the dictatorship's post-1982 export strategy. Nevertheless, they do indicate how state institutions continue to play a key role in organising the export sector of the Chilean economy.

Within this socio-economic context, new trends in the pattern of global capital accumulation in the early 1990s combined to strengthen the export boom. Deteriorating profit rates in the core countries of the US, Europe and Japan led to an abundance of capital without sufficient profitable investment opportunities. This shift conspired to alter the pattern of capital investment on a global scale. With the advanced industrialised countries of the capitalist core mired in recession and rapidly lowering interest rates, the early 1990s were marked by a proliferation of financial flows to preferred locations in the global South (Lemco and MacDonald 2001: 86). This was a trend that grew exponentially over the first half of the decade as capital looked for preferential rates of return from various forms of investment in the South, including foreign portfolio investment, mergers and acquisitions, and greenfield site investment (Soederberg 2004). Chile appeared as a particularly favourable option owing to political stability through the 'protected democracy' fashioned by the military, a well-disciplined labour force with few legal rights, a government that offered significant benefits to foreign capital operating within its borders, not to mention the wide range of investment opportunities afforded by Chile's uniquely rich natural resources, its burgeoning financial markets and the ongoing privatisation process. Not only does the wide variation in Chile's temperate zones provide opportunities for a full range of agro-export activities, including fishing and lumber alongside fruit and vegetables, the Chilean Andean region is considered the world's primary copper deposit, with around 40 percent of identified global reserves (Larraín et al. 2000).

Given these preconditions Chile experienced huge inflows of foreign investment in the early and mid-1990s that spurred on productive activities and technological upgrading in resource extraction (particularly copper) and agro-export sectors. The influx of capital swelled the value of financial assets on financial markets and paved the way for significant investments in the service sector by North American and, notably, Spanish capital (Fazio 2000). Foreign direct investment (FDI) specifically targeted the dynamic and profitable export-orientated sectors of the Chilean economy, with copper extraction leading the way. As Graciela Moguillansky (2001: 190) indicates, the narrow range of activities that attracted FDI ensured that the primary export sector continued to flourish without contributing to a diversification of Chilean production into industrial areas with more value added. Concurrently, financial flows of a more short-term and speculative nature also increased, although remaining below the levels of FDI.

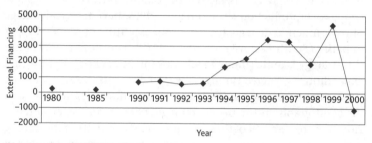

(Data drawn from CEPAL 1999: 502–3)

Figure 6.1   External Financing – Net Direct Investment (US$ millions)

New privatisation initiatives contributed to the attractiveness of fresh sites for foreign investment and facilitated a sharp increase in FDI, particularly given the high rates of return guaranteed by government contracts and flexible forms of regulation (Bitran and Serra 1998). For example, transnational capital in the construction sector has grown from minimal levels at the end of the 1980s to a situation in which 50 percent of investment is foreign and where companies backed by foreign capitals take some 72 percent of public works contracts (Fazio 2000: 36). These initiatives increased the prospects of foreign investment and offered the state considerable, albeit short-term, income through the transfer of assets. Not only has governmental privatisation opened new areas for foreign investment, but also continuing processes of tax incentives, deregulation and exchange rate manipulation throughout the decade helped promote foreign investment. An exemplary case is the booming copper sector, where FDI in the 1990s boom was profoundly superior to all other sectors of the economy, partially owing to the initiation of several 'mega-projects' that explored rich new reserves through the deployment of new technology. Moreover, the attractiveness of investment in copper extraction was increased by the relatively high price of copper in the early and mid-1990s alongside significant tax breaks offered to transnational capital that guaranteed the achievement of high profit rates (Lagos 1999: 32).

In offering significant tax deductions to foreign capital entering mineral extraction sectors, which at 15 percent were the lowest in Latin America, the regime even placed the profitability of the state-owned copper sector at a relative disadvantage (Miller Klubock 2004b: 242). Tax breaks, however, have not been the only incentive offered by the state. Foreign firms, faced with declining prices owing to global copper overproduction since the mid-1990s, have taken advantage of governmental de-regulation to begin exporting unrefined copper in bulk to South-East Asia (Lagos 1999: 30). The motivation behind this strategy is quite simply to take advantage of cheaper processing expenditures garnered through lower labour costs in Asia that more than compensate for increased transportation expenditure, and fits comfortably in the neoliberal logic of comparative advantage. However, the removal of these labour-intensive aspects of the mining process has contributed to an absolute decrease in the number of mining sector jobs in Chile despite the massive levels of foreign investment outlined above (Agacino et al. 1998).

Indeed, the Chilean export boom of the 1990s is replete with contradictions that are often not acknowledged by proponents of the Chilean neoliberal 'miracle'. The following three sections highlight some of the primary tensions that emerged within this period; namely, (1) economic dualisation between the monopoly and competitive sectors, (2) pronounced social inequality, and (3) tendencies to overproduction in key export industries.

CONTRADICTIONS OF THE EXPORT BOOM 1: ECONOMIC DUALISATION

One of the primary effects of neoliberal policies in the Pinochet period, as detailed in chapter 3, was the collapse of many industrial sectors cultivated since the 1930s and the concentration of capital into primary commodity export sectors under the aegis of large financial groups. In the late 1980s, the new export conglomerates operating in these sectors entered into a boom phase, with exports of copper, fruits, lumber and other commodities growing exponentially. These trends were aided by the reduction of tariffs, a suppressed exchange rate, and promotion of free trade agreements by the Concertación, which further encouraged the concentration of capital within Chile within the export sectors. Heavy foreign direct investment in copper and, to a lesser extent, agro-export and forestry also spurred on this process. Lowering tariffs on inputs into the production process facilitated the importation of technology and other inputs into these sectors. Simultaneously, lowering tariffs on domestic consumption items reduced the cost of living and therein played a role in moderating wage increases and suppressing the price of labour for Chilean exporters. Large inflows of foreign capital and the availability of international credit were used by the economic conglomerates to implement technological improvements that increased productivity in the export sectors. Whereas in the 1984–89 period productivity growth per worker was negligible, in the 1990–95 period annual productivity increases reached 4.3 percent (Rosales 1998: 219). Productivity transformation in this manner was most prolific in the core regions of the export sectors, particularly mining but also agro-export, and lumber and seafood processing. Likewise, financial services and, to a lesser degree, commerce and transport also witnessed large increases in productivity over the 1990–96 period (Rosales 1998: 218; Ossandón 2002).

A more problematic result of this strategy, however, has been the accentuated dualisation of the Chilean economy, which is split between a high technology, oligopolistic export sector that is controlled by the large Chilean economic conglomerates and foreign transnational corporations; and a low technology, low wage competitive sector of small and medium firms in the Chilean industrial sector (Parrilli 2004). The former, oligopolistic sector of the economy, displays extremely concentrated ownership characteristics. In addition to the influx of foreign corporations into mining, electricity and telecommunications, the IMF notes that the 40 large economic groups that consolidated in the late 1980s hold the vast majority of the equity in the 500 firms that comprise the Chilean corporate sector (IMF 2002: 81).

In contrast, the competitive sector of small and medium firms provides the majority of Chilean employment yet has few direct links to the dynamic export sectors and must compete with unhindered foreign competition owing to the ongoing liberalisation of trade (Parrilli 2004). Given the low technology status of these firms and the barriers that prevent them from accessing affordable credit, the tendency is for them to compete with foreign competition on the basis of low labour costs, high work intensity, long working weeks, and the subcontracting out of services. Micro-enterprises, employing fewer than five workers, accounted for 40.6 percent of total employment in 1996, and this figure rises to 46 percent if enterprises of five to nine workers are included (Escobar 1999a: 31–2). Informalised work relations are common within these enterprises, with only 30 percent of micro-enterprise workers having a fixed contract. As such, high levels of precarious employment characterise this sector, entailing that workers confront unstable employment relations with a short-term horizon owing to substantial risk of ejection (Escobar 1999a; González 1999: 99). A similar trend is visible in rural Chile, where analysts such as Warwick Murray (2002: 267) have analysed the consolidation of a 'two-track' agricultural system comprised of 'successful large and medium export-orientated growers on the one side, and small-scale inward orientated peasants and rural labourers on the other'.

It should be noted that, although the share of manufacturing in GDP grew at a sustained rate during the boom period, this did not represent the initiation of a second 'phase' of the export-promotion industrialisation strategy, as heralded by the Concertación governments since 1991. The second phase was intended to involve a strong diversification of exports into non-traditional goods that required labour-intensive production with higher value added (Seinen 1996: 153). Additionally, such a transition was projected to require an important role for state institutions, both through an industrial policy that provides incentives for the creation of new industries, and through the creation of an educated and disciplined labour force with wide-ranging skill sets. A specific focus of state intervention in the Concertación period – and particularly in the Lagos presidency – has been to orientate state financing facilities towards small and medium firms, with the intention of improving technology and productivity, and better linking the latter into the export sector (Phillips 2004: 201). In basing production on higher levels of human capital and technology, and therein by increasing exports of finished products, it was believed that Chilean accumulation could overcome its strong dependence on finite primary exports and initiate a virtuous circle of investment in workers leading to stronger exports. In so doing, the projected formation of tightly linked networks of large, medium and small firms was anticipated to overcome the dualisation of the Chilean economy (Rosales 2000).

Nonetheless, the promised transition has been muted. On the one hand, the 1990s saw an increasing number of vertically linked industries involved in the light processing of Chilean raw materials. As discussed below, these industries were not labour intensive and have often involved particularly flexible forms of labour relations, with marginal productivity gains over the decade that belie the idea of a transition to high value-added production reliant on increasingly skilled labour (Ossandón 2002: 12). Where labour-intensive Chilean industry does enjoy regional competitiveness – in metalwork and light manufacturing such as plastics and containers – the lack of state support has hindered technological and skills upgrading (Cypher 2003: 14). On the other, in certain instances, such as that of copper as discussed above, the Concertación responded to deteriorating global conditions for key products in the late 1990s by certifying the export of unprocessed primary materials in order to maintain investment, thereby removing labour-intensive processing stages from copper production in Chile (Lagos 1999). As Table 6.2 demonstrates, copper had regained its position as the most dynamic export growth area by the end of the decade, whereas the rate of growth of non-traditional exports has fallen continuously.

Table 6.2 Quantum Growth of Exports by Period

	1986–89	1990–94	1995–2000
Copper	3.3	5.1	13.4
Non-Copper Traditional	9.0	7.1	3.3
Non-Copper Non-Traditional	21.7	16.3	9.7
Total Exports	**8.8**	**8.7**	**9.4**

To the extent that it has occurred, therefore, the impact of a 'second phase' of Chilean export-promotion industrialisation has not recreated the experience of the East Asian newly industrialising countries (NICs) through a transition into more complex, high value-added goods. The expansion of export manufacturing has been limited primarily to light processing of primary products. For example, in 1997 brute raw materials still constituted 44 percent of exports; moderately processed raw materials, such as fishmeal, processed frozen fish, wood chips, pulp and planks, accounted for 26 percent; and fully manufactured goods constituted only 10 percent (Castillo 1997: 44). Although proponents of the Concertación's development strategy preferred to laud over eight years of straight growth as evidence of the 'jaguar' status of the Chilean economy that placed it on par with the East Asian 'tigers', critics pointed out major problems with such a comparison. In the words of Peter Winn: 'it was absurd to claim equality with Taiwan or Korea – with their steel, electronics and autos – on the basis of exports of copper, fruits, fish and forest products with little value added in Chile to the raw material' (Winn 2004b: 55). A further indication of the limits to second-stage growth is the lack of development in research and development (R&D). Even former proponents of the Chilean model such as Felipe Larraín, Jeffrey Sachs and Andrew Warner have shed considerable doubt on economic sustainability at current trends of R&D. The latter suggested at the turn of the millennium that: 'Chile shows continuing relative weaknesses in education, science, and research and development, the social spheres that will prove to be most important in Chile's task of a broader-based, more diversified national economy, and one that is more tightly integrated with the advanced economies' (Larraín et al. 2000).

CONTRADICTIONS OF THE EXPORT BOOM 2: ENDURING INEQUALITY

A second important element of post-dictatorship Chilean society has been the enduring polarisation of income distribution. The latter has occurred alongside the positive effects of the Chilean boom in terms of rising aggregate real wages and the reincorporation of the unemployed masses into the Chilean workforce. It is common for advocates of the Chilean model to present the figures for rising real wages as proof of the virtues of the development strategy (cf. Chacón 1999: 222). However, presenting the aggregated trends of real wage changes in an undifferentiated fashion clouds the asymmetrical composition of changing wage levels amongst specific occupational strata within the social division of labour. Over the boom period, for example, the highest wage rises went to professionals and technicians who were largely incorporated within the oligopolistic export sector or financial services. The majority of unskilled labourers, in contrast, received below average wage increases (Escobar 1999a: 43–4). The outcome of such trends is the perpetuation of the highly unequal distribution of income that was forged in the Pinochet period, with considerable divergence in wages related to both the branch of production and position within the division of labour. Over the course of the decade there occurred a consolidation and slight deepening of income inequality within Chile, which remains highly polarised, even by the unenviable standards of Latin America.

Table 6.3   Distribution of Income by Decile, 1990–2000

Decile	1990	1992	1994	1996	1998	2000
I	1.4	1.5	1.3	1.3	1.2	1.1
II	2.7	2.8	2.7	2.6	2.5	2.6
III	3.6	3.7	3.5	3.5	3.5	3.7
IV	4.5	4.6	4.6	4.5	4.5	4.5
V	5.4	5.6	5.5	5.4	5.3	5.7
VI	6.9	6.6	6.4	6.3	6.4	6.5
VII	7.8	8.1	8.1	8.2	8.3	7.9
VIII	10.3	10.4	10.6	11.1	11.0	10.5
IX	15.2	14.8	15.4	15.5	16.0	15.2
X	42.2	41.9	41.9	41.6	41.3	42.3

(From MIDEPLAN 2001b: 23)

As such, and notwithstanding the Concertación's repeated motif of 'growth with equity', the outcome of the export-led boom was growth coupled with stagnant or deteriorating income inequality (refer to Table 6.3). The latter is testament to the pervasiveness of social polarisation forged through the contemporary structure of Chilean social relations. Advocates of the Chilean model, however, often downplay escalating inequality by emphasising the positive impact of the export boom upon wages and poverty reduction (Aninat 2000). Nevertheless, when viewed from a medium-term perspective, rather than against the negative social trends fashioned in the 1973–85 restructuring period, these gains in wages and poverty reduction merely represent a long delayed reversion to trends established in the 1960s and 1970s.

With respect to wages, the significant increase in the demand for labour helped to tighten labour markets and push wages upwards in a sustained manner during the first half of the 1990s. The demand for labour during the mid-1990s was great enough to generate labour shortages in peak months in some export industries, thereby forcing employers in regions of labour scarcity – such as the southern coastal fish processors – to offer improved conditions to attract casual workers (Schurman 2001: 20; Barrett et al. 2002: 1957). Unemployment, although manifesting sizeable variations within the course of a given year owing to the seasonal nature of work in the agro-export sector, subsided from the high of 29 percent in the early 1980s to 6.4 percent in 1994, thereby returning to a level just above its historical average of around 6 percent in the post-war period (Stallings 2001: 51). Similar to trends in the late 1980s, a considerable portion of the new employment resulted from the expansion of construction, commerce and of light manufacturing, aimed either towards domestic consumption or concentrated on low value-added transformations of primary extracts for export. Owing to job creation in these latter two areas, employment in the primary sector increased from under 22 percent of total urban employment in 1986 to 27 percent by 1994 (Escobar 1999a).

The outcome of tight labour markets was therefore a notable increase in wages. In 1992 real wages recovered to their pre-debt crisis level and then rose consistently by around 4 percent annually in the boom years of the mid-1990s, slowing only with the crisis of 1997–98 and the subsequent economic stagnation (refer to Table 6.4). In spite of this appreciation, even by the year 2000 real wages were only 28 percent above their 1970 value, which represents an increase of less than 1 percent per year. The process of rising wages was also bolstered by the political decision of the Concertación consistently to make small raises in the level of the minimum wage, although the impact of the latter political decision has been far less dramatic than the accusations of organised business would suggest. Only in 1997 did the minimum wage regain its 1982 level in real terms, and still lagged below that of 1970 (Coloma and Rojas 2000: 511). Moreover, the insecurity of work and barriers to collective bargaining stemming from prevailing labour institutions, as discussed in the following chapter, served to stem the rate of wage rises.

Table 6.4   Index of Real Wages (1970 = 100)

Year	1986	1988	1990	1992	1994	1996	1998	2000
Index	83.8	89.1	92.4	101.3	110.3	119.0	124.0	128.0

(Data drawn from Fazio 2001a: 217)

Rising wage levels had an important impact on poverty. With the re-integration of the unemployed masses into employment during the late 1980s and early 1990s, official poverty levels declined from the 1990 level of 38.6 percent to just over 20.3 percent in 2000, with extreme poverty falling from 12.9 percent to 5.7 percent over the same period (refer to Figure 6.2). Although a notable and positive trend, this seemingly dramatic reduction in poverty represents a return to levels consistent with the longer trend of poverty reduction in Chile over the second half of the twentieth century. Although methodological questions over survey data and processing remain, analysts estimate that poverty levels in 1970 were within the range of 25 to 30 percent (cf. Graham 1991; Raczynski 1999). In this respect poverty reduction during the 1990s is a success only in respect to the drastically *increased* levels of poverty induced by the social restructuring processes occurring between 1975 and 1985. Trends over the 1990s therefore continue the trajectory established in the 1960s and early 1970s before the ruptures of the Pinochet period.

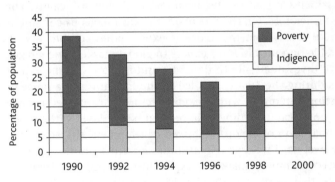

(Data drawn from MIDEPLAN 2001a: 4)

Figure 6.2 Evolution of Poverty and Indigence, 1990–2000

CONTRADICTIONS OF THE EXPORT BOOM 3: OVERPRODUCTION AND THE ASIAN CRISIS

Increasing investment and productivity rises in the monopoly export sector characterised the boom years of 1990–97, yet these trends would generate their own contradictions by the end of the decade. Growth in gross capital formation between 1990 and 1996 averaged 8.3 percent (Escobar 1999a: 24), and GDP grew by 7.8 percent over the same seven-year span (refer to Table 6.1). Whereas economic expansion in the late 1980s involved the re-absorption of the cheap and disciplined reserve labour army into production and the re-utilisation of unused capacity, the early 1990s witnessed heavy investment in technology in the export sectors partially owing to increasingly tight labour markets. Processes of sustained technological improvements would dramatically increase productivity in key branches of production, culminating in tendencies towards overproduction and the displacement of workers from production. The later trend, as indicated below, led to the partial replenishment of the reserve labour army and, by the end of the decade, unemployment returned to above 10 percent. This trend would slow the growth of wages that resulted from tight labour markets, yet technological investment would raise productivity to a level that threatened key industries with overcapacity vis-à-vis the extent of the market.

In this way, of singular importance for the Chilean export-led model is the emergence of global overproduction and subsequent heightening competition within the branches of primary production upon which Chilean capital accumulation relies so heavily. The process is twofold. On the one hand, the advantageous conditions of production within the dynamic export poles combined with favourable opportunities for export to global markets encouraged massive investment – both domestic and foreign – in the export sectors during the 1990s. This led to the formation of a range of competing enterprises within export sectors that invested heavily in technological upgrading to improve productivity. On the other, the propagation of export-orientated development strategies on a global level has increased opportunities for firms aiming at similar Western consumption markets to exploit new competitive advantages in alternative countries in the global South. During the 1990s global capital sought to exploit market opportunities through investment in these same branches of production in other spatial locations within the global division of labour.

Unlike the projections of neoclassical theory, increased competition does not lead to the smooth elimination of inefficient producers and the return of equilibrium. On the contrary, each individual enterprise tends to react to increased competition by introducing technological improvements, funded through credit, and by intensifying the exploitation of labour through increasing the hours or intensity of work. The tighter the market gets, the more pressure is placed upon capitals to reduce production costs and to increase the mass of products produced in order to adjust to falling prices. As a result, the very response of capitals faced with overproduction tends to exacerbate the trend at a social level, therein further accentuating overproduction until a destructive crisis emerges (see chapter 2 and

Clarke 1990). This process of escalating overproduction is particularly clear in the copper industry, which remains at the core of Chilean export-led growth. In terms of a percentage of world copper exports, Chile soared from 26.1 percent in 1990 to 39.6 percent in 1998 owing to the expansion of mines and technological enhancement, driven by large amounts of foreign investment (Lagos 1999: 28). With respect to volume, total copper exports more than doubled between 1990 and 1998. This represented an 11.1 percent average annual increase whereas the US$ value of those exports only increased by 6.4 percent yearly, therein highlighting the decreasing price of copper on global markets (Lagos 1999: 29–31). By 1999 overproduction combined with recession in key importing countries meant that copper prices hit their lowest level for 40 years and remained stagnant into the new millennium (IMF 2000: 105), until growing demand from China led to a recovery by 2003. Accounting for some 40 percent of export earnings, overproduction in the copper industry threatens accumulation in Chile with particularly grave ramifications.

Whereas the overproduction of copper constituted a particularly grave threat owing to its pivotal role in Chilean accumulation, similar processes were nonetheless manifesting themselves in other export sectors. In the fishing sector, for example, six of the eight principal marine fishes of commercial value are currently between full and over-exploitation owing to overcapitalisation, therein threatening the very reproduction of the industry (Aguilar Ibarra et al. 2000: 510). Likewise, other key export industries such as salmon, cellulose, grapes and wine have been marked by decreasing rates of profit through a combination of Chilean overproduction and the arrival of new competitors on the world market (*La Otra Ecónomia* 2002). Notably, by 2003, even the OECD (Organisation for Economic Co-operation and Development) – in spite of its praise for Chilean economic governance over the entire neoliberal period – had raised the possibility of the exhaustion of the export-driven growth model (OECD 2003). In response to rising labour costs and escalating overproduction in key Chilean industries, the large economic groups responded by borrowing huge amounts of foreign capital in order to continue the process of technological upgrades and to acquire assets in other parts of South America. Even the IMF (2000: 98) has expressed concern over the soaring level of private external debt in Chile, which doubled between 1995 and 1999 and in 2004 still amounted to the equivalent of 36 percent of annual GDP (refer to figure 6.3).

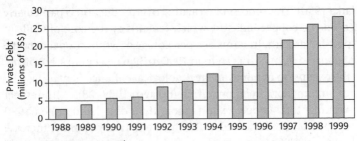

(Data drawn from Fazio 2000: 26)

Figure 6.3   Private External Debt

These contradictions in Chilean capital accumulation came to a head in 1998. Deep integration into the world market brought export opportunities and inflows of foreign investment. The inverse side of this integration, however, is a reliance on fickle and volatile capital flows to provide sustained investment. Much as neoliberal policy advocates are keen to relate every unforeseen negative occurrence to exogenous factors and external shocks, the latter are an inevitable dimension of a strategy that mandates integration into global capital circuits. Nonetheless, regime ideologues were confident that the possibility of crisis owing to this manner of external dependence was minimal. They championed the pragmatic use of capital controls and the seeming immunity of Chile to the 'Tequila Effect' that spread contagion across Latin America following the 1994/95 Mexican Peso Crisis.

In spite of this confidence, significant vulnerabilities of Chilean accumulation were starkly revealed in 1997 following the financial crisis that erupted in East Asia and spread to Russia and Brazil. First, inflows of capital during the mid-1990s caused the Chilean peso to appreciate in value by 16 percent between March 1995 and October 1997 in spite of government attempts to suppress its value (Ffrench-Davis 2002b: 8). This led to a further restraint on the competitiveness of the export sectors to add to those examined in the previous section. Second, rising wage rates affected the profit margins of a range of industrial sectors, a tendency that increasing labour flexibility could only partially compensate. Third, in the wake of the East Asian crisis, export industries were faced with the disruption of markets that had grown to absorb one-third of Chilean goods by the mid-1990s. In conditions of spreading financial panic, investors baulked at the prospect of financial collapse in 'emerging markets' and some US$2.1

billion of capital fled from Chile (International Monetary Fund (IMF) 2000: 99). Together, these factors plunged the Chilean economy into recession, with negative growth registered in 1999 for the first time since the debt crisis and was followed by a period of relative stagnation in the subsequent three years.

Table 6.5   Annual GDP Increase (percentage)

Year	1998	1999	2000	2001	2002	2003
GDP change	3.2	–0.8	4.5	3.4	2.2	3.7

(Data from Banco de Chile online statistical database, accessed December 2003. <http://si2.bcentral. cl/Basededatoseconomicos/>)

Ironically, given the Concertación's previous emphasis on the need for capital controls to maintain macroeconomic stability and a stable capital account, the state response to crisis involved rapidly removing existing capital controls and other impediments to the free mobility of capital in order to attract capital back to Chile. In circumstances of crisis, installing confidence in investors by facilitating their ability to exit easily under any future adverse circumstances took precedence over instruments of financial management. Subsequently, as part of a 2002 free trade agreement signed with the US, the Lagos administration has legally committed itself to maintaining a fully open capital account, thereby forgoing the possibility of implementing any future capital controls (Stiglitz 2003).

Although the outbreak of the Asian financial crisis was a trigger for recession in Chile, the downturn of 1998 and the subsequent stagnation also revealed serious problems within the primary-export model of Chilean accumulation. Signs of tension were already visible before the crisis hit, as manifested by a fall in the rate of growth of manufactured exports from 32 percent in 1991 to 8.2 percent in 1997 (Weyland 1999: 81). Similarly, the terms of trade for Chile had deteriorated by the mid-1990s, and the current account deficit reached 6.3 percent of GDP in 1998 before the onset of crisis (Escobar 1999b: 18) and remained mostly negative until 2004. Notably, as soon as falling commodity prices and capital flight brought an end to the boom in 1998, the Frei and subsequent Lagos governments quickly jettisoned the emphasis on fiscal prudence and reverted to a more Keynesian-inspired approach of running fiscal deficits to counteract cyclical downturns, thereby suggesting that fiscal prudence is as much a consequence as a cause of economic growth. Nonetheless, the relative stagnation of the non-export sectors prompted a new rise in unemployment, which reached 10 percent nationally in 2000 and has remained around this figure into 2003 despite the reintroduction of emergency work programmes for the first time since the mid-1980s. The latter have been introduced by the Concertación and provide direct employment for 100,000 people any time unemployment exceeds 9 percent (CEPAL 2001b: 140).

On a political level, the emergence of the threat of declining commodity prices owing to overproduction, and not any substantial change in Concertación policies, is one of the primary reasons that organised business relaxed its toleration of the Concertación's 'growth with equity' programme and became particularly hostile towards the later Concertación governments, and particularly the Lagos administration (Silva 2002). Specifically, as discussed in depth in the following chapter, the organised bodies of capital became belligerent in their campaign to prevent any substantial reforms to the existing labour code that would give workers more rights and power to engage in collective bargaining. Notably, business interests decried even the compromise of relatively minor amendments in 2001 as a 'grave danger to the Chilean economy' (El Mostrador 2001a). Inversely, the growing crisis of export-orientated accumulation also threatened the ability of the state to increase social expenditures that formed the lynchpin of its political and social strategy in the 1990s. These two themes are taken up in the following two chapters respectively. Prior to that, however, the following section examines shifts in economic policy that followed the Asian crisis period. With the deep crisis afflicting the processes of capital accumulation inherited from the dictatorship, would the Lagos administration have the political will and facility to begin shaping an alternative macroeconomic strategy?

AFTER THE CRISIS – NEW POLICIES FOR AN UNCERTAIN FUTURE?

Following the 1998–99 crisis and during the 2000–02 stagnation, the government of Ricardo Lagos looked for ways to reinvigorate the Chilean economy by selectively adapting and deepening various tenets of the neoliberal model. For example, despite being suspected as the least likely of the Concertación administrations to conform to fiscal discipline owing to its socialist heritage, the Lagos government adopted a strategy of strictly linking government budget levels to macroeconomic indicators in order to both submit to the discipline of monetary movements while allowing flexibility in downturns (CEPAL 2001b: 135). Although the government was therefore able to run a slight deficit in the period of relative stagnation, this had to be compensated for by budget surpluses in upswing periods. The OECD (2003) applauded this move as 'locking in' the credibility built up in the 1980s and 1990s.

Moreover, trade agreements signed with the US and the European Union in the early years of the new millennium were widely heralded as a significant accomplishment for Chilean producers and consumers. With legally binding trade agreements, the Concertación regime sought to ensure a varied set of international options for the export of Chilean products and consolidate the expansion and divergence of export markets ongoing since the 1980s. Contrary to a previous concentration of exports to North America and Europe, by the mid-1990s Chile export destinations were substantially diversified, and East Asia consumed a greater quantity than either the NAFTA or EU blocks with 35 percent of exports in 1997 (Ffrench-Davis 2002b: 13). Latin America also became a more important destination for Chilean products, with 24 percent of exports and – importantly – the largest composition of industrial products rather than raw materials or lightly processed goods.

Whereas such efforts were presented as proactive initiatives to integrate Chile into the global economy to 'embrace development opportunities' (Aninat 2000), these measures were desperately pursued by the Concertación under pressure from Chilean conglomerates as a short-term attempt to reinvigorate the ailing export sector. As such, they are also likely to prolong economic dualisation within Chile by temporarily revitalising the oligopolistic export sector while further opening the country to foreign imports of technologically enhanced goods and cheap agricultural staples. Attention also needs to be placed on the way such agreements affect power structures within Chile. For example, the 2002 free trade agreement concluded with the US further enshrines the legal rights of foreign corporations vis-à-vis the Chilean state. Substantially modelled after the NAFTA chapter on investment which pertains to investment in all industries and public sector contracts at all levels of government, the agreement covers measures including the equal rights of foreign corporations to bid for government contracts as their Chilean competitors. Additionally, the agreement provides new institutions by which investors can pursue claims against the host-country government (investor–state dispute settlement) should they feel their rights have been aggrieved (UNCTAD 2004: 22).

A second aspect of the post-recession political economy was a series of incentives granted to investors aimed at revitalising the flow of FDI into Chile and directing it towards higher technology industries. Similar to the relaxing of neoliberal fiscal policy and its replacement with a more Keynesian-inspired deficit financing in years of slow growth, these new initiatives represented an increasingly active set of industrial policies. For example, subsidies were offered through the state industrial promotion agency CORFO for on-the-job training of workers. Likewise, research and development funds were made available for trade-related activities. In this vein, the city of Valparaíso was promoted as a new hub of hi-tech industry, and the government championed the success of attracting Motorola to establish a mobile-internet technological centre under this new initiative (UNCTAD 2004: 55). Simultaneously, the Government launched a campaign in early 2003 to promote the programme 'Chile: a platform for new markets'. Building upon Chile's reputation for a good business environment, corporations were offered income tax exemptions to select Chile as the hub for Latin American operations (UNCTAD 2004: 20).

Although these initiatives are a notable development of the export-promotion initiatives used by the Pinochet regime and the first Concertación governments, and represent an attempt to emulate the successes of East Asian economies, there are several specific limitations. At the outset, they remain relatively limited programmes operating within the structures of a heavily liberalised economy and which are unlikely to fundamentally alter prevailing patterns of investment by, for example, creating new high value-added industries that can link the oligopolistic export sector and the small and medium firms in which employment is concentrated. Whereas the state industry-promotion body CORFO has increased loans to small and medium firms for technological upgrading, observers have suggested that these initiatives will not offer serious transformative potential unless they, first, are extended to cover more than the current 10 percent of firms; second, supply a greater amount of funding for technological upgrading; and, third, are generalised to either sectoral or regional levels to overcome fragmentation and facilitate the development of linked networks of higher value-added producers (Alarcón and Stumpo 2000; Parrilli 2004). As such, this policy transformation has not precipitated a qualitative break from earlier strategies and does not represent a transformation to a 'neo-structuralist' economic strategy that some observers have suggested is the future of Latin American economic policy (Gwynne and Kay 2001). Industrial policy remains within the neoliberal framework of correcting market failures rather than attempting to promote and deepen industrial sectors through building institutions that would facilitate systematic and strategic intervention, as was prominent in the East Asian experience (cf. Deraniyagala 2001).

THE RETURN TO EXPORT-LED GROWTH

In 2003 capital accumulation in Chile began to accelerate again. Unsurprisingly, the resulting economic growth has been predicated on primary commodity exports, with economic recovery in the US and new demand from China inflating the price of exports. While high unemployment and stagnant demand for basic consumer items remains (Soto 2004), the price of copper on world markets rose by 15 percent between the summer of 2002 and 2003 and provided a significant boost for domestic and multinational exporters in Chile (Lifsher 2003). The dramatic nature of these increases was exemplified in 2004, when the value of mining exports doubled in the space of a year (refer to Figure 6.4). Indeed, Chilean economic expansion in the period following 2002 is closely related to a rise in primary commodity prices on global markets and the reinvigorated interest of foreign capital to invest once again in these sectors (Mulligan 2005).

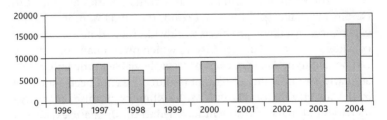

(Data from Banco Central de Chile, accessed June 2005.
<http://si2.bcentral.cl/Basededatoseconomicos/>)

Figure 6.4   Value of Mining Exports (millions of US$)

The emergence of China as a major destination for Latin American primary commodity exports across the continent is noteworthy. China has risen to be Chile's third most important export destination, absorbing 7 percent of exports in 2003 as opposed to just 2.3 percent in 1999. Significantly, China is expected to overtake Japan as Chile's second most important export destination by 2006 and account for over 10 percent of Chile's exports, two-thirds of which are composed of copper and copper derivatives. In the summer of 2004, the two countries were moving a potential free trade agreement into fast-track mode to formalise the new trading relationship. This relationship, however, reaffirms Chile's status as a primary commodity exporter and an importer of finished goods. It may provide the export sector with a new lease of life in the short term but is unlikely to help transform Chilean productive structures in the medium term. Given the new role of China as a major importer of Chilean goods, moreover, the regularly predicted threat of a hard landing for the Chinese economy could spell the end of the post-2002 recovery (on the contradictions of China's growth, see Hart-Landsberg and Burkett 2005).

Although the new export surge has temporarily suspended the immediate economic contradictions of the primary resource based economy, a continued reliance on processed and unprocessed natural resource exports leaves Chile vulnerable to the long-term ecological contradictions that such a path leads toward (Claude 1999). For example, the booming aquaculture commerce that grew up around salmon and other types of fish farms faces notable ecological challenges in the form of growing water pollution and diseases. In this respect, Rachel Schurman (2004: 326) suggests that: 'When these environmental risks and vulnerabilities are added to the already challenging economic conditions and low profit margins experienced by salmon producers worldwide, they create a situation of considerable risk and uncertainty, in which no company or industry can be said to be stable or even necessarily viable in the long term.' Similarly, sustainability of natural resources has not been addressed in the forestry sector. Thomas Miller Klubock surmises that large increases in foreign investment have led to the dramatic expansion of the industry yet without a framework that can mediate the social and environmental dislocations caused and ensure the sustainability of what remains of Chile's temperate rain forests (Miller Klubock 2004b: 380).

The expansion of the market through increasing demand from China and new trade agreements with the US and EU has staved off the immediate problems in Chilean capital accumulation without ameliorating the underlying social tensions. Whether this new demand can provide any more than a short-term solution for Chile's dualistic and primary-resource based economy, however, is doubtful, with even former advocates of the Chilean model expressing concerns about the lack of technology based industrial upgrading. Still less is it likely to transform the dark side of the export model, with inequality remaining trenchant and workers trapped in precarious employment relations. For the Concertación, whose members had widely critiqued such factors in the Pinochet period, it was not possible to address the underlying configuration of social institutions and class relations directly. Instead, they placed a firm emphasis on the renewal of social reform as a solution to these ills. As the next two chapters examine, the Concertación proposed to make significant changes to the institutions of welfare provision and labour relations, and these initiatives would form the heart of their renovated social democracy – or 'Third Way' – approach. Whether this programme of social reforms could adequately mediate the underlying social relations that reproduced vast inequalities within Chilean society, however, remained to be seen.

SUMMARY

In contrast to neoliberal arguments that strong economic growth in the 1990s can be attributed to good policies and good political environment, it is necessary to examine the deeper social context from which economic trends emerge. In this respect, the chapter argued that the primary export boom of this period must be understood in the context of prevailing social institutions that solidify profoundly uneven power relations between social classes and between economic organisations and the state. In this respect, the restructuring undertaken during the Pinochet period created strong class polarisation, manifested in a cheap and disciplined labour force, and unprecedented power for large Chilean corporations to expand their export operations which carried over into the post-dictatorship age. Three primary contradictions emerged from this conjuncture of social relations. First, a pervasive dualisation of the Chilean economy has been strongly reinforced, therein intensifying the gap between oligopolistic export-orientated firms owned by financial conglomerates and a competitive sector composed of small and medium firms that are disadvantaged by the neoliberal macroeconomic framework. Second, class divisions have become increasingly acute, with capital enjoying exceptional political and economic influence and income distribution remaining as polarised as in the Pinochet period. Third, the Chilean economy remains vulnerable owing to its continued dependence on primary commodity exports. This weakness became marked in the 1998–2002 period when global commodity prices led to a recession and stagnant growth. Following that period, surging demand for copper products from China has led to recovery and the beginnings of a new export boom that may temporarily alleviate the tendency towards overproduction of primary commodities that emerged in the late 1990s. However, from a medium-term perspective, it is likely only to exacerbate the existing social, environmental and political contradictions that characterise the contemporary Chilean political economy.

7
Labour Institutions and the Politics of Flexibilisation

Given that Chile has repeatedly been held up as a model of successful neoliberal reform, it is not surprising that the pervasive transformation of labour institutions would garner international attention. With the failure of neoliberal restructuring to deliver on its promise of sustained economic growth across the global South in the 1980s, some of the key architects of the reforms began to reconsider the institutional prerequisites for successful structural adjustment. As part of the reformed neoliberal prescription emergent in the 1990s it was argued that, for economic liberalisation to succeed, greater emphasis had to be placed on the social and political institutions that affected market outcomes. This led to a new focus on the so-called 'second generation reforms', of which one of the elements raised was the necessity of sufficiently flexible labour institutions that could ensure an efficient distribution of labour across economic sectors (cf. Krueger 2000). To address this issue, in 1994 the World Bank published what it considered to be a best-practice prescription for governments seeking to establish market-friendly labour institutions necessary for a successful market-driven economy (World Bank 1994b).

Notably, the World Bank's best-practice model for labour market reform closely resembled the prevailing institutions regulating employment relations in post-dictatorship Chile. As with its neoliberal macroeconomic agenda, Chile was once again seen as providing an ideal-type worthy of emulation elsewhere in the developing world. The World Bank was not alone in this opinion. At the end of the 1990s Chilean economists working at Santiago's Catholic University claimed that Chile enjoyed labour laws that were advanced by world standards. They pointed to the deregulation and flexibility imparted by these laws as one of the main reasons for the country's economic growth during the decade (Coloma and Rojas 2000). Similarly, several years into the new millennium, the *Financial Times* (2003) heralded Chile's labour institutions as Latin America's 'most modern labour code'.

Accolades of this nature, however, tend to occlude the status of labour reform as one of the most contentious issues in post-dictatorship Chile. Although the World Bank presents reforms to labour institutions as simply a technocratic question of economic efficiency, the underlying issues are inherently political. Labour institutions constitute the rules and expectations governing employment and the work-process and, as such, they provide legal and political frameworks that structure many of the basic, yet necessarily antagonistic, social relations of capitalist society (cf. Edwards and Belanger 1994). While the dynamics of capital accumulation constantly compel firms to restructure their labour force and production techniques in order to maximise profits, this tendency has given rise historically to the collective organisation of workers aimed at providing job security and greater control over the conditions of work and wage levels. Labour institutions attempt to formalise the rules under which these conflicts can proceed and, as such, directly affect issues ranging from productivity, competitiveness and profits, through to worker rights and the distribution of income. In this manner, labour institutions have an immediate impact upon the trajectory of capital accumulation at sectoral, national and global levels and, as a result, they repeatedly become the target of political conflicts between social actors who seek to alter the existing character of production and distribution.

Such dynamics have been particularly evident in post-dictatorship Chile, where they have coalesced into struggles over a process known as 'the flexibilisation of labour'. The latter concept is something of a misnomer, for it is not labour that enjoys flexibility. Rather, the term denotes a series of changes to labour institutions that enhances the flexibility of firms to hire and fire workers and to set the conditions of labour. As chapter 3 argued, the institutions created by the Pinochet regime in its 1980 labour code dramatically increased flexibility by profoundly restricting worker rights. This transformation was central to the subsequent recovery and expansion of capital accumulation in Chile following the 1982 debt crisis as it provided a framework under which capital could restructure according to profitability criteria and dramatically increase the hours and intensity of work. However, the degree of flexibilisation introduced by the labour code was also blamed for exacerbating the social ills of the dictatorship period including mass unemployment, low wages, the intensification of work, income polarisation and widespread worker abuses. As a consequence, the reform of labour institutions (known as '*reforma laboral*', or 'labour reform') rapidly became a major political issue following the collapse of the dictatorship. Various unions, social movement activists and many within the governing parties stipulated that legislation to strengthen worker rights and fortify the power of organised labour was central to any attempt at changing the deep social inequities that stratified Chilean society. Contrarily, the bodies of organised business interests strongly opposed any substantive changes to the existing labour code arguing that, by impinging on labour market flexibility, reforms would undermine the social foundations of capital accumulation to the detriment of all Chileans.

In this manner, the issue of labour reform reflects concretely the general paradox facing the Concertación: that is, the contradictions in reproducing the conditions for capital accumulation whilst managing the social and political antagonisms inherent to the latter. Neoliberal labour reform was intended to resolve this contradiction through a process of depoliticisation to be achieved by subordinating all actors to the impersonal impositions of market forces. Although this strategy was indeed effective in breaking down established institutional structures of political agency and demand articulation that characterised the populist period and which had entered into profound crisis, it could not resolve the underlying tensions of capitalist production relations. On the contrary, divisions within the sphere of production were aggravated and conflicts were merely juxtaposed into different realms and recomposed in new forms. As this chapter demonstrates, the issue of labour reform has provoked social and political tensions that successive Concertación governments have been unable to resolve. However, before examining the trajectory of reforms in the post-dictatorship period and analysing their social implications, it is useful to highlight briefly the theoretical issues that underpin debates over labour flexibility.

LABOUR FLEXIBILITY – THEORETICAL DIVISIONS

Within neoclassical economic theory, which provides the primary analytical justification for the project of labour flexibilisation, the labour market is conceptualised as a market like any other. It is thereby assumed to operate according to the laws of supply and demand and to tend towards equilibrium. Within this paradigm, the removal of external influences on labour markets – such as state regulations and collective bargaining frameworks – provides the conditions under which the supply and demand for labour may equilibrate through the benign interplay of market forces. This process of flexibilisation allows the labour market to achieve a harmonious state in which labour is optimally distributed across the economy. Labour market 'clearing', as this process is known, should result in minimal unemployment with wages set at market rates according to the productive input of the particular worker. As a consequence, labour flexibility is suggested to facilitate a virtuous circle in which flexibility increases employment; economic liberalisation promotes growth; and faster growth leads to higher wages (Weeks 1999; Palley 2005).

On this basis, advocates argue that labour flexibility is in the interest of workers themselves and that companies should be able to hire, fire and set wages without constraints beyond those stemming from the market itself (OECD 2003). The suggestion that flexibility benefits workers may seem counter-intuitive. For example, by allowing employers the flexibility to dismiss at will or to contract on a purely temporary basis, job security will necessarily become more precarious. However, neoclassical theory contends that overall efficiency gains will lead to more rapid economic growth and a greater number of total jobs at a higher average wage. Those workers that are released from one branch of production will simply move into another according to supply and demand, thereby avoiding 'misallocations of workers and human capital investments ... that seriously retard development' (Schultz 2000: 295). Similarly, restricting collective bargaining will tend to lower wages in industries characterised by strong unions. In neoclassical theory, however, collective bargaining is considered to be a monopoly situation that induces distortions on the natural market rate of wages to the detriment of those workers outside of collective agreements. Eliminating such distorted wage rates is considered to remove inefficiencies that suppress the level of wages in the economy as a whole (Pencavel 1997).

There are multiple ways, however, in which the neoclassical approach does not recognise the complexity of the subject at hand. Labour markets are idiosyncratic social institutions that are not equivalent to other markets and should not be analysed as such. First and foremost, employers do not merely adjust wages and employment levels according to changing supply and demand for labour on a national basis. Rather, they make decisions based on a complex series of relations that transcend the domestic labour market. Specifically, employer actions are conditioned by, first, the dynamics of accumulation and competition that are global in nature; and, second, the need to maintain a cohesive productive force within the firm that is buffered from short-term economic fluctuations and hierarchically structured according to productivity requirements. In this manner, the forces that determine the macro-structures of employment and wages are not intrinsic to the labour market itself.

The accumulation of capital is a process characterised not by the smooth equilibrium projected in neoclassical models, but by constant disequilibria between different sectors and regions that tend to escalate into destructive crises. This uneven development of capital results in constant periods of 'rationalisation' in which, under the omniscient pressures of competition, firms shed workers either to replace them with labour-saving technology or simply to liquidate assets. Such dynamics are most brutally demonstrated in crisis periods – including the 1974–75, 1982–84 and 1997–98 recessions in Chile examined in chapters 3 and 6 – yet they are a constant feature of capitalist social relations. Whether or not labour will be subsequently reincorporated into productive processes depends on a complex conjuncture of global factors that affect the profitability of firms, including the shifting technological parameters of production, changes in market structures, available skills and relative wage rates. For example, it is increasingly possible for capital to relocate to alternate points in the international division of labour if such sites offer significant advantages.

As such, the essential dynamics of global capitalism ensure that employment trends in specific locales are in a state of constant flux and are shaped by forces that extend far beyond the labour market itself. As Simon Clarke (1999: 11) indicates in his study of labour markets in Russia: 'The labour market is not primarily the arena within which the interaction of supply and demand determines the level of the wage and the number of jobs available, but is the sphere within which people are allocated to jobs, the number, terms and conditions of which are determined elsewhere.' On this basis, the neoclassical predication for analysing labour markets as self-equilibrating around 'natural rates' of employment has been compared to 'trying to understand the nature of the ocean in terms of average sea levels rather than its ebb and flow' (Fine 2003: 89). Within these dynamics, labour flexibility is certainly beneficial for capital as it enables firms to rapidly dispose of unwanted workers in periods of restructuring. However, to suggest that flexibility facilitates an optimal rate of employment is to position mistakenly the labour market as the primary cause of employment trends, rather than an institution that is itself structured within the wider trajectory of capital accumulation. For example, following the crisis of 1997–98 and the subsequent restructuring of capital, Chile has been stricken with sustained levels of high unemployment despite possessing the most flexible labour markets in Latin America.

Furthermore, our conceptualisation of flexibility should not be limited in the manner of neoclassical economics to the operation of labour markets alone. This would be to overlook how labour institutions influence a wider spectrum of relationships in the capitalist enterprise and in society more generally, such as the structuring of the labour process and collective representation within and beyond the enterprise (Edwards and Elger 1999: 5). By restricting the scope of state regulation and collective organisation, processes of labour flexibilisation serve to reconfigure the relationship between employer and employee into an increasingly individualised relationship in which the power of the employer over the terms and conditions of work are amplified. This trend became particularly evident in the Pinochet period during which the length and intensity of the working day increased dramatically at the same time as wages fell. Whereas collective organisation and state regulations have historically played a major role in mitigating the vulnerable position of individual workers vis-à-vis an employer, flexibilisation processes curtail these forms of protection under the pretext that the harmonising operations of efficient markets render all such conflicts obsolete.

The inherently divisive nature of these issues were well understood by all sides in the Chilean debate over labour reform, thereby setting the scene for a particularly bitter political conflict. Whereas the Pinochet dictatorship used overt and unstinting repression to stifle opposition to its labour code, there was significant uncertainty concerning how the newly elected Concertación government that rested on an electoral base rooted in the working class would respond.

THE CONCERTACIÓN AND LABOUR REFORM IN THE 1990s

Given the strong political linkages between the labour movement and the political cadre of the anti-dictatorship movement, the possibilities for a dramatic reform of the Pinochet era labour code seemed very real. In their election campaign of 1989 the Concertación pledged to:

[I]ntroduce profound changes in the juridical position of organised labour in order that this provides workers with fundamental rights and allows the strengthening of labour organisations; so that the latter can transform themselves into an efficient tool for wage earner interests and become a substantial influence in the social life of the country. (cited in Henríquez Riquelme 1999: 93)

The Concertación's proclaimed rationale was that, if the state was to observe the general tenets of a market-orientated approach, and therein refrain from sustained intervention in the economic realm, a greater degree of labour organisation had to be permitted in order for workers to protect effectively their own interests in the sphere of production. This would be necessary because the state intended to allow labour relations to assume the form of negotiations between two freely contracting social actors. As the incoming government of Patricio Aylwin suggested:

It is the involved social agents, through balanced, free and democratic relations, that will set the conditions of work. The state has the role of guaranteeing that the system functions and to generate permanent and stable rules so that the actors proceed adequately ... the state is not a third actor in labour relations. (cited in Ruiz-Tagle 1993: 142)

With organised labour strengthened, the argument proceeded, unions could increase their bargaining prowess and thereby ensure a more equitable distribution of the increased revenues that economic growth would bring. Moreover, by introducing new legislation, it was expected that the worst abuses of worker rights, such as the arbitrary firings that had been sanctified under the dictatorship's 1980 labour code, would cease. It was with recourse to such justifications, within a climate of elevated popular expectations, that the Aylwin government undertook a first attempt at labour legislation following its assumption of power in 1990.

Nonetheless, the Concertación government quickly encountered the determined resistance of the organised bodies of the capitalist class. These included the Sociedad de Fomento y Fabril (SOFOFA), which represented the interests of industrial capitals, and the Confederación de Producción y Comercio (CPC), which represented a wider agglomeration of capitalist interests. Representatives from these groups were actively involved in government-sponsored dialogues and claimed that any reforms that significantly bolstered the strength of labour, and particularly those that hindered the ability of capital to fire workers with relative ease, threatened to undermine the industrial stability that lay at the heart of the economic boom ongoing since the mid-1980s. Applying neoclassical labour market theory, they vigorously defended a position that suggested the interest of the common good was best served by a regulatory code that assured the utmost flexibility for business. The latter, they claimed, would ensure the optimal allocation of labour within the economy and provide the most favourable levels of employment and wages without such factors becoming repoliticised and reigniting the industrial conflicts of the 1960s and 1970s.

Under pressure from both organised capital and labour, and working within the confines of the post-transition institutional framework, the Aylwin regime carefully engineered a compromise solution by altering some of the content of labour legislation to offer more defensive rights to workers, whilst maintaining the basic form of labour institutions established by Pinochet. As such, the primary aim of Aylwin's changes to the existing labour code was to establish a 'labour institutionality' that would ensure long-term stability owing to the self-adherence of the major social actors through cooperation between capital and labour within the formalised structures of the adjusted labour code. 'Institutionality', therefore, was an attempt to construct an industrial pact by providing a framework wherein organised labour acknowledged private ownership and investment as legitimate bases of the Chilean economy and recognised the need for stability and the suppression of ideology in negotiations. Confronting capital or the state through industrial action in order to realise worker needs was deemed obsolete. Conversely, the private sector would accede to the necessity of moderately raising the minimum wage and, at a more general level, accept an augmented tax burden to allow for increases in pensions and social welfare to attain a more equitable division of the social product (Muñoz Gomá and Caledón 1996: 198). In this fashion, the general hue of production relations created during the dictatorship could be left untouched whilst the burden of material compromise would be passed into the realm of social policy. It was on these grounds that, during the process of renovating the labour code, and despite the concerns raised by the private sector, the government remained adamant that reform would not fetter the flexibility of the labour market.

Furthermore, at the same time as negotiations over the labour code reform were ongoing, growing antagonism between government and the labour movement reached new levels with the eruption of strikes in copper, steel, coal, public health and state education sectors. Although these industrial actions were manifested primarily within the public sector, framed within a paradigm of grievances accumulated from the dictatorship period, and relatively long-lasting; the state remained firmly opposed to the strikes and they attained few of their material demands. To justify their rejection, the Aylwin regime claimed that, first and foremost, accession to the strikers' demands would affect its ability to maintain control over inflation (Epstein 1993: 60). Subservience to the discipline of sound money and the refusal to set a precedent of acquiescence to the direct demands of labour were clearly determining priorities for the new Concertación regime and the defeat of the labour movement in these strikes did not bode well for the substantive content of the labour reform.

THE FIRST REFORMS, 1990–93

Beyond the abstract rhetoric of a social pact for industrial peace the reforms implemented between 1990 and 1993 led to few substantive changes in the relationship between state, capital and labour. Within the institutions created by the 1980 labour code, employers had been granted the right to dismiss workers without giving reasons. The Aylwin government's new code stipulated that a reason for dismissal had to be provided. If a sacked employee believed the reason to be unfair, then he or she could attempt to pursue the issue within labour tribunals and, if successful, would receive compensation. Compensation for unfair dismissal, in turn, was increased under the provisions of the reformed code. These measures appeared to improve the defensive mechanisms available to workers who had been made redundant for spurious or political reasons. However, the legislation was rendered largely ineffective as employers were allowed to use the vague and all-encompassing phrase '*necesidad de la empresa*' (need of the company) as the reason for dismissal. Given the wide-ranging deployment of this justification, the reform reproduced the legal conditions for highly arbitrary practices of job termination. As a recent government report confirms at length, employers still routinely sack workers who have sought to create unions, either using the above loophole to justify the sackings or simply stalling or refusing to pay the fines if they are imposed by the overworked labour commission (Preinforme 2001). Unsurprisingly, the International Labour Organisation repeatedly decried such activities throughout the decade; profoundly deploring the anti-union conduct of firms in Chile and highlighting many cases of union persecution (Mostrador 2001).

The reformed labour code also continued to support the establishment of numerous competitive unions within a firm, the results of which have been to reinforce the trend towards smaller, less powerful unions that are in competition with each other within particular corporations. Although the new code granted unions increased rights to form regional or national federations, no collective bargaining has been allowed to proceed above the level of the individual union vis-à-vis the firm in question. This decentralisation of union activity implied a heavily reduced status for the national bodies of organised labour such as the primary national union organisation, the Central Unitaria de Trabajadores (CUT). National federations of this ilk, although receiving formal recognition by the Concertación, are reduced to acting as political pressure groups vis-à-vis the state. They can endeavour to establish national agreements regarding pay or labour rights but these will not stand unless there is multilateral agreement between themselves and capitals in a particular sector over the terms of such agreements, a possibility that has not occurred owing to the intransigence of capital, which would prefer to deal with smaller unions on an individual level. Similarly, the right to strike was re-established, but with the proviso remaining that the firm is permitted to hire replacement labour (*rompehuelgas*) to replace strikers for the duration of the action, thus depriving labour of its most effective form of collective action.

Finally, given the Concertación's insistence on consensual agreements between capital and labour at the level of the firm, it also maintained the institutional grounds for forms of self-regulating labour relations called '*convenios*'. Occurring primarily within the branches of production where labour organisation was historically strongest, the technique of *convenio* has given added strength to employers seeking a more flexible relation with the workforce. A *convenio* signifies a situation where employer and employees give mutual consent within a non-regulated dialogue to a binding agreement on labour regulations and practice that falls outside of the institutionalised code. It creates an isolated relationship between employer and small groups of workers and generally forbids collective action and striking. Research indicates that *convenios* are nearly always formed on the suggestion of the employer and, often, their signing can involve coercion or can form a prior condition for workers to gain employment (Henríquez Riquelme 1999: 104). The principal results of *convenios* are to satisfy the employers' desire to diminish the possibility of industrial conflict and insulate workforce regulation from external interference whilst maintaining the tenor of the relationship with labour forged under the dictatorship.

FLEXIBILITY IN PRACTICE

The new labour code did not fundamentally alter the processes of labour flexibilisation that had been introduced by the Pinochet regime. With the legislation serving to stifle forms of collective action and offering only minimal protection to workers on an individual basis, much of the labour force continued to be drawn into forms of employment that offered little security over the length and conditions of work. In the boom years of 1994 to 1996 it is estimated that half of all new jobs created were ones without contract. These jobs were not only extremely precarious in nature – and many would disappear when the boom ended in 1998 – they also tended to be poorly remunerated. Gross wages paid to temporary staff in 1996 were 59 percent lower than to those with open-ended contracts (UNDP 2002: 95). Notably, average weekly work hours would remain high, with a 48 hour working week still the average in 1996, and with over 35 percent of the population working above this norm (MIDEPLAN 1998: 35).

These trends have been particularly explicit in the key export sectors such as the agro-export sector, one of the much-championed 'dynamic poles' of the new economy. In this sector employment is both highly precarious and characterised by low wages. For close to 40 percent of the rural labour force – largely female in its composition – work is typically categorised by three modes of temporary employment: work paid by piece (e.g. price per volume picked); work paid by task; and work paid per harvest (Cid 2001: 11). This enables agro-industries to absorb large quantities of labour-power in the summer and autumn picking seasons and eject it for the winter and spring. Concurrent to flexibilisation, there is little labour regulation in terms of working conditions and levels of pay, and there are no social security contributions by employers (Tinsman 2004). After completing individual jobs workers are perpetually uncertain of future employment and must move between agro-enterprises within the region in order to find successive contracts. Owing to the impermanent and mobile nature of the work, the collective organisation of the workforce faced significant challenges, a situation reinforced by the Concertación's reluctance throughout the 1990s to undertake legal initiative, such as permitting unionisation of temporary workers, that might endanger the continuing growth of agro-forestry exports (Gwynne and Kay 1997: 9). After a decade of bitter grassroots struggles aimed at both informal organisation techniques amongst the workforce and campaigns directed at the government, the labour legislation enacted by the Lagos administration in 2001 – as examined below – finally provided seasonal workers with the legal right to form unions. Despite this victory, structural impediments still mean that union activity in such sectors presently remains low.

Similarly, the forestry sector has witnessed the adoption of extensive subcontracting strategies in order to maximise productivity and to maintain the rationalisation of enterprises. The forestry sector is archetypal in this respect where subcontracting practices have become pervasive. By enabling larger economic units to contract out tasks to small firms, sometimes organised at the level of the family, the former are able to reduce labour costs, avoid many regulatory aspects of formal sector employment and avoid dealing with organised labour, thereby skirting the responsibilities that they would have to assume were the employees hired directly by the company. At the same time, subcontracting also permits an easy shedding of unusable labour in times of economic slowdown. As a consequence, the Chilean forestry sector has become characterised by levelled practices of subcontracting whereby the first level of subcontracted firms continue to pass specialised tasks out to their own subcontractors (Escobar and López 1996: 102). In this fashion, pyramids of hierarchical subcontracting practices, resting on relations of dependency running from the central contractor down each level, form an 'economic mattress' that cushions the central levels from adverse shocks by allowing them to transfer costs further down the structure. Precarious forms of employment have created a situation in which the reserve army in the forestry sector is both sizeable and in a state of constant flux. Notably, the provinces where the forestry sector is most present have some of the highest levels of under-employment and poverty (Escobar 1999a).

The mining sector, an area of considerable union activity that even the Pinochet regime could not repress, has seen a different flexibilisation strategy attempted by capitals. This has involved the shedding of labour employed by the main mining enterprise and its replacement with subcontracted labour. The percentage of subcontracted employees in the mining industry rose dramatically from 4.6 percent to 40 percent between 1985 and 1996 (Preinforme 2001). In their seminal study of the post-authoritarian period Chilean mining industry, Agacino, González and Rojas (1998: 216) demonstrate that subcontracting practices have resulted in 'extended working days, illegal introduction of continuous work systems, higher vulnerability of the worker, lack of legal protection, temporality of work and income, etc'. There also tended to be a path-dependent effect of these changes owing to their tendency to undermine collective solidarity within mining communities. As Thomas Miller Kluboch indicates in his study of class and community in the El Teniente copper mine, 'workplace solidarities, community ties, and political networks that were once the basis of miners' powerful class identity and collective actions were disrupted by new labor systems, flexibilisation, downsizing, the growth of cultures of individualism and consumerism, and the fragmentation and dispersal of residential neighbourhoods' (Miller Klubock 2004a: 211).

This strategy has been complemented by the transnational relocation of labour-intensive stages of the production process with an increasing amount of ores extracted in pre-processed form in Chile and transported to South-East Asia for refining. The latter is a practice sanctioned by the Chilean government, which has preferred to keep the sector vastly unregulated rather than risk losing investment (Lagos 1999: 31). As such, the increasing capital-intensive nature of mining, alongside the migration of labour-intensive processes to other parts of the international division of labour, has caused a substantial ejection of living-labour from the production process. Despite huge foreign investment and the opening of new 'mega-projects', the number of jobs in the Chilean copper industry during the 1990s declined from 104,000 to 92,000 (Agacino et al. 1998: 215). Ironically, owing to these processes, poverty has also risen amongst those working in the mining sector. Whereas the mining sector still offers some of the highest wages amongst the skilled working class, subcontracting and the emergence of a pool of reserve labour ejected from the transnational mining companies yet able to use its skills to mine small, low quality ores, has led to a situation in which between 1990 and 1995, the number of miners whose households were below the poverty line rose from none to 16 percent (León and Martínez 1998: 301).

These forms of labour relations are not exclusive to key export sectors. For example, a government-commissioned report in 2001 highlighted the abusive practices undertaken by such firms as the water-treatment giant Essel. The latter assumed control of numerous public assets following privatisation of water-treatment in 1999 and took advantage of the laxities of the labour code to sack a substantial number of employees only for the new owners to rehire them as subcontractors under markedly worse conditions (Preinforme

2001: 4). Other observers have highlighted that for important tasks in the construction sector – which accounted for the third-largest increase in employment between 1990 and 1998 – the majority of labour now is performed via subcontracting to micro-firms, creating a growing tendency toward precarious labour in this key employment sector (Wormald and Ruiz-Tagle 1999: 67).

THE POLITICAL RAMIFICATIONS OF LABOUR FLEXIBILISATION

The consequences of the tepid nature of labour reform in the immediate post-dictatorship period had manifold implications for the strategy of the labour movement at a national level. In this respect, the lack of a strong reaffirmation of the legal rights of the working population severely frustrated the formation of a robust national labour movement, both in terms of the number of union affiliates and the strength of the main national federations. In terms of union membership, organised labour numerically remains little above dictatorship levels. After a brief spurt of union growth in the first two years of Concertación, which followed the momentum gained by the labour movement during the immediate pre-transition period, union membership and the incidence of collective negotiation has tailed off considerably. This depreciation is related to the anti-union tactics of employers, the practice of *convenio*, and a general cynicism towards the effectiveness of unions within the current framework. As a United Nations Development Programme survey in 2001 indicated, over 50 percent of respondents suggested that labour relations had worsened over the previous decade (UNDP 2002: 96).

Table 7.1   Evolution of Unionisation, 1988–96

Year	Number of union affiliates	Percentage unionisation of salaried workforce	Percentage unionisation of occupied workforce	Rate of collective negotiation	Number of unions	Average number of union members
1988	446194	15.8	10.5	10	6446	69
1990	606812	19.8	13.4	13.4	8861	69
1992	724065	21.9	15.1	15.1	10576	69
1994	661966	19.3	14	14	12109	55
1996	655579	17.7	11.8	11.8	13528	49

(Data drawn from De la Maza 1999)

Considering that the Concertación ideologues had placed the creation of a stronger labour movement that exercised greater potential for collective negotiation at the centre of their schema to achieve greater social equity, failure to support organised labour seriously undermines their proposed 'Third Way' strategy. Those within the CUT have consistently sought the raising of the minimum wage to above the poverty line and a stricter enforcement of matching productivity increases with wage rises. Moreover, stronger unions at the level of the enterprise could have reduced such employer strategies as imposing *convenios*, arbitrary or politically motivated firing practices, and exploitative subcontracting techniques. Nevertheless, at no stage over the 1990s did the CUT have the institutional strength to achieve these aims, nor was it able to mobilise a general strike to force the government's hand.

In this manner, the effects of the tenacious repression of organised labour undertaken by the dictatorship were not easily overcome, leaving the political strength of the union movement restricted and compromising its ability to pressure the Concertación. Given the leading role played by organised labour in the anti-dictatorship movement, the CUT and other labour groups were dismayed by the institutionalisation of a marginalised role. Frustration within the labour movement over this situation led to a growing radicalisation and combativeness, with the Communist Party becoming the leading political force within the CUT and the emergence of a more antagonistic relationship with the government. Far from disappearing with the legislation of the early 1990s, further labour reform remained a major goal of union movements. The following sections examine how social conflict over labour reform continued to escalate during the decade.

THE LAGOS GOVERNMENT AND THE 2001 REFORMS

In spite of the weaknesses of organised labour in Chile and an oft-cited political apathy manifested in low election turnouts in the mid-1990s, the current pattern of labour relations and the associated polarisation of income distribution have not been passively accepted. There was growing political tension in the latter half of the Frei administration as the bitter winds of the East Asian crisis whipped Chile and the much-championed economic 'miracle' of the previous seven years turned into negative growth and mounting social disquiet. The immediate outcome was the first significant shift of popular support away from the Concertación since the fall of the dictatorship, as displayed by the momentum gathered by Joaquín Lavín's right-wing populist campaign for the 2000 presidential elections. Simultaneously, at the turn of the millennium, industrial action has gathered pace, with the workers in the telecommunications sector employed by Telefónica CTC Chile holding a widely supported strike to protest layoffs and flexibilisation processes (El Mostrador 2002).

In response, Eduardo Frei Ruiz-Tagle's Concertación government attempted to regain popular support by reactivating labour legislation that had been languishing in Congress for the previous five years. Frei hoped that the initiative would give a boost to Concertación candidate Ricardo Lagos's presidential campaign by manoeuvring the parties of the right into an overt anti-worker position. The proposal included a motion to strengthen unions by allowing some bargaining to proceed above the level of the individual firm. Additionally it would restrain the practice of importing replacement, non-unionised labour in the event of a strike (Angell and Pollack 2000: 369). The attempt backfired. Business groups quickly mobilised for a strenuous attack on the proposed changes, arguing that they would be bad for business at a time when capital accumulation appeared to be extremely fragile. Ultimately, the government struggled to retain the support of its own senators and proved unable to win the necessary independent votes to secure the legislation.

Despite this failure, the Concertación won an extremely narrow election victory in January 2000. Ricardo Lagos became the first Chilean president from the Socialist Party since Salvador Allende, raising the expectations of some labour activists that a more sympathetic government had arrived. Additionally, while the Aylwin and, to a lesser extent, the Frei administration had seen their respective labour reforms moderated as they passed through the post-transition institutional system designed by the military regime, by the turn of the millennium the institutionally embedded power of the political right had lessened. Notwithstanding raised expectations, however, by the summer of Lagos's first year many labour leaders were expressing considerable disappointment over a lack of change in the Concertación's policy orientation and were frustrated by a perceived lack of receptive ears within the government. The government itself was dealing with continued troubles following the Asian crisis fallout and was undertaking closed meetings with business leaders over how to reactivate the economy.

In spite of these reservations, Lagos had placed labour reform high on his election manifesto agenda and the looming December 2001 parliamentary elections offered a stern test for the Concertación. Alongside the spectre of a difficult election battle ahead, the emergence of increased labour and social activism and mounting denunciations of labour abuses by both large and small firms from a multitude of domestic and international sources pushed the administration into activity. A sharp increase in illegal strike activity and the 1 May 2001 protests in which some 30,000 workers gathered in Santiago calling for, among other things, a general strike to pressure the government into labour reforms displayed a rising combativeness within the labour movement, particularly within the public sector. Furthermore, in order to expand markets for Chilean goods the Lagos government aimed to conclude free-trade agreements both with the NAFTA countries (Canada, Mexico and the US) and with the European Union. However, various governments and labour organisations within these blocks expressed concerns over the lack of worker rights in Chile. In particular, the Canadian government, fearing competition based on extreme levels of exploitation, demanded further labour reform as a condition for any agreement.

Lagos himself was unequivocal that reform was necessary in order to attain social peace: 'You have to be competitive and efficient [but] you also have to have a society organised in such a way that it does not have permanent divisions' (*Financial Times* 2001). In this respect, his government intended to send a clear message to capitals operating in Chile that the worst abuses would have to stop in order to ensure social stability and continue the momentum of Chile's integration with Western trading blocks. Business leaders in the CPC and the political right, however, rejected the government's stance and bitterly decried the initiative, arguing that it was against the interest not just of capitals but also of workers because a more rigid labour market would mean fewer jobs and lower wages (El Mostrador 2001a). Once again, political struggle resulted in a tentative compromise enshrined in a new reform to the labour code that became law in 2001.

STRENGTHS AND LIMITS OF THE 2001 LABOUR REFORM

The 2001 reforms constituted a step forward by increasing the size of the Labour Department to improve the processing of worker grievances and by raising the monetary fines imposed upon firms involved in illegal labour practices. They also required employers to create contracts for part-time workers and to extend coverage to previously excluded sectors such as notaries, archivists and conservationists. This was a timely change as it gave a legal boost to the attempts of activists to form unions within the seasonal agro-export sector. Notwithstanding these positive changes, however, the amendments continued to ignore the primary demands of the labour movement – namely, the unimpeded right to strike and to bargain collectively. Firms were still permitted to hire replacement labourers in the event of a strike, a condition that severely compromised the potency of industrial action. Likewise, the reform maintained profound weaknesses in the right to collective bargaining, which was confined to the level of the individual firm. The latter is particularly onerous for workers in firms of fewer than 20 employees, who often lack the strength to challenge the firm at an individual level but enjoy no recourse to sectoral or national-level bargaining.

More generally, the new code continued to hinder the ability of regional and national-level labour federations to build stronger organisations and overcome their political marginality. On paper the reforms did not mark a significant break in the trajectory of the labour code under the successive Concertación governments. The new amendments were once again primarily defensive in nature, operating in an individualistic and juridical framework rather than through the support and promotion of collective action. They gave workers better access to protective mechanisms when their rights were abused but did not provide the legal grounds for organised labour to become a serious counterweight to the power of employers either at the level of the firm or in the national political ambit. The sole positive measure of the reforms in this respect was the lowering of the initial quorums necessary for workers to establish unions within a firm.

THE END OF LABOUR REFORM?

The precise impact of these latest reforms upon labour relations will only become fully evident in the course of day-to-day struggles in Chile, both within enterprises and within the wider political environment. Nevertheless, political conflict over the legislation continues. The reforms have been comprehensively and virulently denounced by organised capital on the pretext that, despite their moderation, they nonetheless raise barriers to the accumulation of capital. In this way, the Concertación has acted to discipline capital, forcing firms to operate within a stronger regulatory framework that it believes can ensure social stability for the greater good of accumulation over and above the desires of particular capitals to act with impunity with regard to labour practices. Labour activists, however, have been disappointed by the Concertación's reluctance to push through more decisive measures, especially considering the lowering of previous political and institutional barriers (El Siglo 2001). Although some in the labour movement had been hoping to use these reforms as a stepping stone toward more extensive measures under the Lagos administration, Labour Minister Ricardo Solari had a strong rebuttal, claiming that: 'I believe that at the end of this process we will have a code that will close the discussion and enjoy legitimacy' (El Mostrador 2001b). The deliberate boycott by both labour and business leaders of the ceremony marking the passage of the new laws, however, suggests that the issue is far from resolved.

Militancy within the main national labour federation (the Central Unitaria de Trabajadores, CUT) has continued to gain strength, and culminated in the successful undertaking of Chile's first mass workers' protest in 17 years on 13 August 2003. The action took the form of a general strike in the public sector, with teachers, health workers and transport workers being the largest groups to participate. Specifically aimed at protesting the flexibilised labour conditions and low wages throughout the public sector and highlighting the continuing abuses of worker rights, CUT claimed that 80 percent of business activity had been stopped in the capital (*Financial Times* 2003). Although the Lagos administration declared that the strike was an unproductive anachronism, many within the Socialist Party expressed sympathy towards the strike, suggesting that the growing social tensions are reflecting themselves politically within the increasingly tenuous Concertación coalition.

Such militancy is directly connected to the failure of flexibilisation to achieve even its most basic goal – stable rates of low unemployment. As we have seen in the previous chapter, the influx of capital that fuelled the economic boom of the early and mid-1990s led to a substantial reincorporation of the reserve labour army back into waged employment, leading to the reduction of unemployment from above 30 percent in the debacle years of the early 1980s, back to the pre-neoliberal era average of around 6 percent in the mid-1990s. However, the dramatic crash of the export boom in the late 1990s catapulted unemployment levels back above 10 percent in spite of heavily flexibilised labour markets. Indeed, flexibilisation improved the ability of capital to shed jobs during the crisis, but the former has proved far less willing to reabsorb labour back into production and services following the recovery. For the capital region of Santiago, unemployment has remained between 11 and 15 percent of the economically active population for over six years between 1999 and 2005 (figures from Banco Central de Chile online statistical database, accessed 5 March 2005).

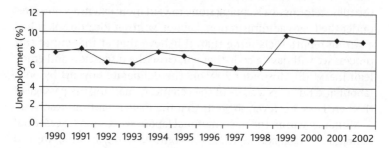

(Data drawn from Banco Central de Chile online statistical database, accessed May 2003. <http://si2.bcentral.cl/basededatoseconomicos/900base.asp?usuidioma=e>)

Figure 7.1   National Unemployment Rate (% of economically active population)

SUMMARY

Restricting the rights of the working population had been an explicit goal of the dictatorship and it was widely expected that substantial changes to the Pinochet era labour code would form an integral part of the Concertación's promised re-democratisation process. This is because labour institutions were recognised to influence the basic social relations that underpin the production and distribution of resources in a capitalist society. However, the limited potential of the post-dictatorship state to deliver a thorough process of social democratisation was reflected in the Concertación's restrained approach to the labour issue. Successive attempts at reforming the labour code were shaped within the threefold context of (1) the Concertación's unwillingness to disrupt the established neoliberal form of capital accumulation, (2) the structural and political weakness of the organised labour movement, and (3) the active struggles of the Chilean capitalist class to ensure moderation. The policy outcomes emerging from this conjuncture resulted in provocative rhetoric from successive administrations alongside labour reforms that disappointed the proponents of reform. Although changes to the labour code undoubtedly provided welcome legal provisions for workers whose rights had been abused, the hyper-flexibilised model of labour relations created by the dictatorship was not fundamentally altered. As indicated in the previous chapter, utilising the opportunities provided by flexibilised labour institutions became an important element in capitalist strategies to overcome economic recession in the later 1990s and new millennium. Before continuing that line of investigation, however, the following chapter examines the second major facet of the Concertación's 'growth with equity' programme – a renewed emphasis on welfare institutions.

8
Growth with Equity?
Social Policy and Anti-Poverty
Programmes, 1990–2003

When examining the transformation of social policy institutions in Latin America in the mid-1990s, Evelyne Huber suggested that the continent stood at a crossroads. The option, as she presented it, was between: 'market-determined, private, individualistic and inegalitarian models on the one hand, and market-correcting, public, solidaristic, and egalitarian models on the other' (Huber 1996: 141). Although her analysis suggested that countries were split between a slow creep and a headlong rush towards the former, neoliberal, pole, her conclusion remained upbeat. She suggested that the return of democracy in many Latin American nations might prompt recognition that universalistic forms are desirable on grounds of both ethics and efficiency. In many respects, such expectations applied strongly to the return of democracy in Chile and, in particular, they reflected the newly elected Concertación government's repeated emphasis on a need to move towards social equity through social policy reforms.

By the close of the decade, however, such expectations in Chile and elsewhere on the continent seemed to have been frustrated. Observers affirmed that a comprehensive transformation of welfare institutions was being consolidated in Latin America, converging upon a neoliberal model with four cornerstones: *selectivity* and targeting in place of universalism, *privatisation* of service provision, *decentralisation* of remaining state responsibilities, and *compensation* for the social costs of structural adjustment through anti-poverty programmes (Raczynski 1998; Garland 2000; Sottoli 2000; Székely 2001). These four pillars of reform, moreover, closely mirror established World Bank wisdom on the subject, and Chile under the Concertación can be considered a paradigmatic example of this approach (World Bank 1990; 1993b; 1994a; 2000; 2001; 2002; 2003). As chapter 4 detailed, during the dictatorship welfare institutions were categorically reshaped to privatise, selectivise and decentralise service provision. Over the 1990s and into the new millennium, the Concertación has maintained these institutional forms while emphasising the need to increase public expenditure and to target these expenditures on marginalised groups. Further, where possible, marginalised groups were expected to play an active role in social policy design and delivery, a strategy that the World Bank would subsequently label 'empowering the poor' (World Bank 2000).

This approach to social policy constitutes a central axis of the Concertación's 'growth with equity' strategy and the current chapter examines the implications and limitations of this approach. In so doing, two primary arguments are raised. First, although increasing social expenditure over the course of the 1990s undoubtedly aided the ailing systems of welfare provision, the impact of greater resources and targeted delivery were muted owing to their containment within the institutional forms created by the dictatorship. Second, the Concertación's social policy initiatives are unable to provide a sustainable strategy for equitable development owing to their embedding within the context of deep class divisions in the realm of production; specifically, the existence of heavily flexibilised labour markets, precarious job security, little scope of collective bargaining and sharp income differentials. Ongoing tensions therefore exist in this attempt to mediate vast inequalities in the realm of production through a more ambitious provision of welfare services.

SOCIAL POLICY AND THE 'GROWTH WITH EQUITY' STRATEGY

As chapter 4 argued, the authoritarian government of Augusto Pinochet had placed the profound transformation of the welfare institutions at the heart of its social restructuring strategy. The ensuing reforms sought to break down existing institutions and replace them with decentralised, individualistic, market-driven modes of provision. The latter formed one part of a depoliticisation strategy that sought to recast public social welfare obligations as private relationships between individuals and firms. Although global institutions such as the World Bank often cited these reforms as best-practice templates for reforming pensions, health, education and anti-poverty strategy, the results of such reforms frequently differed greatly from the those forecast by their advocates. The deployment of market mechanisms in service provision by the Pinochet regime was suggested to provide a neutral institution that could improve efficiency and personal choice by inducing competition between providers (Huber 1996; Duhau 1997). Nevertheless, the essential presupposition of privatisation is that efficiency, personal choice and the provision of services can all be subordinated to profitability without compromising the rationality of service provision across the breadth of the population. In Chile this did not occur, with privatised health, social security and education systems significantly stratified along the lines of social class. In spite of a period of economic growth in the latter half of the 1980s, close to one-half of all Chileans remained under the poverty line while the deep cuts made by the dictatorship to public expenditures in health, education and social security had created widespread debilitation across the breadth of state welfare provision, particularly in the realm of healthcare and pension provision. Moreover, the partial commodification of welfare services had created dual systems of competing private and public service provision. By strengthening the link between household income levels and the quantity and quality of services available, the reforms exacerbated inequalities between social classes.

During the 1980s, the disciplinary forms of social restructuring undertaken by the dictatorship were strongly resisted through significant levels of mobilisation within the worst affected communities (Oxhorn 1995; Roberts 1998b). The latter sought to provide communally organised forms of provision, such as soup kitchens and basic neighbourhood health services, and also to challenge the dictatorship's political legitimacy through various methods of protest. Given that this mobilisation provided the political momentum for the defeat of the dictatorship and the core of the Concertación's support, the subsequent legitimacy of the Concertación governments was in no small measure staked upon their promise to promote a more equitable form of neoliberal development (Paley 2001). To this end, on assuming power President Aylwin emphatically pronounced that:

Chile needs positive state action to move towards equity ... A moral imperative demands that Chile moves increasingly towards social justice. (cited in Barton 2002: 369)

However, in spite of these intentions, the political options of the Concertación government were constrained within a matrix of political, institutional and material limits that were examined in chapter 5. Operating within such restrictions, the Concertación has pursued a policy approach that does not directly challenge the major institutional forms created under the Pinochet regime. Rather, it has attempted to address equity concerns primarily through sustained social expenditure increases in combination with enhanced targeting mechanisms that direct a greater proportion of resources towards the most underprivileged sectors of society. First and foremost, the Concertación increased social expenditure at a sustained rate throughout the decade. Between 1989 and 2000 public social expenditure was almost doubled (Figure 8.1) and the increases have been, partially at least, targeted towards the lower-earning sectors of the population. The most dramatic increases were in health and education, the annual resources of which were increased by 135.4 percent and 165 percent respectively between 1990 and 2000 (Table 8.1). Not only did increased expenditures mark a significant break from the dictatorship's repeated retrenchments, but also the style of social policy reform in the Concertación period would gain attention in international circles and, particularly from the World Bank, as proof that neoliberalism was not inimical to equity concerns (Taylor 2003).

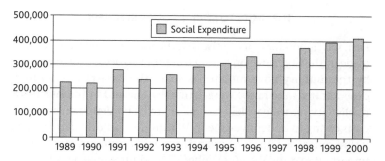

Figure 8.1   Public Social Spending Per Capita, 1989–2000 (in 2000 pesos)

Although the increases in social expenditure indeed appear spectacular and affected the distribution of resources across Chilean society, there are three main issues that need to be explored in order to gain a fuller perspective on the possibilities of attaining social equity through post-dictatorship social policy reform. Respectively, (1) the increases were built on very low bases after almost two decades of underinvestment; (2) owing to the context of profound social polarisation rooted in production relations, the reforms have had more ambiguous effects on social equality than their proponents suggest; and (3) individual areas of service provision remain characterised by notable structural disequilibria as a result of tensions between the dualised public–private systems. These three factors are analysed below, before a more focused examination of education, health, pension and anti-poverty policies is undertaken.

Table 8.1   Public Social Expenditure by Sector, 1989–2000

	Average Annual Increase (%)	Cumulative Increase (%)	% of total Public Social Expenditure (1998)
Health	8.1	135.4	17.9
Housing	3.9	52.7	7.4
Social Security	5.7	84.8	40.8
Education	9.3	165.0	24.5
Monetary Subsidies	5.9	87.3	4.0
Others (inc. FOSIS)	11.7	238.7	5.5
Total	7.1	112.4	100.0

(Data drawn from MIDEPLAN 2001b)

THE LIMITS TO SOCIAL POLICY REFORMS

First, it is important to recognise that the social expenditure increases made by the Concertación followed almost two decades of reductions by the military government. As such, the base rates on which expenditures were raised were extremely low and in the late 1980s public services were widely recognised to be bordering on a state of crisis owing to underinvestment. Within the authoritarian regime's vision, privatised forms of provision would assume an increasingly important role and therefore public expenditure could be reduced to avoid crowding out the private sector. As chapter 4 indicated, however, the private sector did not assume the dominant position expected owing to the lack of profit-making opportunities in the provision of services to the economically marginalised. As a result, the majority of the Chilean population were left dependent on under-resourced public provision of health, education, and to a lesser extent, social security. Sustained reinvestment in these sectors was vital in the post-dictatorship period not just to reinvigorate failing infrastructures of service provision, but also to increase salaries of those working in the public sector. The latter experienced a process of chronic deterioration over the course of the dictatorship. As a consequence, a significant proportion of the expenditure increases in education and health were used to raise teacher and doctor salaries, rather than to contribute directly to infrastructure (Martins and Mulder 2003).

Second, in order to judge their effectiveness and sustainability, it is important to recognise the social context in which the Concertación's reforms take place. The initial step in the Concertación strategy was the negotiation of a small tax increase on corporate profits with business associations led by the *Confederación de Producción y Comercio* (CPC). Greater revenues, it was argued, were necessary to increase the resources devoted to existing health and education systems and also to initiate several new programmes aimed at transferring resources to low-income sections of the populace (Lahera and Cabezas 2000: 1097). However, changes to the tax system established in the Pinochet period were minimal and funding for social expenditure programmes would be derived primarily from surpluses accruing from economic expansion rather than any redistributive measures. In consequence, the taxation system remains heavily regressive with close to 75 percent of revenue raised through indirect means, primarily sales tax. Notably, the top 10 percent of Chilean earners pay only 11.8 percent of their incomes to tax, compared with the bottom 10 percent who pay 14.4 percent (Fazio 2001b).

Given the inability of the Concertación to effect changes in taxation structures that would impart a significant redistribution of income between social classes, the decade-long expenditure increases remained tightly correlated to the primary material export boom that lay behind the posting of an average GDP growth rate of almost 8 percent between 1990 and 1997. Fortunately for the Concertación, the primary export boom led to increased taxation revenues, not least those garnered from the incredibly profitable state copper company, CODELCO. This period of expansion, as examined in the preceding two chapters, was predicated on high prices for Chilean primary exports, large inflows of foreign capital, and the continued suppression of labour through pervasive flexibilisation processes. While recession at the end of the decade brought the average rate of economic expansion for 1989–2000 down to 6.3 percent, this figure for economic expansion is greater than that of increases in total state expenditure (5.5 percent) within which social spending was increased at a greater rate, the average annual increase being 7.1 percent.

As a result of the Concertación's commitment to maintaining expenditure within the threshold of fiscal responsibility without a greater redistributive component, the growth of social expenditure is heavily dependent upon a continued trajectory of rapid capital accumulation (OECD 2003). On the one hand, chapter 6 questioned whether the raw material export boom is either economically or environmentally sustainable in a long-term perspective. The ultimate stagnation of the primary export economy, which has been predicted by observers from various political positions, would fundamentally challenge the material basis of the 'growth with equity' strategy. On the other, as examined in the previous two chapters, the success of the neoliberal accumulation strategy in boosting profit rates rests upon the sharp class distinctions including a highly flexibilised system of labour relations that accentuates income polarisation and leaves a substantial majority of the population below or within one minimum wage of the poverty line. In this sense, the underlying contradiction within the Concertación's 'growth with equity' strategy is the tension-laden relationship between the existing relations of production that rest on and reproduce deeply inequitable social structures, and the attempt to mediate resulting tensions by channelling a percentage of the social surplus into social policies without fundamentally challenging these deep inequities.

To acknowledge this contradiction is not to dismiss the salience of the Concertación's reforms. Where expenditure has been directed at service provision, the introduction of greater targeting within this process has certainly been to the benefit of the bottom quintile of income earners. For example, although representing a small percentage of the Concertación's total social expenditure, monetary subsidies such as family allowances, social aid pensions and new pieces of a social safety net, such as winter supplements, were increased and directed specifically to the lowest-earning decile of Chilean households. Similar to the targeted subsidy policies operated by the dictatorship, these policies helped to sustain the social reproduction of those in extreme poverty and compensated a portion of those marginalised by two decades of social restructuring. Nonetheless, the Concertación has tended to overemphasise the scope of targeting and its ability to fundamentally alter the prevailing and highly unequal social structures. As MIDEPLAN (Ministry of Social Planning) vigorously specifies, if the distribution of social expenditure is quantified in pesos and added to household 'autonomous' incomes according to quintiles of wage earners, an average household in the bottom quintile of wage earners receives a social service value equivalent to almost 85 percent of its conventional income (refer to Figure 8.2). In this schema, 'autonomous' income refers to the market gained income, whereas the 'total' income includes the peso value of education, health and monetary transfer services received from the state.

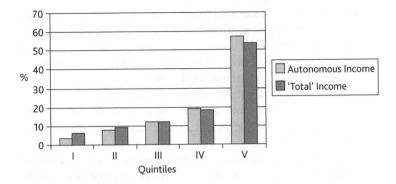

(Data drawn from MIDEPLAN 2000: 52).

Figure 8.2   Distribution of Autonomous and 'Total' Income by Quintile, 1998

In celebrating the targeting of expenditure at the poor, however, the Concertación is making a virtue out of necessity. The bottom three deciles of Chilean income-earners receive a greater proportion of government expenditure precisely because they are marginalised from the superior quality privatised systems owing to prohibitive costs. They therefore rely on public provision of health, education and pensions. Contrarily, the top 20 percent of income earners tend not to use the public health system nor subsidised state municipal schools, and therefore do not benefit from these forms of government expenditure (cf. Martin 2000: 319). This invocation of 'targeting', therefore, is not an active form of redistribution but rather the passive outcome of the dualised forms of service provision in Chile. Additionally, on a technical level, it is also worth noting the statistics provided by MIDEPLAN to demonstrate the progressive nature of public social expenditure exclude those expenditures devoted to pensions. This is significant because, on the one hand, pension provision is the most regressive form of state expenditure; and, on the other hand, it remains the largest component of state social spending, encompassing over 40 percent which corresponds to 6.11 percent of GDP (refer to Table 8.1). One-fifth of social security expenditures go directly to the pensions of the armed forces, who were not forced to join the privatised system, and close to three-fifths are accounted for by payments to those who remained within the public system and the initial transfers into the private system. These recipients are largely within the top 50 percent of income earners. Only the remaining fifth could be described as 'progressive' expenditure, as it is channelled towards raising the value of the state emergency pension to compensate those facing impoverishment owing to their exclusion from the privatised system. As such, if these sizeable and regressive forms of spending had been included in MIDEPLAN's income distribution figures they would significantly alter the progressive description of social expenditure.

Finally, although expenditures have been increased with positive ramifications throughout the social services, there remain acute structural problems owing to the dual system of private and public service provision forged within the Pinochet era. Placed within the larger institutional conjuncture, which must be traced back to the recasting of these sectors under the Pinochet regime, it is possible to comprehend why, despite the sizeable increases in public spending, it was still common at the turn of the millennium for analysts to talk of manifest problems across the sector. Rather than assess these tensions at a general level, such issues are better explored through an examination of the specific impact and limits to education, health, pension and anti-poverty reforms. The latter are addressed in turn in the following four sections.

REFORMING THE EDUCATION REFORMS

As discussed in chapter 4, the authoritarian regime embarked on a partial commodification of education provision through which a version of Milton Friedman's voucher scheme was established. Within this system the state provided funding on the supply side, with schools receiving payments based on the number of students they could attract and parents having a choice of schools in which to enrol their children. Guided by a prevailing belief that market forces and municipal governments could be left to efficiently manage the country's education system, an important element of the restructuring was the establishment of private schools that compete with municipal-run schools for state funded students. These reforms, however, took place alongside large quantitative reductions in public education expenditures, leading to a decrease of aggregate resources in the education system and a significant drop in teacher salaries.

In contrast to the dictatorship, the Concertación repeatedly championed the role of education as an integral aspect of improving the country's productive structure and in providing for greater equality between citizens (Solimano et al. 2000). This is reflective of the liberal dimension of 'Third Way' social democracy, which steadfastly emphasises equality of opportunity rather than equality of outcome (Keaney 2005). However, despite the extremely welcome state increases in education funding – a significant proportion of which has gone to improve school teacher wages after years of relative decline (Castiglioni 2005: 98) – the most important structural reform undertaken by the Concertación has been to allow privately owned yet state subsidised schools to charge a supplementary 'co-payment' for each attending student (Raczynski 1999). Despite the fact that this reform has allowed these private yet state subsidised entities to increase their resources and pedagogic quality, it has been at the cost of increasing polarisation between schools.

In theory, any school is allowed to levy a co-payment. However, the tendency has been for a stratification of schools according to geographic location differentiated along class lines. Those schools that have been able to levy greater extra charges are those that are located in middle or upper class areas and service a clientele that is able to afford the increased costs. With greater resources, these schools are then able to ride a virtuous circle of improving standards and increased student attraction, leading to greater revenues. This polarising tendency is partially reinforced by performance based pay increases for teachers, with a merit based increment for teachers at institutions displaying the highest levels of academic performance (Castiglioni 2005: 98). Moreover, some studies strongly indicate that the higher achieving schools deliberately seek to discourage less educated, working class parents from enrolling their children in the belief that this might lower standards and compromise profit maximisation (Carnoy and McEwan 2000: 14).

Conversely, schools in working class neighbourhoods are commonly state schools, but sometimes privately-owned schools, that suffer from a lack of resources. In the words of several analysts, they risk becoming 'waste-basket' schools (Carnoy and McEwan 2000; Helgø 2002). For the latter, the circle is a vicious one and the only way of maintaining the school within the competitive environment of the semi-privatised system has been to borrow money. Jaime Gajardo suggests that, in order to keep schools solvent, certain municipal education authorities have been forced to borrow money leading to a substantial increase in municipal debt (Gajardo 2002). Significantly, the decentralisation of funding responsibilities leaves poorer neighbourhoods with notable conflicts in spending priorities between education, health and other services. In this respect, Gustavo Rayo and Gonzalo de la Maza (1998: 431) have argued that:

Poor municipalities face serious difficulties in maintaining significant social programmes, not only because of structural financial restrictions, but also for the deficit in programme financing inherited from the previous decade.

Consequently, and somewhat counter-intuitively given the Concertación's political heritage and rhetorical posturing, the new reforms have taken the commodification of education a step further than that accomplished under the dictatorship. In reinforcing the dualised education system, sharp distinctions in quality between private and public education and between those that charge co-payments and those that can't, continue to permeate the entire spectrum of educational provision. These trends have consolidated rather than contravened the educational stratification of Chilean society. Certainly, there have been several programmes created by successive Concertación regimes to try and target extra money towards some of the poorest schools. The P-900 programme initiated by the Aylwin regime aimed to supplement material and financial resources in the most impoverished and underperforming 900 primary schools in Chile, and this was subsequently expanded to encompass 2,300 schools. Such forms of intervention, however, are made all the more necessary by a structural imbalance that promotes consumer choice in education therein transferring resources and students into a discretionary private sector, at the expense of equality. In this respect, by 1997 44 percent of students were enrolled in private yet state-voucher funded schools (Castiglioni 2005: 98).

Despite the rhetoric of the Frei administration concerning the levelling forces of education provision within Chile, such polarisation is notable in the following tables that give a clear picture of education stratification in that period. Table 8.2 shows that the percentage of students receiving the various levels of education remains highly stratified according to income, and Table 8.3 demonstrates that the quality of education varies greatly according to the same income factor. Under the dual system the class dimension of educational achievement is reinforced as children from low-income families attend lesser quality schools whereas the children of the richest families monopolise the highest achieving schools.

In contrast to the suggestion that a high-quality education would be available to all Chileans as part of the 'growth with equity' programme, reinforcing market incentives and tightening the link between choice and income in the reformed education system has perpetuated deep inequalities in the provision of education in Chile.

Table 8.2   Percentage of Educational Coverage by Income Quintile 1996

Education (child age)	Quintile I	Quintile II	Quintile III	Quintile IV	Quintile V
Pre-School (2–5)	22.3	26.8	30.0	36.8	48.4
Primary (5–13)	96.5	98.4	98.0	99.4	99.7
Secondary (14–17)	75.3	81.0	89.3	95.3	97.2
Further (18+)	8.5	15.1	21.5	34.7	59.7

(Data drawn from FNPSP 2000)

Table 8.3   Percentage of Income Quintile in Schools Ranked in Quintiles According to Success in State Mathematics Tests (Metropolitan Region, 1996)

Per Capita Income Quintile	Quintiles of School Performance (ranked according to Simce Results)				
	I	II	III	IV	V
I	32.9	27.3	22.0	14.0	3.8
II	23.2	22.3	24.9	20.2	9.4
III	18.9	20.6	20.2	23.1	17.2
IV	8.7	14.1	18.3	31.0	28.0
V	3.7	8.3	10.8	16.2	61.0

(Data drawn from FNPSP 2000)

These inequalities, moreover, both reflect and reproduce the general polarisation of Chilean society. Some authors on the right of the political spectrum suggest that the failures of semi-privatised education relate to failures of information resulting from the unfamiliarity of low-income parents with the system, and therein their inability to make rational decisions in relation to the education of their children (Beyer 2000). However, to posit such an argument over 20 years since the introduction of the first reforms and in disregard of the manifest structural problems and class-based stratification associated with the dual system is hardly sustainable. In short, the element of choice and quality within the education system remains significantly reliant on income. This necessarily entails that those that have gained most from the improvements in educational provision are precisely those who are able to pay for their children to attend the better schools. Although this outcome may not be surprising, it is a stern corrective to some of the Concertación's rhetoric concerning the Chilean education system as a force for equality rather than an institution reflective of existing stratification.

HEALTH PROVISION WITHIN THE DUALISED SYSTEM

Similar problems also remain in healthcare provision owing to the contradictions fashioned by the dictatorship's disinvestment and privatisation processes. Having pledged during the transition period to reinvigorate the deteriorated health system, the new government set out to solve some of the problems of health provision through sustained increases in the resources destined to the public sector (FONASA). This reinvestment included a particular emphasis on improving hospital services and health-sector pay. However, the overall structure of the health system has been left predominantly unchanged and increased expenditure proved unable to mitigate the systemic failures during the 1990s. In spite of a doubling of public healthcare expenditure between 1989 and 1997, there remains a common sentiment that the system is strongly polarised in favour of private service providers and their patrons, and that public provision is beset with financing and operational problems (Castiglioni 2005; *The Economist* 2002).

As elaborated in chapter 4, the major deficiency that plagues the neoliberal re-institutionalisation of healthcare is that new forms of privatised provision have created a strong structural bias against the state system. To re-cap, while Chileans are theoretically allowed to choose between public or private healthcare providers, entrance into the private system remains heavily structured by class, gender and age. Older women and men, and particularly women who fall in the age range deemed statistically probable to become pregnant are faced with prohibitively increased premiums or, in some cases, are simply rejected by the private health insurers (ISAPREs). On the other hand, middle age high-income (and low-risk) males are targeted by the sales representatives of ISAPREs and are their major contributor. The fiscal implication of this is that, despite incorporating only a minority of the population into private healthcare, the elevated economic position of ISAPRE members means that ISAPREs absorb the majority of total health-insurance contributions. By the turn of the millennium, the ISAPREs were accumulating two-thirds of total payroll contributions to service just one-fifth of the population (Titelman 2001). Concurrently, ISAPRE expenditures per beneficiary are of the nature of four times that of the public sector, thereby underscoring their greater quality healthcare (Barrientos 2002). As a result, the profit-making private health funds continue to absorb the population statistically less likely to need health services alongside the greater part of mandatory contributions. In contrast, the public system receives only a third of health contributions yet must provide services for almost 80 percent of the population, including those sections most likely to require sustained health services.

To compound this situation, observers note that many members of the ISAPRE system prefer to use the public health system for most non-serious medical treatment in order to protect their 'no-claim bonuses'. In the mid-1990s the Concertación began to enforce transparency processes upon the ISAPREs in an attempt to counter such practices, although the proposed computerisation of hospital registers is expected to have a more profound effect in this regard (Barrientos 2002). Further, there are no limits on people switching back to public healthcare and many ISAPRE subscribers tend to revert to the public system to avoid paying higher premiums in the case of, for example, the more costly forms of medical attention associated with childbirth and old age (Cid Pedraza 2001: 5). As such, the public system continues to operate as an insurer of last resort that absorbs cases that the ISAPREs prefer not to insure and therefore subsidises the profits of the private health sector.

By 2000, the number of subscribers to ISAPREs had risen to 23 percent of the population. Concurrently, the private sector assumes double the amount levied by mandatory contributions as compared to FONASA (i.e. a ratio of two-thirds to one-third). Even when the Concertación's increased expenditure is taken into account, the result is still that the ISAPRE system monopolises 46 percent of total health resources to serve 20 percent of the population (Cid Pedraza 2001: 6). Unsurprisingly, the standard of care within the private system is still considered to be vastly superior and, moreover, the higher salaries paid within this sector continues to attract the better-qualified medical staff. Aside from issues concerning the quality of care, a further consequence is long waiting lists for treatment within the public sector (Martins and Mulder 2003).

Both decentralisation and participatory forms of health provision were intended to overcome some of these shortcomings by improving the efficiency and responsiveness of local healthcare providers to their consumers. On the one hand, however, decentralisation has placed financial burdens on municipalities that some are unable to manage effectively, as discussed in the case of education above (cf. Gideon 2002: 207–10). On the other, participatory processes have served not primarily to increase the control of health provision by the recipients, but rather to incorporate social movements into the management of basic healthcare services designed and budgeted elsewhere (Paley 2001). In particular, this arrangement has seen voluntary and unpaid healthcare groups making up the shortfall of health provision in poorer municipalities, therein covering the ground where the private sector will not engage and the public sector lacks funds. As Jasmine Gideon (2002: 213) indicates, healthcare reforms in the Concertación period 'do not overcome social exclusion, but rather "include" people in ways consistent with pre-existing hierarchies and the overall neo-liberal project'.

The imbalances highlighted above are not contingent outcomes but represent the logical result of the neoliberal dualisation of health provision and its reassertion of the cash nexus into service provision. Although the Concertación has ameliorated these contradictions by channelling increased funding into the state sector, particularly to subsidise those with the lowest income levels, the underlying causes of these ruptures have not been challenged. This is not to dismiss the effects of the Concertación's expansion of healthcare spending. It is evident that the introduction of more resources has aided the public system's partial recovery from the calamitous effects of the dictatorship's retrenchment. Nevertheless, even in September of 2002 *The Economist* judged that, despite the threefold increase in health expenditure since 1990, the public system had not overcome two decades of under-investment and suffered from considerable overstretch (*The Economist* 2002). The results of the Concertación's increased funding, therefore, have been well below what had been hoped for in terms of improvements in the quantity and quality of services offered by the public sector (Raczynski 1999: 39).

To address these issues, in May of 2001 President Ricardo Lagos announced a 'profound' reform of the healthcare system that would involve the creation of a solidarity fund called '*Plan Auge*'. The latter would be partially state-financed and partially funded by compulsory contributions, thereby in theory ensuring a basic minimum package of healthcare services would be offered to all Chileans. Even though Congress passed the measure at the end of 2002, concerted debate was ongoing as to the probable effectiveness of the reform. Notably, the Medical College has criticised the initiative, claiming that by refusing to instigate a stronger role for the state in the provision of health the new plan is unlikely to have any significant effect on the profound inequalities existing within the current system. On the other side, the gains of the Plan Auge system were threatened within the Congress, where various representatives from both the parties of the right and the Christian Democrats were suggesting that fiscal responsibility should take precedence over the new taxes needed to raise the necessary annual expenditure of US$230 million. This not only threatened the intended gradual expansion of the number of illnesses whose treatment would be included in the plan, but also the basic resources that underscored the tenuous ability of the public system to provide the new coverage. The Lagos administration was successful in raising value added tax by 1 percent in 2003 to help cover healthcare costs, although this represents a regressive means of financing and part of the money raised would merely cover the loss of revenues incurred by lowering trade tariffs with the European Union and United States (OECD 2003).

PENSIONS AND SOCIAL SECURITY

The authoritarian regime's privatisation of the Chilean pension system was widely applauded as a model to be emulated not just in the developing world, but in the core Western countries as well (Mesa-Lago 2002; Madrid 2005). Indeed, George Bush suggested that Americans had much to learn from the Chilean model in modernising their own social security system, and his administration has drawn upon the direct advice of Jose Piñera, architect of the Chilean reforms and currently senior fellow at the Cato Institute (Cato Institute 2005). Chapter 4 indicated the major tenets of the Chilean pension privatisation scheme, which forced all new entrants into the workforce to pay a defined percentage of their salaries into a personal pension scheme to be managed by a pension company (AFP) of their choice. Unfortunately, despite considerable acclaim, the Chilean pension reform has only proved a success for a relatively small part of the Chilean population and this should raise significant concerns about its global propagation. In the following paragraphs four shortcomings of the privatised approach are highlighted.

First, the privatised system is exclusionary. The number of participants in the privatised system rose from 50 percent of the economically active population in 1990 to slightly fewer than 60 percent by the turn of the millennium. When added to those still covered by the old system, the total percentage of the workforce with pension coverage is 70 percent (Acuña and Iglesias 2000: 456). In the first respect, this means that some 30 percent of the Chilean labour force is still not part of the AFP system, nor is it involved in the legacy of the old system. This section is mostly made up of informal sector workers and the self-employed, including micro-enterprises and small subcontracting firms alongside certain craftspeople, family farmers and small workshop owners. For such independent workers, affiliation to the AFP system is optional and most do not subscribe owing to the low and transitory incomes that are prevalent throughout these sectors. Excluded from the pension system owing to their peripheral position in the Chilean labour force, these workers can expect no more than the state support pension which, as observers from various normative positions concur, is insufficient to meet basic needs despite increases by the Concertación (Huber 1996: 166; Fazio and Riesco 1997; Hiscock and Hojman 1997: 357).

Second, one half of those formally belonging to an AFP are only nominally part of the system. By 1998 the percentage of those actually contributing to the system respective to those not paying inputs, either through retirement or other reasons, registered 52.8 percent (Acuña and Iglesias 2000: 456). Those who do not contribute with regularity – and thereby fail to make the minimum of 240 contributions – will only receive the money they have paid in to the account, plus the state support pension. This latter section comprises one-quarter of all AFP members. It includes many lower class women who tend to move in and out of work for child-rearing purposes and owing to their disproportionate involvement in temporary and precarious forms of work. Furthermore, another one-quarter of all AFP members do indeed make the necessary tally of contributions, but their accumulated fund will not reach a state-designated minimum pension and, thereby, the latter once again must intervene to raise their fund to the minimal level.

Neoclassical economists, such as Rodrigo Acuña and Augusto Iglesias (2000: 482), relate the lack of AFP contributions primarily to the irresponsibility of workers and therefore advise the augmentation of disciplinary elements for non-contributors (fines, higher fees, etc.). This point of view, however, ignores the huge polarisation of the Chilean working class effected by the neoliberal economic reforms. In spite of sustained economic growth between 1990 and 1997, the benefits of economic expansion for different sections of Chilean society were clearly asymmetrical with profound social polarisation, as evidenced by colossal discrepancies in income and, therein, disproportionate ability to pay regular AFP contributions. While the top 10 percent of Chilean earners absorb 42.3 percent of national income, the bottom 70 account for just 32.2 percent (MIDEPLAN 2001b). Precarious and low-income work is the staple for over 40 percent of the Chilean labour force, and non-payment of pension contributions by large sections of the working population, rather than being reducible to individual pathologies, is a direct result of the structural features of Chilean labour markets in the neoliberal period. Ironically, in 2003 the OECD stated that the exclusionary nature of Chile's model pension reforms entailed that the government may be forced to retreat from the existing defined contributions system and re-establish and fund a universal support pillar within the overall pension system (OECD 2003). This would represent a humiliating defeat for those who have promoted the Chilean privatisation of pensions as a best-practice model for global propagation.

Third, although privatising pensions was intended to introduce competition mechanisms to improve efficiency and product choice, pension fund markets are highly monopolised by a handful of companies. Chapter 4 demonstrated how channelling worker savings through the financial system aided the activities of the large economic conglomerates that dominate the Chilean economy. Moreover, it is also important to note that the emergent private pension funds (AFPs) themselves are almost universally subsidiary parts of these large economic conglomerates. This was inevitable given the large start-up costs and requirements and has led to a situation of virtual monopoly in the AFP market. In spite of the rhetoric of competition between AFPs, three funds exercise a profound dominance over the market by taking 70 percent of contributions. Concentrated market control has not been predicated on preferential service or rates of return as all funds offer virtually identical portfolios and charges. Rather, analysts attribute it to the greater advertising power exercised by the larger groups alongside a ruthless competition war undertaken by the latter in the 1990s that has concentrated the number of independent firms from 22 to seven (Fazio and Riesco 1997: 94; Hiscock and Hojman 1997: 356). The concentration of capital within the AFP sector has helped assure high rates of return for the oligopolies that survived the competition of the 1990s. Despite the failures of privatised social security institutions for the majority of Chileans, the six AFPs are the most profitable firms in Chile, with some estimates attributing returns of close to 50 percent on capital invested during the period 1999–2003 (Riesco 2005).

Finally, in spite of the projections that privatisation of the pension system would free the state from considerable expenditures – lauded as one of the greatest virtues of neoliberal reform – the necessary commitment to maintaining the remnants of the old system, alongside providing minimal state-support pensions to the large number of non-AFP affiliates, means that social security has remained the single major component of total state social expenditure. As outlined above, even 20 years following the establishment of the privatised system, expenditure on pensions amounted to 40.8 percent of total public social expenditure, a figure that corresponds to 6.11 percent of GDP. This total represents a relative cost to the state double that of the pre-reform system in 1981 (Borzutzky 2001: 297). Although the long run trend is projected to be a diminution of this amount to an estimated 3.3 percent of GDP in 2040 as the number of those who initially declined to join the private system diminishes, this merely suggests a return to pre-privatisation levels of state social security expenditure.

FOSIS – THE PROTOTYPE ANTI-POVERTY POLICY

The Fondo de Solidaridad y Inversión Social (Solidarity and Social Investment Fund – FOSIS) was the lynchpin of a series of measures introduced by the Concertación that had the objective of transferring resources to the poorest sections of Chilean society. Established in 1990, it came into full operation in 1991 under the direction of the Ministry of Social Planning (MIDEPLAN). The first notable aspect of FOSIS is that, despite its claim to be the 'child of democracy', its roots lay in the community-based groups and non-governmental organisations that formed during the dictatorship in order to cope with mass unemployment and impoverishment. The guiding principles of FOSIS are those common to social funds seen elsewhere in Latin America: namely targeting, de-centralisation, cost-efficiency, complementing but not duplicating traditional social policies, and involving the public sector, private sector, NGOs, and communities in partnerships (Sottoli 2000; Tendler 2000). In this respect, the forms of anti-poverty policy introduced by the authoritarian regime in the 1970s were undoubtedly an influence. Certain aspects of FOSIS's general design, however, are more specific to the needs of the Concertación in the immediate post-dictatorship period.

Firstly, FOSIS operates on the tenet that poverty should be tackled through integrating the income generation strategies of the poor to the mainstream of the Chilean economy. Secondly, FOSIS was not to be a temporary measure but rather was estimated to become a permanent fixture in the government's poverty alleviation strategy. Thirdly, FOSIS was not to be solely reliant on state funding but the projects should seek to mobilise funds from other sources, principally the recipient communities themselves and the network of NGOs established in the dictatorship period. Finally, the primary method for selecting both the projects to be financed and the intermediaries to undertake them is through public bidding. In this way FOSIS operates through a competition system in which communities and/ or individuals and NGOs put forward their projects into a national competition. In somewhat idiosyncratic fashion, those proposals adjudged by a panel of experts to be the best are awarded the resources while unsuccessful communities must wait for the following competition to resubmit.

There exists a small but detailed problem-solving literature on the technical issues that confront FOSIS (Barrientos 1999; Parker et al. 1999). Fixing technical problems within FOSIS is clearly an important concern for those involved in the programme. However, the following paragraphs highlight two key dimensions of a wider critique. It is undeniable that, over the decade of the 1990s, the resources provided by FOSIS programmes have indeed helped many individuals and communities mired below the extreme poverty line in Chile to improve their material circumstances (cf. <www.fosis.cl>). However, when conceptual concerns are raised concerning FOSIS as a means of regulating poverty, it can be seen how FOSIS fits neatly within the wider neoliberal paradigm of disciplinary societal restructuring.

Firstly, at a technical level, it is important to note the limits of the FOSIS as an anti-poverty programme. Despite its 'anti-poverty' label, FOSIS is not designed or intended to impact upon the wage poverty that, even after a decade of economic growth, afflicted over 20 percent of Chilean workers in the new millennium. In contrast, FOSIS is targeted at the population living in conditions of indigence (extreme poverty) that are generally marginalised from formal economic structures. The distinction between non-poverty, poverty and indigence is inherently subjective and open to statistical manipulation (cf. Székely 2001). However, in this respect the chapter follows the designations of the Chilean government, with the poverty line defined as a household income level necessary to be able to satisfy the basic needs of the household through the purchase of a standardised basket of goods. Indigence is a situation whereby even basic nutritional needs cannot be satisfied (cf. Chacón 1999: 183). In this respect, FOSIS cannot be satisfactorily considered an anti-poverty programme according to the government's own categories. It is best conceptualised as a programme that aims to raise the extreme poor up to the level of salaried poor. It attempts, therefore, to provide the means through which the most isolated and marginalised communities can rejoin the category of employable wage labour and reinsert themselves into the hyper-flexibilised Chilean labour markets.

FOSIS therefore is very much a neoliberal form of social policy in that it does not offer a form of decommodification in the manner suggested by social policy theorists such as Gøsta Esping-Andersen: namely, a mediation between individual and market that reduces the dependence of the former on the latter (cf. Esping-Andersen 1990). In contrast, FOSIS aims to provide the physical and human infrastructure to remove barriers from market participation as a means of development. As such, the programme aims precisely to integrate marginalised populations more fully into capitalist social relations thereby inserting the extreme poor more closely into the disciplines of the labour market. FOSIS therefore exists as a prototype for current World Bank programmes that proclaim to 'empower' the poor (cf. World Bank 2000; cf. Taylor 2004). The contradictory dimension of this process is that, in the name of empowerment, individuals are inserted into impersonal globalised market relations over which they have no control and which repeatedly and necessarily enter into frequent crisis periods that marginalise significant portions of the population. While in the early 1990s, the dramatic expansion of capital accumulation and the resulting expansion of employment opportunities appeared to negate such considerations, the return to crisis and a rapid expansion of un- and under-employment in the later 1990s has highlighted some limits to the philosophy underlying the FOSIS strategy.

In spite of its 'anti-poverty' label, therefore, FOSIS is more accurately understood as part of a framework of institutions intended to regulate, rather than resolve, poverty. Even within the Chilean Ministry of Social Planning (MIDEPLAN), there is an open recognition that the primary anti-poverty mechanisms operate through the government's macroeconomic policy (interviews conducted with MIDEPLAN directorate, May 2002). Indeed, the levels of funding through FOSIS are restricted and account for less than 5 percent of the social expenditure budget (refer to Table 8.1 above). These limited resources mitigate the possibility of FOSIS programmes having a large-scale impact that could influence the greater structural trends of inequality and impoverishment, both in relative and absolute terms. In fact, following the period of rapid economic growth in the 1990 to 1996 period, the percentage of the population that exists in conditions of indigence remained static, and even experienced a small increase in the late 1990s, therein confirming the limited ability of the Concertación's initial social policies to ameliorate even extreme poverty. Indeed, more cynical critics (e.g. Petras and Leiva 1994) suggest that the primary function of FOSIS is to provide a series of showcase projects. This argument, however, would seem to deny that such programmes can have any beneficial effects while simultaneously ignoring their role in regulating the relations between state and societal groups, as discussed below.

Secondly, on a political level, the form of the FOSIS programme selection process, which obliges potential recipient communities to compete for resources by subjecting their project proposals to a regional competition, involves a strong disciplinary mechanism. The process of allocating resources starts at the centralised level, with the programme directors in MIDEPLAN distributing the available funds proportionally to the regions they feel are most in need of programmes. They then indicate to the regional authorities what they feel are the specific communities within these regions that should be targeted. Subsequently, the regional government establishes a working committee that includes municipal authorities and other public service groups who disseminate the information concerning the sums of FOSIS money available to the communities. The latter then are encouraged to design projects within the threshold of the stipulated aims of the FOSIS programme. Subsequently, these proposals are submitted to the working committee, which selects the 'winning' proposals at an open meeting. This process of successive decentralisation was considered as essential to responding to the specific needs of the poor in particular locales and to facilitating their greater participation within the formulation, design and undertaking of projects (Barrientos 1999; Raczynski 2000; Angell et al. 2001). In this respect, FOSIS is once again an important forerunner of World Bank participatory development projects that aim to make sizeable gains in efficiency and legitimacy as compared to centrally created programmes. Moreover, once the projects to be funded are established, bidding between service providers (private or NGO) for contracts can take place if this wasn't already stipulated in the project blueprints.

The competition form of FOSIS anti-poverty delivery clearly undercuts any notion of universal welfare or social rights. For example, close to a third of the FOSIS budget is directed towards 'capacity building' to enable poor communities to implement projects to improve their local living infrastructure. That communities have to compete to receive funds for basic infrastructure, including the installation of street paving, lighting and drainage, runs against the political articulation of the popular movements that emerged in the dictatorship period. The latter claimed the universal right for communities to receive these basic services and amenities (cf. Salman 1994; Oxhorn 1995; Paley 2001). Activists and analysts have suggested that because communities now have to compete against each other for access to FOSIS resources to undertake basic infrastructure initiatives trans-movement and community solidarity has been fragmented (Rayo and De la Maza 1998; Taylor 1998: 210). In this respect, FOSIS can be suggested to have contributed to the reformulation of community social movements, a process that Ton Salman (1994: 85) highlights as characterised by 'disintegration, withdrawal from the public realm, and individualistic strategies for integration'.

Similarly, if an acceptance of the limits to post-dictatorship politics could be successfully imposed, the Concertación saw the possibility of transforming the swathes of grassroots movements that combined political opposition to the dictatorship with communal self-help into willing technical facilitators of social programmes such as FOSIS (cf. Paley 2001: 169). The institutional form of FOSIS required both communal social movements and wider non-governmental organisations to play the leading role in project design and, often, implementation (Barrientos 1999; Parker et al. 1999). As Joe Foweraker has suggested in a provocative analysis of social movements in post-dictatorship Chile, the latter have been largely displaced by or transformed into apolitical, problem-solving non-governmental organisations (NGOs) that are often financially and technologically dependent upon, and therefore increasingly influenced by, specific foreign agencies and institutions. The original aims of grassroots movements to act as a significant motor of social change, therefore, have been considerably marginalised by this process. Where they have chosen to interact with the state, they have been commonly subordinated as instruments of state policy with limited political influence beyond the technical issues of project implementation. Concurrently, where avoiding interaction has often led to marginalisation and ineffectiveness (Foweraker 2001: 845–9; Greaves 2005).

In this manner, when considered in its wider socio-political context, the character of FOSIS as one moment of the larger trend towards depoliticisation becomes more evident. This is not to suggest that FOSIS is simply an instrumentally designed tool to pacify the masses and secure the legitimation of the Chilean ruling classes. On the contrary, the creation of FOSIS accords primarily to the extent of popular mobilisation of the popular sectors in the dictatorship period and the desire both to build upon this mobilisation as well as set formidable institutional limits to its potential directions. Resultantly, as a form of regulating poverty, FOSIS marks a considerable improvement in both technical content and substantive process from the authoritarian programmes that characterised the dictatorship period. As Gustavo Rayo and Gonzalo de la Maza (1998: 431) indicate in the context of several case studies of FOSIS projects, beyond their material aims, social funds such as FOSIS operate as 'a linkage and structure of dialogue between state and grassroots social movements'.

Social funds, like other institutionalised forms of state-relations, are therefore an object of struggle and open to continual challenge and pressures for reform from actors on both sides of the relationship. Nonetheless, given the institutional form of the programme that was established within the confines of the immediate post-authoritarian period, FOSIS closely reflects the Concertación's strategy of diverting the social expectations of the population into the realm of social policy where it envisaged being able to exercise a greater control. Although FOSIS indeed necessitates a specific degree of social mobilisation from recipient communities, the form of this mobilisation is one of intra-community competition and requires communities to focus on performing technical tasks to further their insertion into the market mainstream. It therefore displays significant tensions between, on the one hand, social mobilisation and the attempt to depoliticise; and, on the other, community expectations of empowerment to material betterment and the peculiar character of capitalist development that repeatedly frustrates those aims.

SUMMARY

Increased social expenditure has been central to the Concertación's 'growth with equity' strategy. In this respect, public spending on the full range of social programmes – including healthcare, education, pensions and anti-poverty – has been raised in a sustained fashion. Although, after two decades of retrenchment in the Pinochet era, the base rates upon which this renewed expenditure built were very low, these increases have nonetheless aided a notable recovery in public services from a generalised situation of crisis. However, despite these achievements, several contradictions still permeate social policy in the post-dictatorship era, and these have profoundly limited the Concertación's proclamation of a policy of 'growth with equity'. First, the financial resources for increased social expenditure were and remain greatly reliant on the continued success of the natural resource exports driven accumulation strategy and this, as indicated in the previous chapter, is predicated upon the maintenance of a heavily flexibilised system of labour relations that have helped suppress the level of wages and increase job insecurity and working hours. In this respect, there is an underlying tension within the Concertación's strategy. Moreover, the strategy remains vulnerable to changing global economic conditions, and most analysts suggest that Chile has entered a period of much more modest growth punctuated by periods of relative stagnation. Second, structural problems exist in each of the major areas of social policy owing to structural tensions between the dual public–private systems of service provision. Third, the chapter also re-emphasised, through a focus on the FOSIS anti-poverty programme, how social policies in the Concertación period remain configured within a broader attempt to depoliticise Chilean society and limit opposition to the prevailing institutions that frame neoliberal capital accumulation.

9
The Uncertain Future of Neoliberalism

The previous four chapters have explicated numerous contradictions that suffuse the attempt of the Concertación governments to combine the major tenets of neoliberalism with a commitment to equitable social development in the post-dictatorship era. In contrast to their political rhetoric, the conspicuous failure of the Concertación to reconcile growth with equity remains readily apparent. As the previous chapters demonstrate, inequalities in Chile remain entrenched, not just in terms of the highly unequal distribution of income but also in the institutionally embedded and profoundly uneven power relationships that span Chilean society. The latter are tangible in the relationships between oligarchic corporations rooted in the financial sector and all other economic actors; between workers and employers throughout the realm of production; and in the highly stratified modes of social service provision ranging from social security to education. In addition, we could also focus on the gendered division of labour in Chilean society and the escalating ecological tensions of the export-driven model, although these were not the primary foci of this book. In view of such contradictions, it is pertinent to address the question of why this refined neoliberalism has been unable to meet the primary goals that it established for itself, not least because this is a question that affects the future of progressive politics across Latin America. What are the limits to 'Third Way' neoliberalism such as the Concertación's 'growth with equity' strategy, and what do these tell us about the uncertain future of neoliberalism in Chile and more broadly?

In order to consider such questions, it is worth returning briefly to the underlying nature of neoliberalism that preoccupied the start of this book. Neoliberalism, it was argued in chapter 2, emerged at a time of profound social and economic crisis as a state-led strategy of institutional restructuring that aimed to refashion the basic social relationships through which capitalist societies reproduce themselves. By reinforcing social institutions that consolidate the regulatory power of markets within society, and destroying those that constrain the latter, neoliberalism sought to subordinate individual and collective actions to the impersonal and seemingly neutral impositions of market forces. Although such motivations were particularly evident in Chile, they are the essence of neoliberalism at a global level (see Taylor 2004). As is well known, within the neoclassical canon, the invisible hand of the market is portrayed to optimally distribute resources across society through the unintended interactions of private individuals exchanging goods. On this basis, neoliberalism promised to resolve the repeated crises afflicting capitalist societies by offering a clear route to economic prosperity while simultaneously depoliticising society through the removal of institutions that sanctioned collective social action. Such claims, however, clash with the uneven and conflict ridden trajectory of 'actually-existing' neoliberalism both in Chile and at a global level.

Viewing neoliberalism as a strategy of institutional transformation is expressly important because it allows us to advance beyond an understanding of neoliberalism as simply a question of policy choice. Such a perspective is preponderant within the tradition of economics, which is characterised by a peculiar political-determinism in which the external factor of government policy is seen as the primary influence upon an otherwise universal and static set of relationships that constitute an economy. Good social outcomes are then reduced to an issue of 'getting the policies right'. The political implications of this approach are notable and have been unwittingly absorbed within wider social science perspectives and into political movements. If neoliberalism is reducible to a question of policy, then simply substituting or supplementing neoliberal with alternative or corrective policies can effect substantial social change. The latter corresponds to the Concertación's approach over the last decade and a half, wherein each government has suggested that supplementary policies to impose equitable outcomes upon prevailing social institutions and processes is both possible and desirable.

Comprehending neoliberalism as a process of deep-seated social transformation, however, problematises such assumptions and allows us to explain the Concertación's profoundly uneven results. Neoliberalism was implemented, with relative success, in order to reconstitute the institutionalised social relationships through which society reproduces itself. These basic social relationships were not only transformed but were also embedded within new institutional forms, therein imbuing a systematic and path-dependent quality upon the social interactions, shaping both individual and collective forms of action. On a material level, neoliberalism in Chile obliterated existing productive structures and the relations between capital and workers upon which they stood. De-industrialisation and the shift towards primary commodity exports was not merely a case of 'embracing development opportunities' through correct policies, as proponents would put it, but of systematically undermining the established and conflictual relationships between classes in the realm of production. These were recomposed around new productive structures and on the basis of new labour institutions that systematically disempowered workers from exercising control over the terms and conditions of work. On a political level, the institutional structures that facilitated collective social action were obliterated and replaced with those that promoted individualised market exchanges and a formalistic democratic system that excludes major social questions – such as macroeconomic policy – from democratic influence. On an ideological level, such changes resulted in an emphasis on individualism and strong social pressures to define identities through consumption patterns (Stillerman 2004). In short, neoliberalism constructed a new social fabric upon which human interactions transgress and, in so doing, reshaped the way power is constituted and exercised within society.

Given the magnitude of this social transformation, a simple refinement of policies or the addition of supplementary programmes to address inequalities were always unlikely to have an extensive impact upon the existing institutionally embedded structure of social relations. The Concertación's 'Third Way' neoliberalism, however, has never been a systematic programme of social transformation, but rather represents a politics of expediency. The 'Third Way' genre of neoliberalism has emerged globally as a way for governments and international organisations that operate in heavily stratified power relations to address the contradictions that emerge from such relationships without addressing their underlying social constitution. The emphasis on the necessary role of state measures to ensure sound market activities adheres to the neoliberal emphasis on the fundamental rationality of marketised social relations yet provides a systematic basis to justify selective interventions according to information asymmetries, sporadic market failures, and uneven development. As such, 'Third Way' neoliberalism comprises a sophisticated rationale for the perceived failures of orthodox neoliberalism, supplementary policies to mediate the most explicit symptoms of these failures, and a way to attempt to incorporate social struggles within the threshold of the prevailing relations of production and distribution. The Concertación and their 'Third Way' approach, therein, is the product of the institutionalised power structures of Chilean society rather than their negation. This places the coalition in a tension-laden political position. At one and the same time, the Concertación has been pressured to respond to the contradictions of neoliberal restructuring even as it reproduces the fundamental relationships forged by the neoliberal project.

How these tensions will continue to unfold in Chile – and Latin America more generally – remains unclear and is contingent on a range of social struggles at national, regional and global levels. Even a cursory glance at the contemporary global political economy reveals that the array of social forces committed to upholding neoliberalism at national and global levels is daunting and may lead us to suggest that far-reaching transformations of politics and society are remote. However, it should be borne in mind that, in 1970, one would most probably have been mocked for suggesting that, within five years, Chile would witness the death of Keynesian-influenced national developmentalism and, within ten years, experience the reconfiguration of the country's entire institutional structure in a way that reversed a 50-year trajectory of struggle-driven institution building. The rise of neoliberalism in Latin America was swift, and historical precedents suggest that, as its contradictions continue to evolve, its decline could be equally rapid. It is little surprise, therefore, that within these conditions the spectre of Karl Polanyi's historical account of the earlier rise and fall of the self-regulating market has once again become in vogue (see Munck 2002).

Some signs of a decline of neoliberalism have been evident in Latin America for a number of years. The collapse of the Argentine economy in 2001 brought social devastation to a former poster-child, much in the same way the Peso Crisis had ended neoliberal triumphalism in Mexico seven years previous. As recent events in Brazil, Mexico, Argentina, Bolivia and others demonstrate, the political tide in Latin America is shifting leftwards, causing consternation in the bodies of the US executive and on the pages of journals such as *The Financial Times* and *The Economist*, among others. Even more explicitly, Venezuelan president Hugo Chavez has become a vociferous focal point for anti-neoliberal rhetoric from across the continent, although this in turn expresses the complex social transformations ongoing in Venezuela over the late 1990s and into the new millennium. At the heart of these continent-wide events is a rejection of the insecuritisation of social reproduction and society-wide polarisation that lie at the heart of capitalist social relations and which have become ever more explicit during the neoliberal epoch in Latin America.

In Chile, frustrations over the inability of the Concertación to deliver a more profound process of social transformation have led to tensions between the parties within the governing coalition and to conflicts with its grassroots. More than this, they have provided the momentum for a continuing shift of the political ground towards the left, a process that will see the Socialist Party put forward a second successive presidential candidate for the Concertación in 2006, something unthinkable in the mid-1990s when the Christian Democrat wing represented the most powerful political ground. In this respect, Michelle Bachelet, the Concertación's candidate for the 2006 presidential elections has suggested a need to reinvigorate the equity side of the 'growth with equity' programme. The more precise proposals, however, indicate a further deepening rather than any substantial transformation of this approach. As with previous Concertación reforms, the strategy aims to provide an added yet limited degree of social protection while constraining actors within a framework of individualised market exchanges. Seemingly contingent market failures are addressed in a sporadic fashion, and popular mobilisation is encouraged only in so far as it contributes to eliminating apparent market distortions – as in the FOSIS programme examined in the previous chapter – but is obstructed from proceeding any further.

The full dynamics of political and social change in Chile, however, will only unfold within the context of the trajectory of capital accumulation at a global level. Throughout the first decade of the Concertación, strong capital accumulation was envisaged to provide the Chilean state with the material resources it needed to maintain a tenuous social peace. However, to assume levels of accumulation similar to those of the early and mid-1990s is a significant leap of faith. Not only has the primary-commodity export model looked increasingly unable to fashion a sustainable long-term future for the Chilean populace, but it also remains susceptible to short-term rupture. Neoliberalism has sought to overcome the problems of capital accumulation within Chile by seeking ever-greater integration into markets that are global in scope. Far from resolving the crisis-prone tendencies of capital accumulation, however, this strategy merely juxtaposes the locus of expansion and crisis to a global level. Chile – like much of Latin America – is particularly vulnerable to the euphemistically labelled 'external shocks', whether these take the form of fluctuating global demand, overproduction of staple commodities, or contagious financial crises. In a global political economy that observers from all sides of the political spectrum recognise as characterised by significant imbalances, it is fair to assume that the litany of crises that punctuated the previous ten years is far from over. What the effects of further crisis within Latin America – whose populace suffered from three recessions within the space of a decade between 1994 and 2004 – would have on popular movements for social change is far from clear. Nonetheless, there appears to be a rapidly consolidating political resolve to attempt to re-embed market forces within systems of social protection, and this will necessitate potentially profound forms of institutional restructuring that will need to tackle entrenched power asymmetries, both locally and at an international level. The barriers to such events are multiple and steep, yet they are obstacles that need to be overcome to create better societies for tomorrow.

References

Acker, Joan. 2004. 'Gender, Capitalism and Globalization', *Critical Sociology* 30(1), pp. 17–41.

Acuña, Rodrigo and Augusto Iglesias. 2000. 'La Reforma a las Pensiones', in *La Transformación Económica de Chile*, edited by F. Larraín and R. Vergara. Santiago: Centro de Estudios Públicos.

Agacino, Rafael, Cristián González and Jorge Rojas. 1998. *Capital Transnacional y Trabajo: El Desarollo Minero en Chile*. Santiago: Ediciones LOM.

Agosín, Manuel. 2000. 'Reformas Comerciales, Exportaciones y Crecimiento', in *Reformas, Crecimiento y Políticas Sociales en Chile desde 1973*, edited by R. Ffrench-Davis and B. Stallings. Santiago: Ediciones LOM.

Aguilar Ibarra, Alonso, Chris Reid and Andy Thorpe. 2000. 'The Political Economy of Marine Fisheries Development in Peru, Chile and Mexico', *Journal of Latin American Studies* 32(2), pp. 503–27.

Alarcón, Cecilia and Giovanni Stumpo. 2000. 'Pequeñas y medianas empresas industriales en Chile', Working Paper, CEPAL / United Nations.

Angell, Alan. 1993. 'Chile since 1958', pp. 129–202 in *Chile Since Independence*, edited by L. Bethell. Cambridge: Cambridge University Press.

Angell, Alan and Benny Pollack. 2000. 'The Chilean Presidential Elections of 1999–2000 and Democratic Consolidation', *Bulletin of Latin American Research* no. 19, pp. 357–78.

Angell, Alan, Pamela Lowden and Rosemary Thorp. 2001. *Decentralizing Development: The Political Economy of Institutional Change in Colombia and Chile*. Oxford: Oxford University Press.

Aninat, Eduardo. 2000. 'Embracing Development Opportunities', *Finance and Development* 37(1).

Austin, Robert. 1997. 'Armed Forces, Market Forces: Intellectuals and Higher Education in Chile, 1973–1993', *Latin American Perspectives* 24(5).

Barrera, Manuel and J. Samuel Valenzuela. 1986. 'The Development of Labour Movement Opposition to the Military Regime', in *Military Rule in Chile: Dictatorship and Oppositions*, edited by S. Valenzuela and A. Valenzuela. Baltimore: Johns Hopkins Press.

Barrett, Gene, Mauricio Caniggia and Lorna Read. 2002. 'There are More Vets than Doctors in Chiloé: Social and Community Impact of the Globalization of Aquaculture in Chile', *World Development* 30(11), pp. 1951–65.

Barrientos, Armando. 2002. 'Health Policy in Chile: The Return of the Public Sector?' *Bulletin of Latin American Research* 21(3), pp. 442–59.

Barrientos, Jorge. 1999. *Coordinating Poverty Alleviation Programs with Regional and Local Governments: The Experience of the Chilean Social Fund (FOSIS)*. Washington: World Bank.

Barro, Robert. 2000. 'One Pinochet Legacy That Deserves to Live', *Business Week*, 17 January 2000, pp. 22.

Barton, Jonathan. 2002. 'State Continuismo and Pinochetismo: The Keys to the Chilean Transition', *Bulletin of Latin American Research* 21(3), pp. 358–74.

——. 2004. 'The Legacy of Popular Unity: Chile 1973–2003', *Capital & Class* no. 82, pp. 9–16.

Barton, Jonathan and Warwick Murray. 2002. 'The End of Transition? Chile 1990–2000', *Bulletin of Latin American Research* 21(3), pp. 329–38.

Berger, Mark. 2004. *The Battle for Asia: From Decolonization to Globalization.* New York and London: Routledge.

Beyer, Harald. 2000. 'Entre la Autonomía y la Intervención: Las Reformas de la Educación en Chile', in *La Transformación Económica de Chile*, edited by F. Larraín and R. Vergara. Santiago: Centro de Estudios Públicos.

Bitran, Eduardo and Pablo Serra. 1998. 'Regulation of Privatized Utilities: The Chilean Experience', *World Development* 26(6), pp. 945–62.

Blakemore, Harold. 1993. 'From the War of the Pacific to 1930', pp. 33–86 in *Chile Since Independence*, edited by L. Bethell. Cambridge: Cambridge University Press.

Bonefeld, Werner. 2000. 'The Spectre of Globalization: On the form and content of the World Market', in *The Politics of Change: Globalization, Ideology and Critique*, edited by W. Bonefeld and K. Psychopedis. Basingstoke: Palgrave Macmillan.

——. 2005. 'Europe, the Market and the Transformation of Democracy', *Journal of Contemporary European Studies* 13(1), pp. 93–106.

Borzutzky, Silvia. 2001. 'Chile: Has Social Security Privatisation Fostered Economic Development?' *International Journal of Social Welfare* 10(4), pp. 294–99.

——. 2002. *Vital Connections: Politics, Social Security, and Inequality in Chile.* Notre Dame: University of Notre Dame Press.

Bossert, Thomas. 1980. 'The Agrarian Reform and Peasant Political Consciousness in Chile', *Latin American Perspectives* 7(4), pp. 6–28.

Bresnahan, Rosalind. 2003. 'The Media and the Neoliberal Transition in Chile: Democratic Promise Unfulfilled', *Latin American Perspectives* 30(6), pp. 39–68.

Brohman, John. 1995. 'Economism and Critical Silences in Development Studies: A Theoretical Critique of Neoliberalism', *Third World Quarterly* 16(2), pp. 297–318.

Burkett, Paul and Martin Hart-Landsberg. 2000. *Development, Crisis and Class Struggle: Learning from Japan and East Asia.* New York: St Martin's Press.

Burnham, Peter. 2000. 'Globalisation, Depoliticisation and "Modern" Economic Management', in *The Politics of Change: Globalisation, Ideology and Critique*, edited by W. Bonefeld and K. Psychopedis. Basingstoke: Palgrave Macmillan.

Cademartori, Jose. 2003. 'The Chilean Neoliberal Model Enters into Crisis', *Latin American Perspectives* 30(5), pp. 79–88.

Campbell, John L. and Ove Kaj Pedersen. 2001. *The Rise of Neoliberalism and Institutional Analysis.* Princeton: Princeton University Press.

Campero, Guillermo. 2004. 'Macroeconomic Reforms, Labour Markets and Labour Policies: Chile, 1973–2000', in *International Labour Office Employment Analysis Unit Papers*. Geneva: International Labour Office.

Carnoy, Martin and Patrick McEwan. 2000. 'Does Privatization Improve Education? The Case of Chile's National Voucher Plan', in *Working Paper, International Comparative Education Programme, University of Stanford.*

Castiglioni, Rossana. 2001. 'The Politics of Retrenchment: The Quandaries of Social Protection Under Military Rule in Chile', *Latin American Politics and Society* 45(1), pp. 37–56.

——. 2005. *The Politics of Social Policy Change in Chile and Uruguay: Retrenchment Versus Maintenance, 1973–1998*. London: Routledge.

Castillo, Patricia Olave. 1997. *El Proyecto Neoliberal en Chile y la Construcción de una Nueva Economía*. Mexico City: UNAM.

Cato Institute. 2005. 'Project on Social Security Choice', April 2005. Washington, DC.

CEPAL (Comisión Económica de America Latina y el Caribe). 1999. *Annuario Estadístico 1999*. Santiago: CEPAL.

——. 2001a. *Annuario Estadístico 2001*. Santiago: CEPAL.

——. 2001b. *Estudio Económico de América Latina y el Caribe 2000–2001*. Santiago: CEPAL.

Chacón, Borris. 1999. 'Calidad del empleo y pobreza en Chile, 1990–1996', in *La Calidad del Empleo: La Experiencia de los Países Latinoamericanos y de los Estados Unidos*, edited by R. Infante. Santiago: Oficina Internacional del Trabajo.

Cid, Beatriz. 2001. *Trabajadoras Temporales de la Agroindustria*. Santiago: Universidad de Chile.

Cid Pedraza, C. 2001. 'Algunas Consideraciones Sobre la Situación Actual de la Seguridad Social de Salud en Chile', in *Visiones Económicas*, Santiago: ARCIS.

Clarke, Simon. 1988. *Keynesianism, Monetarism and the Crisis of the State*. Aldershot: Edward Elgar Press.

——. 1990. 'The Marxist Theory of Overaccumulation and Crisis', *Science and Society* 54(4), pp. 442–67.

——. 1991a. *Marx, Marginalism and Modern Sociology*. London: Macmillan.

——. 1991b. *The State Debate*. London: Macmillan.

——. 1994. *Marx's Theory of Crisis*. London: Macmillan.

——. 1999. *The Formation of a Labour Market in Russia*. Aldershot: Edward Elgar Publishing.

Claude, Marcel. 1999. 'Las Miserias del Desarrollo Chileno (una Mirada desde la Sustentabilidad)', in *El Modelo Chileno: Democracia y Desarrollo en los Noventa*, edited by P. Drake and I. Jaksic. Santiago: LOM.

Collier, Simon and William Sater. 2004. *A History of Chile, 1808–2002*. Cambridge: Cambridge University Press.

Coloma, Fernando and Patricio Rojas. 2000. 'Evolución del Mercado Laboral en Chile: Reformas y Resultados', in *La Transformación Económica en Chile*, edited by F. Larraín and R. Vergara. Santiago: Centro de Estudios Públicos.

Cortazár, René. 1997. 'Chile: The Evolution and the Reform of Labour Markets', in *Labour Markets in Latin America: Combining Social Protection with Market Flexibility*, edited by S. Edwards and N. Lustig. Washington: Brookings Institution.

Cypher, James. 2003. 'La Economia Chilena: Trasturnos y muestras del modelo neoliberal maduro', in *Semenario de Flacso*. Santiago, Chile.

——. 2004. 'Pinochet Meets Polanyi? The Curious Case of the Chilean Embrace of "Free" Market Economics', *Journal of Economic Issues* 38(2), pp. 527–36.

De la Maza, Gonzalo. 1999. 'Los Movimientos Sociales en la Democratisación de Chile', in *El Modelo Chileno: Democracia y Desarollo en los Noventa.*, edited by P. Drake and I. Jaksic. Santiago: LOM.

DeMartino, George. 2000. *Global Economy, Global Justice: Theoretical Objections and Policy Alternatives to Neoliberalism*. London and New York: Routledge.

Deraniyagala, Sonali. 2001. 'From Washington to Post-Washington: Does It Matter for Industrial Policy?' in *Development Policy in the Twenty-First Century: Beyond the Post-Washington Consensus*, edited by B. Fine, C. Lapavitsas and J. Pincus. London: Routledge.

DeShazo, Peter. 1983. *Urban Workers and Labor Unions in Chile, 1902–1927*. Madison: University of Wisconsin Press.

Díaz, Alvaro. 1993. *Restructuring and the New Working Classes in Chile: Trends in Waged Employment, Informality and Poverty*. Geneva: UNRISD.

——. 1997. 'Chile: Neoliberal Policy, Socioeconomic Reorganization, and Urban Labour Market', in *Global Restructuring, Employment, and Social Inequality in Urban Latin America*, edited by R. Tardanico and R. Menjívar Larín. Miami: North-South Center Press.

Drake, Paul. 1993. 'Chile, 1930–1958', in *Chile Since Independence*, edited by L. Bethell. Cambridge: Cambridge University Press.

Drake, Paul and Ivan Jaksic. 1999. *El Modelo Chileno*. Santiago: LOM.

Duhau, Emilio. 1997. 'Las Políticas Sociales en América Latina: Del Universalismo Fragmentado a la Dualización?' *Revista Mexicana de Sociología* 2, pp. 185–207.

The Economist. 2002. 'A New Prescription', 14 September, 2002. London.

Edwards, Paul and Tony Elger (eds). 1999. *The Global Economy, National States and the Regulation of Labour*. London: Mansell.

Edwards, Paul and Jacques Belanger. 1994. 'Introduction: The Workplace and Labour Regulation in Comparative Perspective', in *Workplace Industrial Relations and the Global Challenge*, edited by P. Edwards, J. Belanger and L. Haiven. Ithaca: ILR Press.

El Mostrador. 2001a. 'Crece tensión entre Gobierno y empresarios por reforma laboral', 1 September. Santiago, Chile.

——. 2001b. 'Gobierno presentó 15 indicaciones a la reforma laboral', 5 September. Santiago, Chile.

——. 2002. 'Huelga en CTC: Flexibilidad laboral o Despidos Masivos?' 22 July. Santiago, Chile.

El Siglo. 2001. 'Reforma Laboral', 14 September. Santiago, Chile.

Epstein, Edward. 1993. 'Labour and Political Stability in the New Chilean Democracy: Three Illusions', *Economía & Trabajo* 1(2), pp. 47–64.

Escobar, Patricio. 1999a. 'Hacia una caracteriación del mercado del trabajo', in *Trabajadores y Empleo en el Chile de los Noventa*, edited by P. Escobar. Santiago: LOM.

——. 1999b. 'La Crisis de la Economía Chilena: el fin de un largo ciclo de rápida expansion', *Economía & Trabajo* (9), pp. 7–26.

Escobar, Patricio and Diego López. 1996. *El Sector Forestal en Chile: Crecimiento y Precarización del Empleo*. Santiago: Ediciones Tierra Mia / PET.

Esping-Andersen, Gøsta. 1990. *The Three Worlds of Welfare Capitalism*. Cambridge: Polity Press.

Fazio, Hugo. 2000. *La Transnacionalización de la Economía Chilena: Mapa de la Extrema Riqueza al año 2000*. Santiago: LOM.

——. 2001a. *Crece La Desigualidad*. Santiago: LOM.

——. 2001b. 'Sistema Tibutario Chileno', *Visiones Económicas* (01/08).

Fazio, Hugo and Manuel Riesco. 1997. 'Chilean Pension Fund Associations', *New Left Review* (223), pp. 90–100.

Fernández Jilberto, Alex. 1993. 'Chile: The Laboratory Experiment of International Neoliberalism', in *Restructuring Hegemony in the Global Political Economy*, edited by H. Overbeek. London: Routledge.

——. 2000. 'América Latina: el debate sobre los "Nuevos Grupos Económicos" y conglomerados industrials después de la reestructuración neoliberal', *European Review of Latin American and Caribbean Studies* (69), pp. 97–108.

Ffrench-Davis, Ricardo. 2002a. *Economic Reforms in Chile: From Dictatorship to Democracy*. Ann Arbor: University of Michigan Press.

——. 2002b. 'Export Dynamism and Growth in Chile Since the 1980s', *CEPAL Review* (No. 76).

Ffrench-Davis, Ricardo and Babara Stallings. 2001. *Reformas, Crecimiento y Politicas Sociales en Chile Desde 1973*. Santiago: LOM.

Ffrench-Davis, Ricardo and Heriberto Tapia. 2001. 'Políticas Económicas y la Cuenta de Capitales', pp. 61–99 in *Reformas, Crecimiento y Politicas Sociales en Chile desde 1973*, edited by B. Stallings and R. Ffrench-Davis. Santiago: LOM.

Financial Times. 2001. 'Chile's Leader Takes Careful Path to Reform', 1 October, London.

——. 2003. 'Chile Prepares for General Strike', 12 August, London.

Fine, Ben. 2001a. 'Neither the Washington Nor the Post-Washington Consensus', in *Development Policy in the Twenty-First Century: Beyond the Post-Washington Consensus*, edited by B. Fine, C. Lapavitsas and J. Pincus. London: Routledge.

——. 2001b. *Social Capital Versus Social Theory*. London: Routledge.

——. 2003. 'Contesting Labour Markets', in *Anti-Capitalism*, edited by A. Saad-Filho. London: Pluto.

FNPSP (Fundación Nacional Para la Superación de la Pobreza). 2000. *'Propuestas Para la Futura Política Social'*.

Fortín, Carlos. 1985. 'The Political Economy of Repressive Monetarism: The State and Capital Accumulation in Post-1973 Chile', in *The State and Capital Accumulation in Latin America*, vol. 1, edited by C. Anglade and C. Fortín. London: Macmillan.

Foweraker, Joe. 2001. 'Grassroots Movements and Political Activism in Latin America: A Critical Comparison of Chile and Brazil', *Journal of Latin American Studies* 33(4), pp. 839–65.

Foxley, Alejandro. 1986. 'The Neoconservative Economic Experiment in Chile', in *Military Rule in Chile: Dictatorship and Oppositions*, edited by A. Valenzuela and S. Valenzuela. Baltimore: Johns Hopkins Press.

Frank, Andre Gunder. 1969. *Capitalism and Underdevelopment in Latin America: Historical Studies of Chile and Brazil*. New York: Monthly Review Press.

——. 1975. 'Commentary on Chile', *Conference of Socialist Economists Bulletin* (12).

Frank, Volker. 2004. 'Politics Without Policy: The Failure of Social Concertación in Democratic Chile, 1990–2000', in *Victims of the Chilean Miracle: Workers and Neoliberalism in the Pinochet Era, 1973–2002*, edited by P. Winn. Durham: Duke University Press.

Friedman, Milton. 1962. *Capitalism and Freedom*. Chicago: University of Chicago Press.

Fullbrook, Edward. 2005. 'Post-Autistic Economics', *Soundings: A Journal of Politics and Culture* (29).

Gajardo, Jaime. 2002. 'Las autoridades deben reconocer que la reforma educacional ha fracasado', in *El Siglo*, 20 February. Santiago, Chile.

Garland, Allison. 2000. 'The Politics and Administration of Social Development in Latin America', in *Social Development in Latin America*, edited by J. Tulchin and A. Garland. Boulder: Lynne Rienner.

Gaury, Varun. 1998. *School Choice in Chile: Two Decades of Educational Reform*. Pittsburgh: University of Pittsburgh Press.

George, Susan and Fabrizio Sabelli. 1994. *Faith and Credit: The World Bank's Secular Empire*. London: Penguin.

Giddens, Anthony. 1998. *The Third Way: The Renewal of Social Democracy*. Cambridge: Polity.

——. 2003. 'The World Has Not Heard the Last of the Third Way', *Financial Times*, 11 July. London.

Gideon, Jasmine. 2002. 'Decentralization, Participation and Inclusion? Reassessing Primary Health Care Delivery in Chile', in *Social Policy Reform and Market Governance in Latin America*, edited by L. Haagh and C. Helgø. Basingstoke: Palgrave Macmillan.

González, Cristián. 1999. 'El Derecho Laboral en Chile: Situación Actual y Propuestas de Reforma', in *Trabajadores y Empleo en el Chile de los Noventa*, edited by P. Escobar. Santiago: LOM.

Grabel, Ilene. 2000. 'The Political Economy of "Policy Credibility": The New-Classical Macroeconomics and the Remaking of Emerging Economies', *Cambridge Journal of Economics* 24, pp. 1–19.

——. 2003. 'Averting Crisis? Assessing Measures to Manage Financial Integration in Emerging Economies', *Cambridge Journal of Economics* vol. 27, pp. 317–36.

Graham, Carol. 1991. *From Emergency Employment to Social Investment: Alleviating Poverty in Chile*. Washington: Brookings Institution.

Greaves, Edward. 2005. 'Panoptic Municipalities, the Spatial Dimensions of the Political, and Passive Revolution in Post-Dictatorship Chile', *City & Community* 4(2), pp. 189–216.

Green, Duncan. 1995. *Silent Revolution: The Rise of Market Economics in Latin America*. New York: Monthly Review Press.

Gwynne, Robert and Cristóbal Kay. 1997. 'Agrarian Change and the Democratic Transition in Chile: An Introduction', *Bulletin of Latin American Research* 16(1), pp. 3–10.

——. 2001. 'Views from the Periphery: Futures of Neoliberalism in Latin America', *Third World Quarterly* 21(1), pp. 141–56.

Haagh, Louise. 2002a. *Citizenship, Labour Markets and Democratization: Chile and the Modern Sequence*. Basingstoke: Palgrave Macmillan.

———. 2002b. 'The Emperor's New Clothes: Labor Reform and Social Democratization in Chile', *Studies in Comparative International Development* 37(1), pp. 86–115.

———. 2002c. 'Markets and Rights in the Governance of Welfare: Latin America's Market Reforms', in *Social Policy Reform and Market Governance in Latin America*, edited by L. Haagh and C. Helgø. Basingstoke: Palgrave Macmillan.

Hachette, Dominique. 2000. 'Privatiziciones: Reforma Estructural Pero Inconclusa', in *La Transformación Económica de Chile*, edited by F. Larraín and R. Vergara. Santiago: Centro de Estudios Públicos.

Hannon, Brian and Scott Gould. 1987. 'Debt-Equity Swaps Help Latin America Out of its Debt Dilemma', in *Business America*, 19 January.

Harnecker, Marta. 2003. 'Understanding the Past to Make the Future: Reflections on Allende's Government', *Historical Materialism* 11(3), pp. 5–15.

Hart-Landsberg, Martin and Paul Burkett. 2005. *China and Socialism: Market Reforms and Class Struggle*. New York: Monthly Review Press.

Hayek, Friedrich A. von. 1973. *Law, Legislation and Liberty: A New Statement of the Liberal Principles of Justice and Political Economy*. Chicago: University of Chicago Press.

Held, Gunther and Luis Felipe Jimenez. 2001. 'Liberalización, crisis y reforma del sistema bancario, 1974–99', in *Reformas Comerciales, Exportaciones y Crecimiento*, edited by B. Stallings and R. Ffrench-Davis. Santiago: CEPAL / LOM.

Helgø, Camilla. 2002. 'Market-Orientated Education Reforms and Social Inequalities Among the Young Population in Chile', in *Social Policy Reform and Market Governance in Latin America*, edited by L. Haagh and C. Helgø. Basingstoke: Palgrave Macmillan.

Helleiner, Eric. 1994. *States and the Reemergence of Global Finance: From Bretton Woods to the 1990s*. New York: Cornell University Press.

Henríquez Riquelme, Helia. 1999. 'Las Relaciones Laborales en Chile. Un sistema colectivo o un amplio espacio para la dispersión?' in *El Modelo Chileno*, edited by P. Drake and I. Jaksic. Santiago: LOM.

Heritage Foundation. 2003. *2003 Index of Economic Freedom*. Washington: Heritage Foundation.

Hiscock, J. and D. Hojman. 1997. 'Social Policy in a Fast Growing Economy: The Case of Chile', *Social Policy and Administration* 31(4), pp. 354–70.

Hodgson, Geoffrey. 1999. *Economics and Utopia: Why the Learning Economy is Not the End of History*. London and New York: Routledge.

———. 2001. *How Economics Forgot History: The Problem of Historical Specificity in Social Science*. London and New York: Routledge.

Hojman, David and Mark Ramsden. 1993. 'Employment and the Labour Market in Chile: Trends, Fluctuations, and Prospects for the 1990s', in *The Legacy of Dictatorship: Political, Economic and Social Change in Pinochet's Chile*, edited by A. Angell and B. Pollack. Liverpool: Institute of Latin American Studies.

Holloway, John and Sol Picciotto. 1977. 'Capital, Crisis and the State', *Capital & Class* no. 2.

Huber, Evelyne. 1996. 'Options for Social Policy in Latin America: Neoliberal versus Social Democratic Models', in *Welfare States in Transition*, edited by G. Esping-Andersen. London: Sage.

ICFTU (International Confederation of Free Trade Unions). 1997. 'Internationally-Recognized Core Labour Standards in Chile', in *Report for the WTO Genderal Council Review of the Trade Policies of Chile*. Geneva.

IMF (International Monetary Fund). 2000. 'Chile: Selected Issues', S. C. Report: IMF.

——. 2002. 'Chile – Selected Issues', S. C. Report: IMF.

Itoh, Makoto and Costas Lapavitsas. 1999. *The Political Economy of Money and Finance*. New York: St Martin's Press.

Jadresic, Esteban and Roberto Zahler. 2000. 'Chile's Rapid Growth in the 1990s: Good Policies, Good Luck, or Political Change?' *IMF Working Paper* WP/00/153.

Javier, Francisco and Jose Fuentes. 2000. 'The State of Economic Processes', in *Chile in the Nineties*, edited by C. Toloza and E. Lahera. Stanford: Stanford University Press.

Katzner, Donald. 2003. 'Equilibrium and Non-Equilibrium', pp. 126–31 in *The Elgar Companion to Post Keynesian Economics*, edited by J.E. King. Cheltenham: Edward Elgar.

Kay, Cristóbal. 1978. 'Agrarian Reform and the Class Struggle in Chile', *Latin American Perspectives* 3(5), pp. 117–42.

——. 1989. *Latin American Theories of Development and Underdevelopment*. London: Routledge.

Kay, Geoffrey. 1975. *Development and Underdevelopment: A Marxist Analysis*. London: Macmillan.

Keaney, Michael. 2005. 'Social Democracy, Laissez-faire and the "Third Way" of Capitalist Development', *Review of Radical Political Economics* 37(3), pp. 357–78.

Kirkendall, Andrew. 2004. 'Paulo Freire, Eduardo Frei, Literacy Training and the Politics of Consciousness Raising in Chile, 1964 to 1970', *Journal of Latin American Studies* (36), pp. 687–717.

Körner, Peter. 1986. *The IMF and the Debt Crisis: A Guide to the Third World's Dilemma*. London: Zed Books.

Krueger, Anne. 2000. 'Economic Policy Reform: The Second Stage', Chicago: University of Chicago Press.

Kurtz, Marcus. 1999. 'Free Markets and Democratic Consolidation in Chile: The National Politics of Rural Transformation', *Politics and Society* 27(2), pp. 275–302.

——. 2001. 'State Developmentalism Without a Developmental State: The Public Foundations of the "Free Market Miracle" in Chile', *Latin American Politics and Society* 43(2), pp. 1–28.

La Otra Ecónomia. 2002. 'Sobreproducción de Bienes', 14 April.

Lagos, Juan Francisco. 1999. 'Chile exportador de cobre en bruto: una involución en la composición de las exportaciones de su principal riqueza mineral', *Economía & Trabajo* no. 9.

Lahera, Eugenio and Mabel Cabezas. 2000. 'Governance and Institutional Development of the Chilean Economy', *Journal of International Development* 12, pp. 1087–109.

Larraín, Felipe and Rodrigo Vergara. 2000. 'Un Cuarto de Siglo de Reformas Fiscales', in *La Transformación Económica de Chile*, edited by F. Larraín and R. Vergara. Santiago: Centro de Estudios Públicos.

Larraín, Felipe, Jeffrey Sachs and Andrew Warner. 2000. 'A Structural Analysis of Chile's Long-Term Growth: History, Prospects and Policy Implications', Santiago: Report for the Government of Chile.

Lemco, Jonathan and Scott B. MacDonald. 2001. 'Latin America's Volatile Financial Markets', Current History, February 2001, pp. 86–9.

León, Arturo and Javier Martínez. 1998. 'La estratificación social chilena hacia fines del siglo XX', pp. 285–311 in Chile en los Noventa, vol. II, edited by C. Toloza and E. Lahera. Santiago: Ediciones Dolmen.

Lifsher, Marc. 2003. 'Latin America Gets Boost From China's Success', Wall Street Journal Online. New York.

Madrid, Raul. 2005. 'Ideas, Economic Pressures and Pension Privatization', Latin American Politics and Society 47(2), pp. 23–51.

Marshall, Jorge. 2003. 'Fiscal Rule and Central Bank Issues in Chile', no. 20 in BIS Papers: Bank of International Settlements.

Martin, Maria Pia. 2000. 'Integration and Development: A Vision of Social Policy', in Chile in the Nineties, edited by C. Toloza and E. Lahera. Stanford: Stanford University Press.

Martínez, Javier and Alvaro Díaz. 1996. Chile: The Great Transformation. Washington: Brookings Institution.

Martins, Joaquim Oliviera and Nanno Mulder. 2003. 'Chile's Economy: The Way Forward', OECD Observer (240/241).

Marx, Karl. 1973. Grundrisse. London: Penguin Books.

——. 1976. Capital – Vol. 1. London: Penguin Books.

Mesa-Lago, Carmelo. 1989. Ascent to Bankruptcy: Financing Social Security in Latin America. Pittsburgh: University of Pittsburgh Press.

——. 2002. 'Myth and Reality of Pension Reform: The Latin American Evidence', World Development 30(8), pp. 1309–21.

MIDEPLAN (Ministerio de Planificación y Cooperación). 1998. Evolución del empleo en Chile, 1990–1996. Santiago: MIDEPLAN.

——. 2000. Impacto Distributivo del Gasto Social 1998. MIDEPLAN, Santiago, Chile.

——. 2001a. Impacto Distributivo de Gasto Social 2000. MIDEPLAN, Santiago, Chile.

——. 2001b. Indicadores Económicos y Sociales, 1990–2000', MIDEPLAN, Santiago, Chile.

Mies, Maria. 1986. Patriarchy and Accumulation on a World Scale: Women in the International Division of Labour. London: Zed Books.

Miller Klubock, Thomas. 2004a. 'Class, Community and Neoliberalism in Chile: Copper Workers and the Labor Movement During the Military Dictatorship and the Restoration of Democracy', in Victims of the Chilean Miracle: Workers and Neoliberalism in the Pinochet Era, 1973–2002, edited by P. Winn. Durham: Duke University Press.

——. 2004b. 'Labor, Land and the Environmental Change in the Forestry Sector in Chile, 1973–1998', in Victims of the Chilean Miracle: Workers and Neoliberalism in the Pinochet Era, 1973–2002, edited by P. Winn. Durham: Duke University Press.

Mizala, Alejandra and Pilar Romaguera. 2001. 'La Legislación Laboral y el Mercado del Trabajo: 1975–2000', in Reformas, Crecimiento y Políticas Sociales *en Chile desde 1973*, edited by R. Ffrench-Davis and B. Stallings. Santiago: LOM.

Moguillansky, Graciela. 2001. 'Privatizaciones y su impacto en la inversion', in *Reformas, Crecimiento y Políticas Sociales en Chile desde 1973*, edited by R. Ffrench-Davis and B. Stallings. Santiago: LOM.

Mönckeberg, María Olivia. 2001. *El Saqueo de los grupos económicos al Estado chileno*. Santiago: Ediciones B Chile, S.A.

Monteón, Michael. 1998. *Chile and the Great Depression: The Politics of Underdevelopment, 1927–1948*. Tempe: Arizona University Press.

Morris, James. 1966. *Elites, Intellectuals and Consensus: A Study of the Social Question and the Industrial Relations System in Chile*. Ithaca: Cornell University Press.

Mostrador, El. 2001. 'OIT acoge denuncia contra Chile por practicas antisindicales', in *El Mostrador*. Santiago.

Müller, Wolfgang and Christel Neusüss. 1975. 'The Illusion of State Socialism and the Contradiction between Wage Labor and Capital', *Telos* (25), pp. 3–45.

Mulligan, Mark. 2005. 'Latin America is Looking Healthy – For Now', *Financial Times*, 14 March. London.

Munck, Ronaldo. 2002. *Globalisation and Labour*. London: Zed Books.

Muñoz Gomá, Oscar and Carmen Caledón. 1996. 'Chile in Transition: Economic and Political Strategies', in *Economic Policy and the Transition to Democracy: The Latin American Experience*, edited by J. Morales and G. McMahon. New York: St Martin's Press.

Murray, Warwick. 2002. 'The Neoliberal Inheritance: Agrarian Policy and Rural Differentiation in Democratic Chile', *Bulletin of Latin American Research* 21(3), pp. 425–41.

Myers, Jason. 2002. 'Ideology After the Welfare State', *Historical Materialism* 10(2), pp. 171–89.

Neary, Mike and Graham Taylor. 1998. *Money and the Human Condition*. Basingstoke: Macmillan.

Nef, Jorge. 2003. 'The Chilean Model: Fact and Fiction', *Latin American Perspectives* 30(5), pp. 16–40.

Nesvetailova, Anastasia. 2005. 'United in Debt: Towards a Global Crisis of Debt-Driven Finance?' *Science and Society* 69(3), pp. 396–419.

O'Donnell, Guillermo. 1979. 'Tensions in the Bureaucratic-Authoritarian State and the Question of Democracy', in *The New Authoritarianism in Latin America*, edited by D. Collier. Princeton: Princeton University Press.

OECD (Organisation for Economic Co-operation and Development). 2003. 'Economic Survey – Chile 2003', Geneva: OECD.

Oppenheim, Lois Hecht. 1999. *Politics in Chile: Democracy, Authoritarianism, and the Search for Development*. Boulder: Westview Press.

Ossandón, Mario. 2002. 'Mercado Laboral y Pobreza', Concertación Publico-Privada Para El Desarrollo Económico. Presented at Santiago, Chile. 21 November.

Oxhorn, Philip. 1995. *Organizing Civil Society: The Popular Sectors and the Struggle for Democracy in Chile*. Pennsylvania: Pennsylvania State University Press.

Paiva, C. and M. Riesco. 2001. 'Sistema Chileno de AFP, Principales Problemas y Algunas Propuestas de Solución', *Visiones Económicas* (01/10).

Paley, Julia. 2001. *Marketing Democracy: Power and Social Movements in Post-Dictatorship Chile*. Berkeley: University of California Press.

Palley, Thomas. 2005. 'From Keynesianism to Neoliberalism: Shifting Paradigms in Economics', in *Neoliberalism: A Critical Reader*, edited by A. Saad-Filho and D. Johnston. London: Pluto.

Parker, Cristián, Gerardo Rivas and Daniel Causas. 1999. 'Evaluación de Impacto en Programas de Superación de Pobreza: El Caso del Fondo de Inversión Social (FOSIS) de Chile', Santiago: ECLAC.

Parrilli, Mario Davide. 2004. 'Integrating the National Industrial System: The New Challenge for Chile', *Review of International Political Economy* 11(5), pp. 905–25.

Pencavel, John. 1997. 'The Legal Framework for Collective Bargaining in Developing Economies', pp. 27–61 in *Labor Markets in Latin America: Combining Social Protection with Market Flexibility*, edited by S. Edwards and N. Lustig. Washington: Brookings Institution.

Perez-Aleman, Paola. 2000. 'Learning, Adjustment and Economic Development: Transforming Firms, The State and Associations in Chile', *World Development* 28(1), pp. 41–55.

——. 2003. 'Decentralised Production Organisation and Institutional Transformation: Large and Small Firm Networks in Chile and Nicaragua', *Cambridge Journal of Economics* 27, pp. 780–805.

Petras, James and Fernando Ignacio Leiva. 1994. *Democracy and Poverty in Chile: The Limits to Electoral Politics*. Boulder: Westview.

Petras, James F. and Hugo Zemelman. 1972. *Peasants in Revolt: A Chilean Case Study, 1965–1971*. Austin: University of Texas Press.

Phillips, Nicola. 2004. *The Southern Cone Model: The Political Economy of Regional Capitalist Development in Latin America*. London: Routledge.

Polanyi, Karl. 2001. *The Great Transformation: The Political and Economic Origins of Our Time*. Boston: Beacon Press.

Portales, Felipe. 2000. *Chile: Una Democracia Tutelada*. Santiago: Editorial Sudamericana.

Postone, Moishe. 1993. *Time, Labour and Social Domination*. Cambridge: Cambridge University Press.

Pregger-Roman, Charles. 1983. 'The Origin and Development of the Bourgeoisie in Nineteenth-Century Chile', *Latin American Perspectives* 10(2/3), pp. 39–59.

Preinforme. 2001. *Preinforme de la comisión investigadora encargada de analizar los incumplimientos empresariales de la normativa laboral vigente*. Santiago: Gobierno de Chile.

Raczynski, Dagmar. 1998. 'The Crisis of Old Models of Social Protection in Latin America: New Alternatives for Dealing with Poverty', in *Poverty and Inequality in Latin America: Issues and New Challenges*, edited by V. Tokman and G. O'Donnell. Notre Dame: University of Notre Dame Press.

——. 1999. 'Políticas socials en los años noventa en Chile. Balance y desafíos', in *El Modelo Chileno: Democracia y Desarrollo en los Noventa*, edited by P. Drake and I. Jaksic. Santiago: LOM.

———. 2000. 'Overcoming Poverty in Chile', in *Social Development in Latin America: The Politics of Reform*, edited by J. Tulchin and A. Garland. Boulder: Lynne Rienner Press.

Raczynski, Dagmar and Pilar Romaguera. 1995. 'Chile: Poverty, Adjustment and Social Policies in the 1980s', in *Coping With Austerity: Poverty and Inequality in Latin America*, edited by N. Lustig. Washington: Brookings Institution.

Radice, Hugo. 1984. 'The National Economy: A Keynesian Myth?' *Capital & Class* (22), pp. 111–40.

Rayo, Gustavo and Gonzalo De la Maza. 1998. 'La Acción Colectiva Popular Urbana', pp. 427–69 in *Chile en Los Noventa: Tomo 1*, edited by C. Toloza and E. Lahera. Santiago: Ediciones Dolmen.

Riesco, Manuel. 1999. 'Chile, a Quarter of a Century On', *New Left Review* (238), pp. 97–123.

———. 2005. 'Lessons for Proposed U.S. Social Security Reform: 25 Years Reveal Myths of Privatized Federal Pensions in Chile', edited by I. A. Program: International Relations Center, Silver City: NM.

Ritter, Archibald. 1992. *Development Strategy and Structural Adjustment in Chile: From the Unidad Popular to the Concertación*. Ottawa: North-South Institute.

Roberts, Kenneth. 1998a. *Deepening Democracy: The Modern Left and Social Movements in Chile and Peru*. Stanford: University of Stanford Press.

———. 1998b. *Deepening Democracy? The Modern Left and Social Movements in Chile and Peru*. Stanford: Stanford University Press.

Robinson, William I. 1996. *Promoting Polyarchy: Globalization, US Intervention, and Hegemony*. New York: Cambridge University Press.

Roddick, Jacqueline. 1989. 'The State, Industrial Relations and the Labour Movement in Chile', in *The State, Industrial Relations and the Labour Movement in Latin America: Vol 1*, edited by J. Carrière, N. Haworth and J. Roddick. London: Macmillan.

Rosales, Osvaldo. 1998. 'Transformación productiva: competitividad y generación de empleo', in *Chile en Los Noventa: Tomo 1*, edited by C. Toloza and E. Lahera. Santiago: Ediciones Dolmen.

———. 2000. 'Productive Transformation: Competitiveness and Job Creation', pp. 207–32 in *Chile in the Nineties*, edited by C. Toloza and E. Lahera. Stanford: Stanford University Press.

Roxborough, Ian, Phil O'Brien and Jacqueline Roddick. 1977. *Chile: The State and Revolution*. London: Macmillan.

Ruiz-Tagle, Jaime. 1993. 'Desafíos del sindicalismo chileno frente a la flexibilización del mercado de trabajo', *Economía & Trabajo* 1(1), pp. 137–53.

Saad-Filho, Alfredo. 2005. 'Monetary Policy and Social Discipline: From Keynesianism to the New Monetary Policy Consensus', *Mimeo*.

Salazar, Gabriel and Julio Pinto. 1999. *Historia Contemporánea de Chile I: Estado, Legitimidad, Ciudadanía*. Santiago: LOM.

Salman, Ton. 1994. 'Challenging the City, Joining the City: The Chilean Pobladores Between Social Movement and Social Integration', *Bulletin of Latin American Research* 13(1), pp. 79–90.

Sayer, Andrew. 1995. *Radical Political Economy: A Critique*. Oxford [England]; Cambridge, Mass.: Blackwell.

Schamis, Hector E. 2002. *Re-forming the State: The Politics of Privatization in Latin America and Europe*. Ann Arbor: University of Michigan Press.

Schneider, Cathy. 1993. 'Chile: The Underside of the Miracle', *NACLA – Report on the Americas* 26(4), pp. 30–1.

Schultz, T. Paul. 2000. 'Labour Market Reforms: Issues, Evidence and Prospects', in *Economic Policy Reform: The Second Stage*, edited by A. Krueger. Chicago: University of Chicago Press.

Schumpeter, Jospeh. 1975. *Capitalism, Socialism and Democracy*. New York: Harper.

Schurman, Rachel. 1996. 'Chile's New Entrepreneurs and the "Economic Miracle": The Invisible Hand or a Hand From the State?' *Studies in Comparative International Development* 31(2), pp. 83–110.

———. 2001. 'Uncertain Gains: Labor in Chile's New Export Sectors', *Latin American Research Review* 36(2), pp. 3–30.

———. 2004. 'Shuckers, Sorters, Headers and Gutters: Labor in the Fisheries Sector', pp. 298–336 in *Victims of the Chilean Miracle: Workers and Neoliberalism in the Pinochet Era, 1973–2002*, edited by P. Winn. Durham: Duke University Press.

Seinen, Anne. 1996. 'Chile: From Early Liberalisation to "Second-phase Export-led Growth"', in *Latin America's New Insertion in the World Economy: Towards Systemic Competitiveness in Small Economies*, edited by R. Buitelaar and P. van Dijck. New York: St Martin's Press.

Siavelis, Peter. 2000. *The President and Congress in Postauthoritarian Chile: Institutional Constraints to Democratic Consolidation*. Pennsylvania: Pennsylvania State University Press.

Silva, Eduardo. 1996. *The State and Capital in Chile: Business Elites, Technocrats, and Market Economics*. Boulder: Westview.

———. 1998. 'Organized Business, Neoliberal Economic Restructuring, and Redemocratization in Chile', in *Organized Business, Economic Change, and Democracy in Latin America*, edited by F. Durand and E. Silva. Boulder: Lynne Rienner Press.

———. 2002. 'Capital and the Lagos Presidency: Business as Usual?' *Bulletin of Latin American Research* 21(3), pp. 339–57.

Smith, Adam. 1991. *Inquiry into the Nature and Causes of the Wealth of Nations*. New York: Knopf.

Soederberg, Susanne. 2002. 'An Historical Materialist Account of the Chilean Capital Control: Prototype Policy for Whom?' *Review of International Political Economy* 9(3), pp. 490–512.

———. 2004. *The Politics of the New International Financial Architecture: Reimposing Neoliberal Domination in the Global South*. London: Zed Books.

Solimano, Andrés, Eduardo Aninat and Nancy Birdsall. 2000. 'Distributive Justice and Economic Development: The Case of Chile and Developing Countries', in *Development and Inequality in the Market Economy*. Ann Arbor: University of Michigan Press.

Soto, Claudio. 2004. 'Desempleo y consumo en Chile', *Economía Chilena* 7(1), pp. 31–50.

Sottoli, Susana. 2000. 'La política social en América Latina bajo el signo de la economía de mercado y la democracia', *European Review of Latin American and Caribbean Studies* no. 68.

Stallings, Barbara. 1978. *Class Conflict and Economic Development in Chile, 1958–1973.* Stanford: Stanford University Press.

———. 2001. 'Las Reformas Estructurales y el Desempeño Socioeconomico', in *Reformas, Crecimiento y Políticas Sociales en Chile desde 1973*, edited by R. Ffrench-Davis and B. Stallings. Santiago: LOM.

Stiglitz, Joseph. 1998. 'More Instruments and Broader Goals: Moving Toward the Post Washington Consensus', WIDER Annual Lecture. Presented at Helsinki. 7 January.

———. 2000. 'Introduction', in *The World Bank: Structure and Policies*, edited by C. Gilbert and D. Vines. Cambridge: Cambridge University Press.

———. 2002. *Globalization and its Discontents.* New York: W.W. Norton.

———. 2003. 'Fair-Trade Treaties Play Unfair Tricks', *Straights Times.* Kuala Lumpur.

Stillerman, Joel. 2004. 'Disciplined Workers and Avid Consumers: Neoliberal Policy and the Transformation of Work and Identity among Chilean Metalworkers', pp. 164–207 in *Victims of the Chilean Miracle: Workers and Neoliberalism in the Pinochet Era, 1973–2002*, edited by P. Winn. Durham: Duke University Press.

Storper, Michael. 2005. 'State, Community, and Economic Development', *Studies in Comparative International Development* 39(4), pp. 30–57.

Streeter, Steven. 2004. 'Destabilizing Chile: The United States and the Overthrow of Allende', Latin American Studies Association. Presented at Las Vegas. October.

Székely, Miguel. 2001. 'Poverty and Policy: The Story So Far', *Latin American Economic Policies* 14(2).

Taylor, Lucy. 1998. *Citizenship, Participation and Democracy: Changing Dynamics in Chile and Argentina.* London: Macmillan.

Taylor, Marcus. 2003. 'The Reformulation of Social Policy in Chile, 1973–2001: Questioning a Neoliberal Model', *Global Social Policy* 3(1), pp. 21–44.

———. 2004. 'Responding to Neoliberalism in Crisis: Discipline and Empowerment in the World Bank's New Development Agenda', *Research in Political Economy* no. 21, pp. 3–30.

Tendler, Judith. 2000. 'Safety Nets and Service Delivery: What are Social Funds Really Telling Us?' in *Social Development in Latin America: The Politics of Reform*, edited by J. Tulchin and A. Garland. Boulder: Lynne Rienner Press.

Tinsman, Heidi. 2004. 'More Than Victims: Women Agricultural Workers and Social Change in Rural Chile', in *Victims of the Chilean Miracle: Workers and Neoliberalism in the Pinochet Era, 1973–2002*, edited by P. Winn. Durham: Duke University Press.

Titelman, David. 2001. 'Las reformas al sistema de salud: desafíos pendientes', in *Reformas, Crecimiento y Políticas Sociales en Chile desde 1973*, edited by R. Ffrench-Davis and B. Stallings. Santiago: LOM.

Torche, A. 2000. 'Pobreza, Necesidades Básicas y Desigualidad: Tres Objetivos Par una Sola Política Social', in *La Transformación Económica de Chile*, edited by F. Larraín and R. Vergara. Santiago: Centro de Estudios Públicos.

UNCTAD (United Nations Commission on Trade and Development). 2004. 'World Investment Directory: Volume IX Latin America and the Caribbean'.

UNDP (United Nations Development Programme). 2002. 'Human Development in Chile'. UNDP, Santiago, Chile.

US State Department. 2001. 'Annual Country Commerce Report – Chile', Washington: US State Department.

Valdés, Juan Gabriel. 1995. *Pinochet's Economists: The Chicago School in Chile.* Cambridge: Cambridge University Press.

Vergara, Pilar. 1985. *Auge y Caida del Neoliberalismo en Chile.* Santiago: Flacso.

———. 1986. 'Changes in the Economic Functions of the Chilean State under the Military Regime', in *Military Rule in Chile: Dictatorship and Oppositions,* edited by J.S. Valenzuela and A. Valenzuela. New York: Johns Hopkins Press.

Vial, Joaquin. 2000. 'Chile's Development Strategy – Growth With Equity', in *Chile in the Nineties,* edited by C. Toloza and E. Lahera. Stanford: Stanford University Press.

Vitale, Luis. 1990. *Interpretación Marxista de la Historia de Chile – vol. 6.* Santiago: LOM.

Weeks, John. 1981. *Capital and Exploitation.* London: Edward Arnold.

———. 1989. *A Critique of Neoclassical Macroeconomics.* London: Macmillan.

———. 1999. 'Wages, Employment and Workers' Rights in Latin America, 1970–98', *International Labour Review* 138(2), pp. 151–69.

Weyland, Kurt. 1999. 'Economic Policy in Chile's New Democracy', *Journal of Interamerican Studies and World Affairs* 41(3), pp. 67–96.

Winn, Peter. 2004a. '"No Miracle For Us": The Textile Industry in the Pinochet Era', in *Victims of the Chilean Miracle: Workers and Neoliberalism in the Pinochet Era, 1973–2002,* edited by P. Winn. Durham: Duke University Press.

———. 2004b. 'The Pinochet Era', in *Victims of the Chilean Miracle: Workers and Neoliberalism in the Pinochet Era, 1973–2002,* edited by P. Winn. Durham: Duke University Press.

———. 2004c. 'Victims of the Chilean Miracle: Workers and Neoliberalism in the Pinochet Era, 1973–2002', Durham: Duke University Press.

Wolfensohn, James. 1999. 'A Proposal for a Comprehensive Development Framework', World Bank.

World Bank. 1990. *World Development Report 1990: Poverty.* Oxford: Oxford University Press.

———. 1993a. *The East Asian Miracle.* Oxford: Oxford University Press.

———. 1993b. *World Development Report 1993: Investing in Health.* Oxford: Oxford University Press.

———. 1994a. *Averting the Old Age Crisis.* Oxford: Oxford University Press.

———. 1994b. *World Development Report 1995: Workers in an Integrating World.* Oxford: Oxford University Press.

———. 1997. *World Development Report 1997: The State in a Changing World.* Oxford: Oxford University Press.

———. 2000. *World Development Report 2000/2001: Attacking Poverty.* Oxford: Oxford University Press.

——. 2001. *World Development Report 2002: Building Institutions for Markets*. Oxford: Oxford University Press.

——. 2002. *World Development Report 2003: Sustainable Development in a Dynamic World*. Oxford: Oxford University Press.

——. 2003. *World Development Report 2004: Making Services Work for Poor People*. Oxford: Oxford University Press.

Wormald, Guillermo and Jaime Ruiz-Tagle. 1999. *Exclusión Social en el Mercado del Trabajo: El Caso de Chile*. Santiago: International Labour Office.

Index

Compiled by Sue Carlton

labour reform *continued*
　flexibility 152, 153–6, 158, 161–5, 169–70, 177, 196
　impact of 168–70
　and institutionality 158
　Pinochet regime and 65–7, 108, 152, 157
　and unions 157, 159–60, 164
El Ladrillo 84
Lagos, Ricardo 5, 107, 110, 114, 118
　economic policy 134, 143, 144–5
　healthcare reforms 186–7
　labour policy 165–8
Larraín, F. 136
Lavín, Joaquín 166
Leiva, F. 106
Liberal Party 12

marginalist revolution 34–5, 38
　see also utility maximisation
Maritain, Jacques 20
market failure 115, 116, 201
markets 43–4, 45
　and equilibrium 46, 49–50
　invisible hand 122
　and rationality 6, 37, 40, 45
　regulatory role of 2, 6–7
　and state intervention 2, 37–8, 77
Marx, K. 45–6
Maza, G. de la 181–2, 185
MERCOSUR 124
Mexico 200
MIDEPLAN (Ministry of Social Planning) 178, 179–80, 190, 192
mining sector, labour flexibility 162–3
Moguillansky, G. 131
Mönckeberg, M.O. 87
monetarism 3, 43, 54–6, 123
money, social power of 44, 46, 47, 48, 107
Motorola 146
Movimento Democrático Popular (Popular Democratic Movement) 102
Murray, W. 5, 134

NAFTA (North American Free Trade Agreement) 124, 145, 167

national developmentalism 11–29, 30, 33, 39, 51, 54, 55, 77, 82, 88, 200
National Party 12
Nef, J. 110
neoclassicism
　and capitalist social relations 45–51
　and market 43, 49, 122
　roots of neoliberalism 34–8
neoliberalism
　and authoritarianism 42–5
　and capitalism 45–51
　Chilean models 1–5
　and creative destruction 56, 57–60, 80
　decline in Latin America 200–1
　and democracy 42–3
　and economic policy of Concertación 123–6
　future of 197–202
　materialisation in Chile 33–4
　neoclassical roots of 34–8
　neoliberal restructuring 1, 6–7, 38–42, 44–5, 51–2, 112–13, 121, 126–7
　　see also social institutions, restructuring of
　as social engineering 38–9, 43, 45, 56
　and social transformation 6–7, 31, 41, 44, 53, 65, 72, 75–6, 103, 198–9
　and state 7, 42–5, 59, 67, 71–2, 129
New Labour 5, 8
NGOs 109, 191, 194
Nicaragua 101
nitrate industry 12, 13, 14, 34
Nixon, Richard 2, 27

ODEPLAN (National Planning Office) 82–3
O'Donnell, G. 28
OECD (Organisation for Economic Co-operation and Development) 141, 189
Oppenheim, L.H. 27–8
Orrego, F. 2–3